THE CO-CREATION PARADIGM

Venkat Ramaswamy and
Kerimcan Ozcan

STANFORD BUSINESS BOOKS
An Imprint of Stanford University Press
Stanford, California

Stanford University Press
Stanford, California

Special discounts for bulk quantities of titles in the Stanford Business Books imprint are available to corporations, professional associations, and other organizations. For details and discount information, contact the special sales department of Stanford University Press. Tel: (650) 736-1782, Fax: (650) 736-1784

Printed in the United States of America on acid-free, archival-quality paper

Library of Congress Cataloging-in-Publication Data

Ramaswamy, Venkatram, author.

  The co-creation paradigm / Venkat Ramaswamy and Kerimcan Ozcan.
    pages cm
  Includes bibliographical references and index.
  ISBN 978-0-8047-8915-8 (cloth : alk. paper)
    1. Customer relations.   2. Relationship marketing.   3. Product management.   4. Business networks.   I. Ozcan, Kerimcan, author.
II. Title.
  HF5415.5.R354 2014
  658.5'75—dc23

                                                    2013043601

ISBN 978-0-8047-9075-8 (electronic)

Typeset by Newgen in 10/15 Sabon

To Brahman and Swami Krishnananda,
Ishvara and Shivashankar,
Bhumi Devi and Soulmate Bindu,
Prakriti and Joyful Adithya and Lalitha,
Matrudevo Bhava and Pitrudevo Bhava,
And co-creators of the future everywhere.

In loving memory of my father, Shri A. V. Ramaswamy,
whose soul departed this earthly world during the co-creation
of this book.
God bless his soul.
—Venkat Ramaswamy

To Pana for love,
Dora and Jülide for purpose,
Belgin, Gürbüz, and Elbe for encouragement,
And my teachers and students for wisdom and humility.
—Kerimcan Ozcan

CONTENTS

TABLES AND FIGURES

ACKNOWLEDGMENTS

No paradigmatic book can be written without help from and significant dialogue with a large number of individuals as co-creators. We owe a special debt to many people who have given their time and energy to document and share the examples in this book. Our heartfelt thanks go to all of you mentioned in this book and those we may have unintentionally omitted.

We first want to recognize the spirit of the late C. K. Prahalad, who inspired us with his visionary thoughts, insights, teachings, mentorship, and friendship. May God bless his soul. We are also very grateful to the Prahalad family, especially Gayatri, Murali, and Deepa.

We next want to profusely thank Francis Gouillart. Many of the examples in this book originated from the joint work of Venkat Ramaswamy with the ECC Partnership. We thank the consulting clients who believed in the power of co-creation early on and were willing to share their work in documenting these examples. We appreciate the support of Mark Deck and Doug Billings, then at PRTM. We thank Ed Prewitt for his strong case research and editorial skills that helped in shaping the content of several examples. We are also grateful to Kirsten Sandberg and Emily Loose for their editorial guidance and support in the evolution of this work.

We have been inspired by and benefited from several thoughtful senior executives who gave their valuable perspectives as well as their unstinted support: Pablo Armendariz (head of innovation, Caja Navarra), Tim Brown (CEO of IDEO), Bernard Charlès (CEO of Dassault Systèmes), Yasayuki Cho (general manager of Wacoal Japan), Naveen Chopra (senior general manager and head of plant quality, Mahindra & Mahindra), Kris Gopalakrishnan (ex-CEO of Infosys), Subu Goparajau (head of Infosys Labs), S. Karun (head of sustainability, ABB India), Jørgen Knudstorp (CEO of LEGO), Anand Mahindra (chairman and managing director of Mahindra & Mahindra), Katsutoshi Murakami (general manager, NRI, Japan), N. R. Narayana Murthy (founder-chairman and chief mentor of Infosys), Dr. João Polanczyk (CEO of Hospital Moinhos de Vento), David Richards (board member of Orange Telecom), Jay Rogers (CEO of Local Motors), and S. Sivakumar (chief executive of ITC Agri Business).

We also want to thank André Coutinho, Mathias Mangels, and the rest of the team at Symnetics/Tantum Group for being such a strong partner in the evangelization and implementation of co-creation in Latin America. We also want to thank David Moschella (global research director, CSC) and Doug Neal (research fellow, CSC) for exploring co-creation as a next practice through the Leading Edge Forum. We are also very grateful to Richard and Ilse Straub (Drucker Forum), as well as Robert Randall and Brian Leavy (editor in chief and contributing editor at *Strategy and Leadership*) for their support.

In evolving the original manuscript for this book, we are very grateful to Rex Degnegaard (Copenhagen Business School) and Bill Fischer (IMD), who reviewed it early on and provided detailed feedback, critical comments, and valuable suggestions for rewriting and improving it. We also thank Sachin Joshi (CII), S. V. Krishnan (SPI), and Venkatesh Rajah (Oracle) for providing additional comments and feedback on selected portions of the manuscript.

A good editor is a co-creator. We are indebted to Margo Beth Fleming, our editor at Stanford University Press, who sought us out and encouraged us to pursue this paradigmatic undertaking. She went far beyond the role of a traditional editor and truly co-created the book with us. Margo dug into the manuscript incisively, with a keen sense of where the message had to be, and brought clarity to complex arguments. Following the reviews, she provided detailed guidance in reworking the manuscript. She continuously and untiringly urged us to see the forest for the trees, use simple language wherever possible, and clear the underbrush, while still keeping alive the spirit and distinctiveness of this book. Her good nature, persistence, and unwavering commitment helped us immensely. We also thank James Holt for his edits, and the copyeditor, graphic artists, and other personnel at Stanford University Press for their dedicated efforts as "behind the scenes" co-creators.

We also thank the Ross School of Business and International University of Japan for their support and especially M. S. Krishnan (Ross), Toshiro Wakayama (IUJ), and Philip Sugai (Doshisha University).

Finally, we could not have written this book without the unwavering family support of our wives—Bindu and Pana. Their belief in our search and its importance was unwavering. By taking on a disproportionate part of the duties of parenting, they gave us the privilege of time and the peace of mind required for research and writing. Our children—Adithya, Lalitha, Jülide, and Dora—were a constant source of inspiration and encouragement.

We apologize for any unintended omissions in our acknowledgments and are indeed extremely grateful to many who helped us with this book. We alone are responsible for all its shortcomings.

We sincerely hope this book inspires you to become a co-creator in your own life, to help your organization become a co-creative enterprise, and to co-create the future of human experiences in economy and society.

Venkat Ramaswamy
Kerimcan Ozcan

PREFACE

For a long time, people believed that the sun revolved around the earth because it was the sun that rose and set every day. A paradigm shift occurred with the realization that the earth revolved around the sun. Something similar is underway in our social, business, and civic systems. Individuals were seen as revolving around firms and institutions. We were pockets of demand, rising and setting around supply. This is no longer true. Individuals, not institutions, are now at the center of value creation.

Traditional business thinking starts with the premise that the firm autonomously determines value through its choice of products and services. Consumers are assumed to represent demand for the firm's offerings. The implications for business follow from these premises. The firm needs an exchange process to move its goods and services to consumers. This exchange process has long been the locus of the producer's role in extracting economic value from the consumer. Firms have developed multiple approaches to extracting this value: increasing the variety of offerings, efficiently delivering and servicing those offerings, staging goods and services like themed restaurants do, and customizing offerings for individual customers.

These premises and implications manifest themselves in the perspectives and practices of firms in the industrial system. Managers focus on the "chain of activities" that captures the flow of products and services through operations that the firm controls or influences. This "value" chain system essentially represents the "cost build" of products and services. Decisions on what to make, what to buy from suppliers, where to assemble and service products, and a host of other supply and logistics decisions all emanate from this perspective. Employees focus on the quality of the firm's products and processes, potentially enhanced through internal disciplines such as Six Sigma and Total Quality Management. The value creation process of the firm is separate from the market where various parties simply "exchange" this value. Matching supply and demand for goods and services has long been the bedrock of the value creation process. Consumers are often only passively involved in the process of value creation. They are researched, observed, segmented, targeted, marketed at, and sold to by people from the firm, but they are not engaged in any deep, meaningful interaction with the firm, especially on their terms. To use common business terminology, the firm has established "touch points" for them, but these are scarce and brief and are staged from the perspective of the firm. The firm decides what the touch points are and how the relationship with the individual is defined. Individuals do not get to decide what they can share with the firm but instead must answer the questions asked of them at the focus group. They do not participate in the design of the product or service or program, but they are only presented with an offering designed for them by the firm. They do not participate in the marketing of the offering, but they only get to see the campaign aimed at them. They do not actively influence how the firm sells offerings to them or to each other as individuals. They are left with a yes-or-no decision, a modern capitalistic equivalent of Shakespeare's Hamlet: "to buy or not to buy." This firm-centric paradigm of the conventional enterprise has served us well for many years, but it is rapidly becoming outmoded.

Going beyond consumers, networked individuals around the globe are no longer passive and docile recipients of supply, thanks to digitization, globalization, the World Wide Web, advances in interactive communications and information technologies, social media, and ubiquitous connectivity. Rather, all stakeholding individuals expect to be active participants and collaborators in the value creation process as co-creators of value. Individuals today are highly connected and networked, sharing their experiences with products and services. They want to help design the value of the products and services they use, want an ongoing conversation with the companies they do business with and with one another, and want their voices heard. The varieties of interactions that people can engage in have also exploded on an unprecedented scale, with everything from blogs to videos, wikis, podcasts, and a plethora of rapidly evolving engagement technologies.

We are witnessing a paradigmatic shift in value creation, away from a firm-centric, utilitarian view of unilateral value creation to a co-creation paradigm of value creation, as the title of this book suggests. The co-creation paradigm is about:

- interactions as the locus of value creation;

- jointly creating and evolving value with stakeholding individuals;

- harnessing open and social resources of individuals and their skills on the one hand, and enterprise and network resources of multiple private, public, and social sector enterprises on the other, as a joint resource base;

- innovating engagement platforms as the means of connecting joint value creation opportunities with joint resources through agential actions;

- leveraging ecosystems of capabilities based on meshworks of social, business, civic, and natural communities to engender new value creation capacities;

- individuated experiences as the basis of outcomes of value; and

- wealth-welfare-wellbeing as the basis of joint aspirations.

Both this shift and this book have been a long time coming. In 2004, following a series of articles from 1998 to 2003, C. K. Prahalad and Venkat Ramaswamy published *The Future of Competition: Co-Creating Unique Value with Customers* (HBS Press, 2004).[1] That book detailed the shifting of competencies toward an enhanced network of customer communities and global talent outside the firm. It suggested that customer experience was becoming central to enterprise value creation, innovation, strategy, and executive leadership. It offered a series of compelling examples, showing that value was being created jointly by the firm and the customer, rather than entirely inside the firm. The book held that customers seek the freedom of choice to interact with firms through a range of experiences. Customers want to define choices in a manner that reflects their view of value, and they want to interact and transact in their preferred language and style. *The Future of Competition* provided a new frame of reference for jointly creating value through experiences and called for a process of co-creation—the practice of developing offerings through ongoing collaboration with customers, employees, managers, and other stakeholders. Just three years after publication, businesses had begun to capitalize on opportunities anticipated by the book, embracing concepts such as "customer competence," "experience innovation," "experience personalization," and the larger perspective of "value co-creation."

The Future of Competition commenced an ongoing journey for us as authors. From 2005 until 2010, Venkat engaged with thousands of managers globally who had begun experimenting with co-creation, especially following the explosion of digital and social media, convergence of technologies and industries, proliferation of sensors and embedded intelligence, and IT-enabled services. Through a series of articles, Venkat discussed and explored how enterprises were building platforms that enabled "large-scale ongoing interactions" among the firm, its customers, and its extended network.[2] This shift also allowed for the continuous development of new experiences and new opportunities for the firm by way of customer engagement. In some cases, enterprises had gone further in extending their resource base through practices such as crowdsourcing, open innovation, and mass collaboration. In other cases, they were tapping into user communities and social networking among customers. Some enterprises had also begun allowing their customers to personalize products. The fundamental shift managers had to make with the dawn of these changes required them to go beyond a conventional goods-services mindset and develop an experience mindset. Success lay in using people's actual experiences to generate insights and change the nature and quality of interactions in building a co-creative enterprise.[3] In 2010, Venkat and Francis Gouillart published *The Power of Co-Creation* (Free Press, 2010), which showed how enterprises (in the private, public, and social sectors) were leveraging platforms to create new interactions with people everywhere in the system and new forms of value together with individuals through a focus on human experiences. As a result, people and their interactions were becoming central to effective design, innovation, marketing, operations, IT, human resources, leadership, and strategy at large. This called for co-creation among managers inside the organization to support external co-creation with customers and stakeholders.[4]

In 2010, Kerimcan Ozcan joined Venkat on the co-creation journey. A decade after *The Future of Competition*, we feel that the time has come for a deep dive into the fundamental nature of value creation as a co-creation. It has become clear that the world is on the cusp of a fundamental structural transformation of the very nature of value and the process of creating it. It has also became evident that co-creation thinking challenges the nature of enterprises; their organization; governance; the relative roles of private, social, and public sector enterprises; and how economies and societies are shaped.[5]

This book is the result of our joint efforts in attempting to provide a comprehensive paradigmatic framework of co-creation to ground the future of value creation as it is developing. We use a lot of examples as "thinking props" to convey our perspective and key ideas, not to illustrate best practices or prescribe "one best way" or to glorify any one enterprise as the model of the future. Instead, we strive to discover next practices, so no single example could possibly exemplify the concepts underlying the paradigm shift and a synthesized frame of reference we provide. While some of the examples may be broadly familiar to some readers, we have strived to use the examples purposefully to elucidate concepts, components, and particular aspects of our framework. We recognize a wide array of options that individuals can explore and exercise to cope with and capture the opportunities available to everyone reading this book.

We recognize that a paradigm shift occurs over a fairly long period of ferment and that it is not attributable to only a few people. We share the spirit of humility in recognizing the work of many whose shoulders we stand upon. A curated website (cocreationparadigm.com) accompanies this book and expands on the content of co-creation by providing a glossary and links to the works of different authors and related topics—

across multiple disciplines—that cumulatively connect with the co-creation paradigm at large. We synthesize various strands of economics and social sciences, information, design, complexity sciences, natural sciences, psychology and cognitive neurosciences, phenomenology, metaphysics and philosophy, morality and ethics, policy, and organizational and business scholarship that contribute to a progressive, pluralistic, and constructive foundation of a co-creation paradigm of value creation in contemporary enterprises, markets, economies, and societies.

In writing this book, we tried to maximize accessibility for an intellectually curious and academically minded audience by citing only the most salient journal articles, since most of the books we mention contain a plethora of references and our open access website provides an extensive bibliography with aids to further exploration. Moreover, we tried to minimize quotations and inline references as much as possible to make the reading experience smoother, while at the same time remaining cognizant of the dangers of simplification. Achieving this balance was not easy, and we did our best to rearticulate the ideas of original contributors in a way that is accessible without losing its fidelity.

This book is more than an invitation to think differently; it is a clarion call to action—to help create a new world of possibilities together. While we focus primarily on the strategic implications for enterprises, and particularly with a conceptual inclination, we believe that, ultimately, all of us will have to see, think, and act differently—not just as practitioners or academics but as individuals in economy and society—thereby rebalancing the relative influence of the individual and the institutions of private, public, and social sector enterprises. We expect a long but exciting journey through the unfamiliar that will force us out of our comfort zones into a more complex world of co-creation but a journey that is more fulfilling in realizing the potential of humanity and our worldly experiences.

THE CO-CREATION PARADIGM

I INTRODUCTION TO THE CO-CREATION PARADIGM

Propelled by advances in global communication and information technologies, the nature of interactions among individuals and their environments has been changing rapidly, driving an ongoing metamorphosis of value creation in business, economy, and society. The centrality of personal and collective agency with the advent of the Web and the progression of new mobile technologies has accelerated the generation of data through interactions, the communication and exchange of information, and the democratization of value creation.[6] Individuals—whether customers, employees, suppliers, partners, financiers, or citizens at large—are playing out their different interests from both within and outside of traditional enterprises.[7] Nongovernmental and social organizations are taking increasingly assertive roles vis-à-vis corporations. Citizens and communities are engaging local and national governments in the deliberation of policies and the delivery of services. In all these cases, individuals are attempting to push through previously impervious institutional boundaries to express their various demands and expectations. In other words, individuals as active stakeholders want to be more intensively engaged in value creation than ever before.[8]

What is the significance of this new age of engagement? As depicted in Figure 1-1, a fundamental implication is that enterprises—whether private, public, or social sector enterprises and whether established or at the

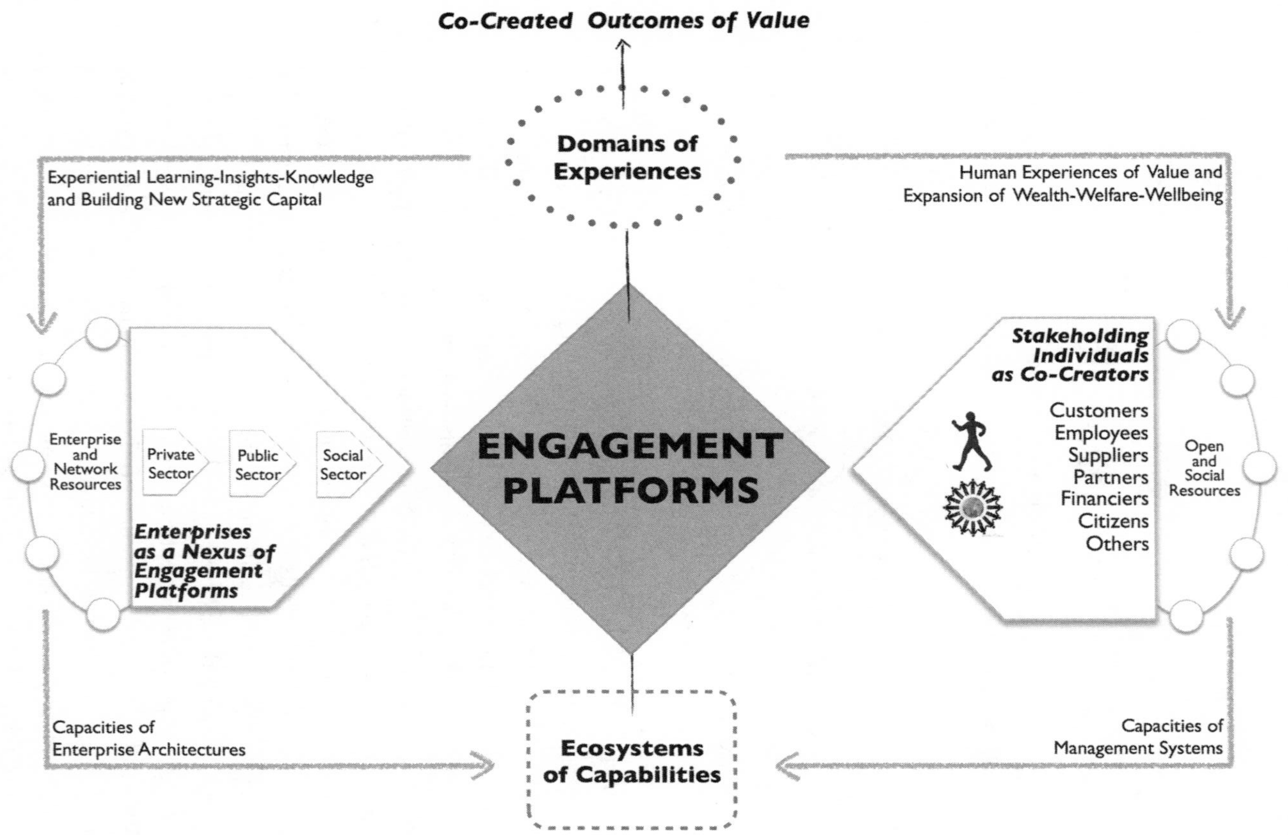

Co-Created Outcomes of Value

Domains of Experiences

ENGAGEMENT PLATFORMS

Ecosystems of Capabilities

Stakeholding Individuals as Co-Creators

Customers
Employees
Suppliers
Partners
Financiers
Citizens
Others

Open and Social Resources

Human Experiences of Value and Expansion of Wealth-Welfare-Wellbeing

Capacities of Management Systems

Enterprises as a Nexus of Engagement Platforms

Private Sector
Public Sector
Social Sector

Enterprise and Network Resources

Experiential Learning-Insights-Knowledge and Building New Strategic Capital

Capacities of Enterprise Architectures

FIGURE 1-1 Value creation as co-creation

start-up stage—must be architected as a nexus of engagement platforms, organizing human agency to create value with, and for, all stakeholding individuals as co-creators.[9]

Using two examples from the private sector, an established enterprise (Nike) and a start-up (Local Motors), let us illustrate:

1. how engagement platforms—assemblages of persons, processes, artifacts, and interfaces—can create value together with stakeholding individuals;

2. how enterprises as a nexus of engagement platforms can connect value creation opportunities with value-creating resources in new "win more–win more" ways; and

3. how private, public, and social sector enterprises have the potential to converge on matters of wealth, welfare, and wellbeing, while positively transforming business, economy, and society in ways we are only beginning to grasp.[10]

CREATING VALUE TOGETHER THROUGH ENGAGEMENT PLATFORMS

In 2006, Nike launched NikePlus, a *running experience platform*, with the communications tagline "Get connected to your running experiences."[11] It consisted of a smart sensor that gathered data (e.g., steps, distance, pace) while you—the "stakeholding individual" of your running experience— enjoyed your run. If you ran with the Apple iPod, then the sensor could be placed inside your shoe, with the data being wirelessly transmitted to and stored on the iPod, which also served as an interface for your runs. The combination of data and music also enabled you to pull up your personal motivating tunes, or Power Songs, just when your energy started to dip. If you didn't listen to music during your runs, then a Nike SportBand, an armband introduced by Nike in June 2009, offered a combined sensor and data storage option, while providing an interface for your running data. Either way, after your run, you could go to the NikePlus website and perform many functions related to your running experience with both your own data and with a community of runners. For example, you could chart your run; track your progress; analyze your performance; map your runs; share data with your family, friends, coaches, or trainers; and even invite and challenge other runners. You could also engage in a whole host of social interactions with other people that would not necessarily revolve around your running data, such as find running buddies, connect with running events that Nike and others organize, or engage in conversations with other runners through the NikePlus-enabled community.

The smart sensor was a required artifact to participate in an assemblage of other artifacts, persons, processes, and interfaces, all purposefully designed with the intent of generating running data-based outcomes of value to runners and other stakeholders both external and internal to the Nike enterprise (e.g., trainers, coaches, and individuals in managerial functions at Nike). The digitization of momentary analog data facilitates linkages between offline and online interactions, between individuals and the community of runners, and between individuals and their trainers and coaches.

The ways in which individuals could affect their running environments—before, during, and after a run—are multiplied. Various domains of human experiences unfold as a function of the involvements of individuals in the environments afforded by NikePlus, such as engaging with music or data while running (e.g., the voiceover of Olympic athletes through the Apple iPod that announces your progress and milestones achieved). In extending the intentionalities of NikePlus engagements, one can imagine Nike taking any of the environments afforded to runners and enabling connections to the environments of other stakeholders (e.g., marathon organizers or fitness instructors), as well as communities of runners in new roles.

Thus, NikePlus is enveloped in a larger *ecosystem of capabilities*—a meshwork of social, business, civic, and natural communities whose capabilities can be leveraged as co-creative resources to afford new value creation possibilities.[12] For instance, the Nike RunReporter platform, which NikePlus links with, attempts to engage nonprofessional runners who can report live from marathon running events (like citizen journalists). These RunReporters can potentially enhance the running environment of a particular runner in a marathon run or the experience of a spectator at the marathon event. The co-creative resource networks not only generate additional value from the perspective of runners (the traditional customer base of Nike Running), but they also represent new value creation opportunities in of themselves. For instance, by looking at NikePlus from a "trainer as customer" perspective, Nike was able to imagine new environments of interactions that connect with NikePlus, such as the ability for a trainer to interact with a group of runners and coach them both individually and as a group, drawing on other resources in the Nike enterprise ecosystem. This, in turn, led Nike to leverage meshworks of running, coaching, and training communities to afford new environments of interactions and potentially new outcomes of value for all involved.

Nike has also leveraged the capabilities of partners into the Nike enterprise ecosystem. First, Nike actively collaborated with Apple in integrating runner engagement with music and data through the iPod interface. After Apple launched the iPhone in 2007, along with its App Store, through which developers in Apple's ecosystem could provide applications, Nike took advantage of the Apple iPhone's built-in accelerometer and GPS to launch its NikePlus GPS app. This app could collect your running data without the need for a separate shoe/armband sensor, provided you did not mind running with your iPhone. This, in turn, led to the development of new assemblages coming together as the NikePlus Fuelband, a wristband that can be worn throughout the day, like a watch. The extended NikePlus Fuelband keeps track of every step you take and every move you make and converts all your daily activities to a common metric called NikeFuel, which helps you set active lifestyle goals and stay motivated throughout the day. Thus, NikeFuel evolved from the NikePlus engagement platform, extending its value beyond running to other sports and making lifestyles as a whole more active.

The new task for managers and employees, as co-creators from within the Nike enterprise, is to pay attention to the embeddedness of NikePlus in the daily experiences of individuals to not only gain a deeper understanding of the involvements of people but also of their contexts of engagements, the events that give rise to their life experiences through NikePlus, and what is meaningful to them. Further, decision makers at Nike have to reflect on and use the insights gained to personally and collectively virtualize the co-creative capacities of Nike's strategic architecture—multiple, linked environments of interactions across the NikePlus extended engagement platform and the meshwork of communities enveloping it in the ever-expanding Nike enterprise ecosystem.[13] Thus, the ultimate goal is to actualize new co-created outcomes that expand value for all participating individuals in *win more–win more* fashion.

Nike's engagement platforms, ultimately, enable its extended enterprise ecosystem to:

- learn directly from the interactions of its customers and other stakeholders;

- get direct input from individuals on their engagement preferences and connect with their experiences;

- build deeper relationships and trust with the communities served and whose resources it depends on;

- foster private-public-social sector partnerships;

- leverage open and social resources, and enterprise and network resources;

- generate new ideas rapidly;

- experiment with new offerings quickly;

- engender stickier brand collateral; and

- enhance new sources of value creation advantage.

Most significantly, Nike's extended enterprise ecosystem is a multiway learning engine, facilitating dialogue with and among stakeholder communities. Nike can continuously identify and act upon new growth opportunities with its enhanced global capability ecosystem. It can enable the combining of consented individual private data, social community data, open public data, and other data sources. For instance, if you were an urban NikePlus user with atmospheric sensitivities—for example, allergic to pollen—you would be able to share fitness and sensor data with others, combine that with open environmental data from your city, and through real-time analytics be able to co-create a running course that did not include high–pollen count areas. This opens up new avenues for innovation in the NikePlus ecosystem.

Besides attracting new adherents to the Nike brand through the largest community of individuals it has ever assembled, the NikePlus ecosystem boosts product sales and enhances returns through the increased motivation and involvement of individuals. By the end of 2007, Nike had sold over 1.3 million NikePlus iPod Sport Kits (at $29 apiece) and over 500,000 NikePlus SportBands (at $59 apiece) and had captured 57 percent of the $3.6 billion U.S. running shoe market, compared with 47 percent in 2006. More than 600,000 runners from more than 170 countries used the NikePlus website in just a year, with over 40 million miles run. Seeing the growth potential, Charlie Denson, president of the Nike brand, set a stretch goal in 2007 of having 15 percent of the world's estimated 100 million runners participate in the NikePlus ecosystem.[14] The subsequent growth was relentless. By the end of 2008, runners had logged 100 million miles on NikePlus. By August 2009, despite a sluggish economy, over 150 million miles had been uploaded by more than 1.3 million runners, burning more than 14 billion calories. By mid-2009, Nike's share of the U.S. running shoe market had increased to 61 percent. By mid-2013, more than 7 million runners were participating in NikePlus, with over 900 million miles run.

With NikePlus, the company shifted its spending away from traditional media like TV networks. Trevor Edwards, Nike's marketing director, remarked, "We're not in the business of keeping the media companies alive. We're in the business of connecting with consumers. NikePlus is a very different way to connect with consumers. People are coming into it on average three times a week. So we're not having to go to them."[15] Instead, Nike began making investments in extending the NikePlus platform further and enhancing its social media capabilities to enable runners to connect with one another and with Nike in new ways. By 2007, Nike's nonmedia spending of $457.9 million surpassed its traditional media spending of $220.5 million. For Nike, the benefits of NikePlus included reducing the cost of marketing through the positive word-of-mouth created, sharing the risk of product-service development with partners by getting them to coinvest and participate, and mitigating the risk of capital investment through enlightened experimentation because it could now pilot major investments through its extended ecosystem.

Hence, through NikePlus, Nike's managers and employees have co-evolved their learning environments with customers and other platform participants. In early 2013, Jayme Martin, vice president of Global Category Running, noted, "The NikePlus Running experience is one of the most personalized and motivational ways we serve the runner. We're introducing a new chapter that will take the running experience to a new level in terms of connectivity, community, social sharing, and data-driven insights."[16] Further, as Stefan Olander, Nike's global director of consumer connections, remarked, "The more we can open up NikePlus, the better. The only reason to close it out is because you actually don't believe that you have a strong enough product for others to want to take it and do good things with it."[17] Indeed, in early 2013, Nike blazed new paths of transformative engagement by opening up the application programming interfaces of the NikePlus platform to other developers to expand the value frontier through new potential applications designed around the data generated through NikePlus. Simultaneously, together with TechStars, Nike also launched a start-up Accelerator program, with the intent of bringing together ten start-ups for an "immersive, mentor-driven" experience through a network of resources that aims to foster innovation and build offerings that "inspire and assist people to live more active, healthy lifestyles."[18]

Now, let us turn to the shoe itself—the traditional artifact designed, developed, and offered by Nike through its conventional chain of enterprise activities. Through another engagement platform, NikeID, the Nike enterprise has now opened up the creative design of the shoe to customers and enthusiasts. Online, you can start with a design from the community at large, one of Nike's in-house shoe designers, or your own, and play with colors and shapes. Offline, at the NikeID Studio Live (e.g., in New York and London), selected athletes can engage with physical materials in crafting unique shoe designs. Nike provides some of the tools it uses internally in its own product design and testing labs. Further, Nike attempts to connect better with NikeID platform users' experiences of personalization, continuously learning about what matters to them—for example, color matching. Its NikeID iPhone app now enables you to take a picture of an object in your favorite color and use the picture rather than the color wheel to specify colors. In April 2013, in partnership with Instagram, Nike launched PHOTOiD, which enables you to take the captured moments of your life and commemorate them on your feet by applying colors from the image to your favorite Nike Air Max shoe. You can then share your design through Facebook, Twitter, Tumblr, Pinterest, Google+, and back to Instagram, or purchase your personalized shoe to arrive within four weeks. The opening up of shoe design enhances the experience and accessibility not only to individuals but also to collectives like a school soccer team designing with a particular set of team colors. In the latter case, the team-locker interface allows individuals to generate and share designs, invite others to comment on them, and facilitate the emergence of a unique shoe design for the team.

Thus, NikeID is a *product design platform* involving not only users of shoes but design consultants, influencers, and decision supporters, as well as people with product design responsibilities within Nike and partners such as R/GA, a digital advertising agency. While NikeID engages a circle of stakeholders distinct from NikePlus, both entail particular states of stakeholder relations, ideation, decision making, and offerings. For instance, the NikeID design engagement platform entails:

- community relations with customers, enthusiasts, and designers (amateurs and professionals alike);

- collecting, sharing, and spreading of design ideas;

- product personalization decisions individually and consensus building decisions collectively (to design a team shoe); and

- product design concepts and custom artifacts such as a NikeID card and the Nike customized shoe itself as offerings.

JOINT VALUE CREATION BASED ON STAKEHOLDER EXPERIENCES

While Nike has innovated impressively in the ecosystem in which it participates, its engagement platforms could be enhanced further to co-create better outcomes. Consider Nike's *wear-testing* platform. Nike has long involved runners in testing its products. Nike brings runners into its laboratories, where it assesses the functional performance of shoes. These labs test friction, wear, and fatigue on the shoes, and they experiment with new materials, involving runners as in-house testers. While lab tests are important for assessing technical performance, Nike recognizes that they provide only limited data on what really counts: the actual experiences afforded by interactions between the runner's body, the running environment, and the shoe. The generation of such highly contextualized information on interactions requires having access to the flesh, blood, and perspiration of real people who are running in real weather and under real road/trail conditions.

So Nike also sends shoes to a subset of self-selecting runners, who are asked to wear the shoes, test them in the natural environment in which they run, and send back their comments. The feedback is given through a website that creates a direct line of communication between the testers and Nike's shoe designers. This interaction has great value for both Nike and the testers, as evidenced by the high demand to become a Nike product tester (visible in many comments on the Web). "Wear testing," as this real-world testing is called, removes the "lab rat" aspect of product testing, allowing Nike to capture customers' experiences with its shoes. Yet, these interactions between Nike and product testers have rarely been co-creative.

Wear testers have traditionally been viewed as passive sources of data to be analyzed by the "shoe experts"—product development teams consisting of analysts, designers, product managers, and manufacturing associates who evaluate features and determine their additional value to the final product. Comments posted on websites and online forums that provide unsolicited feedback on new shoes hitting the market suggest that wear testers have very different opinions from those of shoe experts. Many wear testers do want to help Nike, and their passion for Nike can be infectious. Nike can encourage richer, more meaningful dialogue with individual testers and potentially among a community of testers. Envision wear testers working as a community with Nike's in-house designers, exchanging impressions as a group and codesigning the shoe with a considerably richer and broader set of inputs. The dialogue would be decentered across space and time, with issues originating from the community, centered on the human experiences of individual testers. Such a dialogue would have significant strategic value, with experiential learning, real-time insights, and rapidly created knowledge generating additional enterprise and stakeholder value—internally for Nike analysts and designers and externally for customers.

Nike wear testers typically do not have much transparency into how the data they collectively generate is used by Nike to (re)design shoes. Moreover, wear testers are typically forbidden from discussing the shoes they are testing with anyone, including other testers. This precaution may be to prevent leakage of information to competitors. Nevertheless, providing "feedback on the feedback" would deepen the conversation about the product. Wear testers are not typically trained in shoe design and development and thus do not know the lingo of shoe design. Wear testers can become frustrated when trying to communicate their evaluation of the shoes to Nike in a way that is not only meaningful to testers but to analysts and designers as well.

Access to domain knowledge, tools, and expertise is necessary for wear testers to evaluate shoes and participate effectively in a two-way conversation. For instance, some wear testers modify their shoes to better match their feet or performance needs. How is the observed wear to be interpreted by the analyst? For instance, a person wearing orthopedic supports may remove the insoles of a shoe. Nike could ask wear testers to identify when they modified a shoe and why. Nike could do a foot scan—say, at selected store locations or through mobile smartphones—to get an exact match of the wear tester's foot. In fact, foot scans could become another channel of interaction between the enterprise and the wear testers. Nike could eventually leverage these capabilities in designing shoes customized for personal fit.

Any attempts to make interactions more co-creative must also facilitate reflexivity—that is, individuals being able to "feed back into" the cause-effect engagement loops in the platforms. For instance, some wear testers have a lot of expertise on the particular features they have designed, and their changes could be posted for other testers to see. Wear testers' evaluations could even be made visible to consumers after the launch of the new product. For example, if a wear tester tested a custom option, a future customer considering that same type of customization could benefit from knowing the tester's experience. Testers and consumers alike could, thus, manage their own assessment of risks versus rewards in engaging with Nike (based on why and how Nike makes certain decisions) to create mutual value.

Thus, dialogue, transparency, access, and reflexivity build on one another in the co-configuration of co-creation experiences. The value to Nike goes beyond economic outcomes to the ongoing generation of new *strategic capital*—sources of innovation, value creation, and competitive advantage—by Nike's internal groups capitalizing on experiential learning, insights, and knowledge, from product development to marketing and other functions associated with Nike Wear Testing.

EVOLVING ENGAGEMENT PLATFORMS EVERYWHERE IN THE ENTERPRISE ECOSYSTEM

Engagement platforms can evolve anywhere in the ecosystem in which an enterprise operates. For instance, when it comes to retail sales, one of Nike's challenges is that it does not directly manage the quality of end customer experiences at the thousands of retail stores worldwide that carry Nike shoes. So the company developed an online training platform to engage retail salespeople. Called Nike SKU (Sports Knowledge Underground), this *sales training platform* gives sales associates access to a series of self-learning tools that they can use at their leisure to develop an in-depth knowledge of different sports and the roles that Nike shoes, apparel, and equipment play in those sports. SKU features user-friendly navigation, with the various sports laid out like a colorful "underground" public transportation map (think London Tube or Paris Metro). Each module requires three to five minutes to complete, which is well suited to the busy schedules of salespeople and the short attention spans of the young people who comprise most of the sales force in stores. Sales associates can stop any time in the middle of a module and restart where they left off.

Nike SKU allows the store sales associate, the store manager, and Nike to create the learning agenda together. While the sales associate is the ostensible focus of the SKU platform, store owners also actively participate as stakeholders by being in the associates' learning environment, which also includes other associates in the store. Store owners can customize SKU to the specifics of their store by choosing only those modules pertaining to sports for which they carry the Nike line. They can ensure that sales associates complete certain modules by a certain time. SKU also encourages the sales associates to correlate their skills levels with the amount of their sales, the customer satisfaction these sales generate, and other factors that contribute to overall sales performance. Store associates can learn more rapidly from other associates through collaborative communication tools that foster social interaction. In-depth training through dialogue and transparency is ever more crucial in a new world of retail engagement in which customers (users and enthusiasts) are often more informed and passionate about a sport than the retail salesperson. Nike benefits from sales associates developing their skills and by stores increasing their sales and customer satisfaction. For instance, Nike demonstrated an increase in product sell-through of about 4 percent in pilot tests in 2007 of same-store comparisons with and without SKU.

Going beyond product sales, Nike aims to use sports as a way to accelerate development and drive social change through partnerships with Ashoka (a social organization in the citizen sector) and its Changemakers platform. This *social change platform* seeks to recruit societal stakeholders using sports as an instrument of social change. Nike and Ashoka have jointly hosted GameChanger competitions to find innovative solutions and catalyze a community of Changemakers around the world. Through an open call to all types of individuals and organizations (charitable organizations, private companies, or public entities), they have sought solutions for using soccer as a mechanism for social change. Through such partnerships, Nike is attempting to mesh together co-creative capacities of social and civic communities with those of its business communities. In the past, Nike has been subject to allegations and the activism of human rights stakeholders with respect to child labor in its manufacturing operations. It has since actively addressed these issues, even signing onto the Global Compact and using a "triple bottom line" approach that supplements its economic bottom line with explicit social and environmental responsibilities.

As Mark Parker, CEO of Nike, said in 2010:

In the early days, our "systems" consisted of only those things that helped us build better shoes and shirts, and ads and events. We are, after all, a consumer products company. It took us a while, but we finally figured out that we could apply our two core competencies—design and innovation—to bring about environmental, labor, and social change. We opened the aperture of our lens and discovered our potential to have a positive influence on waste reduction, climate change, managing natural resources, and renewable energy and factory conditions. We saw that doing the right thing was good for business today—and would be an engine for our growth in the near future. With each new discovery and partnership, we willingly gave up old ideas to shift our thinking toward a better, smarter, faster and ultimately more sustainable future—financially, environmentally, and socially.[19]

In summary, engagement platforms can be everywhere in the ecosystem in which the enterprise operates, designed for varying purposes:

- as offerings themselves (e.g., NikePlus);
- encouraging entrepreneurship and decision making (e.g., Nike Accelerator);
- enabling the design of offerings (e.g., NikeID);
- harnessing ideas and insights (e.g., NikePlus, NikeID);
- supporting the delivery of offerings (e.g., Nike Retail Stores);
- facilitating training and marketing (e.g., Nike SKU); and
- expanding the circle of value creation stakeholders (e.g., Nike-Ashoka Changemakers).

THE SHIFT IN THINKING TO VALUE CREATION AS A CO-CREATION

Now that we have seen how co-creation functions in the Nike enterprise ecosystem, let us now summarize the shift in thinking to value creation as a co-creation.

Co-creation is
joint creation and evolution of value *with stakeholding individuals*,
intensified and enacted through *platforms of engagements*,
virtualized and emergent from *ecosystems of capabilities*, and
actualized and embodied in *domains of experiences*,
expanding *wealth-welfare-wellbeing*.

The co-creation-based view of value creation views organizations as creating value together with stakeholding individuals. As depicted in Figure 1-1, co-creation is *both the means and the end*, continuously evolving in a virtuous cycle of "win more–win more" outcomes. There are potentially infinite opportunities of joint value creation. Individuals in their role as managers must rethink the nature of both resources and opportunities, locus of competence, and how access to competence is developed. All stakeholders represent a resource and opportunity base, from consumers to employees at all levels; they are also partners with all other stakeholders. Gaining privileged and timely access to these resources and opportunities, and stakeholder knowledge and skills at large, requires managers to explicitly consider ways in which they can navigate risk-reward relationships in networks. Value creation strategies today call for a new spirit of discovery, involving experimentation, analysis, consolidation of gains, and further exploration. Managing the infrastructure of the ecosystem, with its continual friction between collaboration and competition in co-creation can be a source of competitive advantage. In co-creation, strategy is not a game with knowable rules and finite options. The goal of the strategist is to effectively navigate through the fog of value creation opportunities, connecting them with appropriate value creating resources.[20]

Returning to Figure 1-1, if we represent organizations with the color blue and stakeholders with the color yellow, then co-creation can occur in two fundamental ways: by mixing yellow into blue and/or mixing blue into yellow, both of which yield the color green—the color of co-creation, as it were.[21] The mixing of blue into yellow is a very important distinction, because this represents bringing organizational capabilities to bear in creating a platform that opens up stakeholder activities to co-creation. In other words, stakeholder value comes before enterprise value, as it were. In contrast, the mixing of yellow into blue, as is implied more often in the popular parlance of co-creation, is about extending the enterprise resource base through practices such as crowdsourcing, mass collaboration, and open innovation;[22] tapping into user communities and social networking among customers for outbound marketing and sales activities of enterprises; or allowing customers more variety in customizing products and services from an enterprise menu. In these cases, enterprise value comes before stakeholder value, as it were. From the perspective of the blue side, bringing yellow into blue is about "bringing the outside in"—that is, bringing stakeholders and their capabilities into the enterprise activities of value creation. Bringing blue into yellow is about "bringing the inside out"—that is, bringing enterprises and their capabilities into the stakeholders' activities of value creation. In both cases, this requires engagement platforms. The metaphor of "color-mixing" is important because co-creation goes beyond bringing pieces together as many cooperative (i.e., "co"-operating) or even collaborative (i.e., "co"-laboring) efforts tend to be. Rather, "co-creation" essentially represents a transformation on both the blue and the yellow sides: the blue turns green, as does the yellow. But the green still has blue and yellow side capacities inside of it.

As we expound in detail in this book, the co-creation paradigm requires a shift in our thinking to:

1. engaging stakeholders personally and collectively in creating value together and expanding how the enterprise connects value creation opportunities with resources;

2. conceiving platforms of engagements as purposefully designed assemblages of persons, processes, interfaces, and artifacts, which afford environments of interactions to intensify co-creating actions and generate mutually valuable outcomes;

3. recognizing that actualized value is subjective and varies as a function of individuated experiences of co-created outcomes;

4. leveraging the capabilities of meshworks of social, business, civic, and natural communities in which individuals are embedded to virtualize new co-creative capacities of value creation; and

5. building ecosystems of capabilities together with other private, public, and social sector enterprises to expand wealth-welfare-wellbeing in the economy and in society as a whole.

BUILDING ENTERPRISES AS A NEXUS OF
CO-CREATION PLATFORMS OF ENGAGEMENTS

As should be evident by now, enterprises are no longer just a conventional chain of activities (nor are firms just a nexus of contracts). Rather, as the

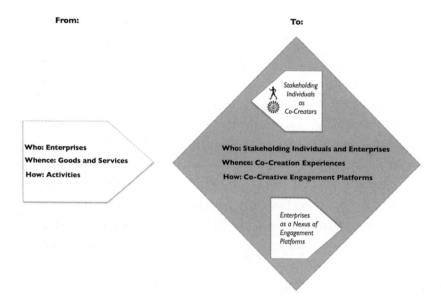

From:

To:

Who: Enterprises
Whence: Goods and Services
How: Activities

Stakeholding Individuals as Co-Creators

Who: Stakeholding Individuals and Enterprises
Whence: Co-Creation Experiences
How: Co-Creative Engagement Platforms

Enterprises as a Nexus of Engagement Platforms

FIGURE 1-2   From conventional enterprises to co-creative enterprises

Nike example suggests, enterprises are now a nexus of co-creation platforms of engagements through which individuals exercise their agency in creating value together based on individual human experiences, as summarized in Figure 1-2.[23]

With this new vision of organization life in mind, let us turn to the example of Local Motors, exploring how it has designed its entire organizational form this way—from the design and development of automotive vehicles to their modification, building, and maintenance. We illustrate how with the power of the Web any enterprise can now architect itself to access open and social network resources globally and turn fixed costs into variable ones that can be scaled up or down, resulting in much lower capital intensity and better risk-reward relationships. Leaner and more flexible than their industrial era counterparts, enterprises like this one must compel co-creating agents to engage and intensify value through purposefully designed engagement platforms.[24]

Local Motors begins with a new view of how to leverage global resources on the one hand and a blank slate for the design, development, manufacturing, delivery, and postdelivery platforms of engagements on the other. It has parceled out some elements of its value creation system to a portfolio of partners, and it has acted as a nodal enterprise in the ecosystem by providing intellectual leadership and by linking together platforms of engagements for design and development, while controlling core elements of manufacturing, delivery, and postdelivery activities. The integration of platforms into the firm's boundaries is a function of the unique arrangement that the firm can co-create with its stakeholders through the global use of resources, knowledge, and skills all along the activity chain.

The strategic architecture of the Local Motors enterprise entails, for example, an automotive *product design platform* that involves a community of over 5,000 (amateur) designers worldwide who participate in its periodic design contests for a new car model. Once a winning design is chosen, it uses an open *supply chain platform* where any supplier of components, parts, or subassemblies can participate as the manufacture of the chosen design is settled upon. Local Motors, however, fabricates only the composite frames in a local micro-factory in which the car is built. As a buyer of the car, you can choose a custom car skin and personalize accessories to your taste from an online website, where the conventional "aftermarket" is now an open "in-market" where anybody can offer accessories for a particular automobile for which component data are available to all. Then there is the micro-factory with a *car-building platform*, where you are the lead builder, with Local Motors providing the training, tools, and support as you build the car over two three-day weekends. You can share the car-building experience live with other participants. Moreover, the automobile itself can be seen as a *product-service offering platform* of engagements involving fleet owners, operators, and communities of truck drivers on the one hand and increasingly sophisticated software, embedded intelligence, and remote interfaces on the other. Together, these components offer new sources of agency and experience-centric opportunities for value creation.

While Local Motors relies on an open and social network of global resources, it must also rely on an enterprise network of partners like Dassault Systèmes, one of the global enterprise leaders in design tools and a key partner and stakeholder in Local Motors' capability ecosystem. As communications and information technologies advance, Dassault Systèmes offers platforms for enabling better design engagement through 3D visualization, simulation, and prototyping tools. Through its Web browser-based, collaborative design platform, which is integrated into the Local Motors platform, participants can visualize and explore new products, and engage in interactions of value to them. The software and interfaces enable more effective social product development, empowering individuals to share their ideas, vote on designs, and give feedback.

Thus, Local Motors leverages capabilities in the meshwork of communities in which it is enveloped, and in which it participates. The Local Motors example suggests how new engagement models can be designed all across the value chain of enterprise activities using engagement platforms as the very basis of enterprise value creation.[25] While rhizomatic organizational forms similar to Local Motors are spreading, at the same time, established enterprises are embracing the essence of such enterprise ecosystems, even indirectly. For example, the U.S. government used the Local Forge engagement platform (provided by Local Motors as a separate service offering in and of itself) to co-create a military vehicle design concept that could support two types of missions: combat reconnaissance and combat delivery-evacuation. More than 12,000 designers and enthusiasts in the Local Motors community participated in this combat-support vehicle design challenge, incorporating and discussing novel concepts and ideas from peers, with more than 150 validated design entries. Dassault Systèmes software tools consisted of 3D design objects in a project ignition kit, packaging and component designs, tools for storing and managing design data, computer-simulated testing and analysis, and tools to simulate the experience of the product—not to mention online and social media integration to foster intensive product design engagement, individually and socially.

In an interesting twist, in the fall of 2012, BMW, an established enterprise, teamed up with Local Motors to put on the BMW "Urban Driving Experience Challenge" through the Local Forge platform. Conducted by Local Motors through its design community, it aimed to stimulate new ideas in developing a city car for the year 2025. This was not a new vehicle design competition, but rather BMW sought to take BMW's Ultimate Driving Machine beyond working for the driver and passenger, "to benefit an area, a community, a city, and the world at large." According to Local Motors, the competition gave its community "the opportunity to identify and design premium vehicle features and functions that enhance the urban driving experience of the future." The objective of the challenge, according to BMW, was to "transform the car into a value-adding socially responsible machine that contributes to our global wellbeing." Doing good in the context of urban environments was the binding theme for the challenge. BMW focused on a set of specific available resources for the challenge, ranging from electric energy storage on board; highly connected telecom and cloud services; augmented reality in the car; windows as display screens; semiautomated driving functionalities; multiple sensors (such as onboard camera, radar, ultrasonic, and laser); drive information sharing between cars, people, neighbors, infrastructure, and the city; an application runtime for connected apps and functionalities within the car; and interfaces to access car functionalities from the outside world. In short, the goal was to use the Local Motors crowdsourcing platform to design a BMW product that would act as an engagement platform itself.[26]

It is worth emphasizing that an engagement platform is only as good as the engagement design of its constitutive components, as we saw in the Nike example. The same holds true for Local Motors. For instance, while Local Motors relies on a crowdsourced design engagement platform that taps into an open, global pool of automotive design talent, the interfaces, artifacts, and processes that underlie this engagement platform must be purposefully designed to actualize value to all co-creating stakeholders. Consider briefly the Peterbilt enterprise, which posed a challenge to redesign its Class 8 RIG truck on the Local Motors platform. To ensure inclusivity, bringing in stakeholders who would otherwise not have been engaged, special CAD tools and software assets had to be developed to enable the integration of an aluminum cab and to meet other required design restrictions. A highly advanced CAD tool might suppress inclusivity of designer talent and also result in fewer technically desirable offerings. Thus, Local Motors also needed to understand the intentionalities of participating individuals to foster creativity in a directed way. Different individuals within the client organization and different clients have different intentionalities, given varying expectations and goals. Local Motors continues to overcome resistance posed by internal development teams in client organizations, who may not view the incursion of Local Motors onto their turf favorably. This may require a new type of design environment and organizational adjustment to the change, including new workflows that involve thinking about design briefs, assets, and tools to facilitate discovery internally and externally. In turn, this may require training and mentoring to guide the behavioral transformation that the Local Motors platform requires. After all, the goal of the assemblage system is to ultimately transform value with, and for, all participating individuals.[27]

STRATEGY AND CO-CREATION THINKING

Following the illustrative examples of Nike and Local Motors, enterprises can now tap into talent and competencies anywhere in the world through platforms for mass collaboration and open innovation.[28] Simultaneously, enterprises can now tap into new sources of value based on individualized human experiences through platform-based product-service offerings. The concept of the co-creative enterprise as a nexus of engagement platforms that co-creates value together with stakeholders is all about connecting these new expansive resource and opportunity spaces. In doing so, it expands the frontiers of the very concept of enterprises, their boundaries, why they exist, how they organize, and how they collaborate and compete in heterogeneous ways.

Nobel laureate Ronald Coase famously argued in the 1930s that firms exist because of some market failure or a "cost to using the price mechanism."[29] Online marketplace firms (e.g., Amazon), as organizational forms, have emerged to further lower the transactions costs (e.g., search, contracting, and coordination) of buying and selling goods and services. This transaction cost–based view of the firm can be applied along every step of the chain of activities from conceiving to producing to delivering goods and services.[30] Further, Coase argued that a given firm would tend to expand its boundary until the cost of organizing within becomes equal to the cost of going to the marketplace. Thanks to the Internet, new firms have emerged all along the traditional value chain that make it efficient for other firms to outsource business processes to the market. Simultaneously, new organizational forms have emerged, as in the Local Motors example, which strategically blend the market with the boundary of the firm.[31]

Let us now step back to briefly review the evolution of value creation in the field of strategy, leading us to the point of co-creation, which is summarized in Table 1-1.[32] The traditional view of resources was primarily financial (cash), physical (plants), and human (labor). The role of managers was seen as allocating resources to competing opportunities within the firm. Implicit in this resource-based view of the firm was that resources are limited to what the firm owns.[33] These resources were assumed to determine the scope of activities inside and outside the discrete set of productive opportunities available to the firm. Subsequently, a wide variety of models were developed for appropriate allocation of resources across a diversified portfolio within the firm. Little or no synergies between business units were typically considered. Further, resource availability was restricted by viewing the diversified firm, for practical purposes, as a closed system of cash flows. In this view, value creation limits aspirations to means. In other words, strategy here is *Aspiration = Resources.*

A breakthrough in this thinking about value creation was developed in the 1990s. A diversified firm, by definition, must add more value than what the standalone businesses in the portfolio can. Corporate managers had to add additional value by the way they managed the portfolio. The whole had to be greater than the sum of the parts. At the same time, another development forced managers to rethink the very meaning of resources. If availability of resources was a source of competitive advantage, why were smaller, resource-disadvantaged competitors able to outperform their bigger rivals? The role of managers in creating a whole that is greater than the parts, and the need to explain the success of the smaller entrants against incumbents many times their size, led to a new conception of resources. Three basic premises emerged from the study of this phenomenon:[34]

- Resources are more than financial and physical. The accumulated intellectual resources (core competence) was equally critical and a new currency for managers to reckon with.

- The concept of resources is fungible. Resources can be expanded if we creatively leverage the resources of others through alliances and joint ventures.

- Most important, managers had to start with the view that "strategy is about stretch" in order to leverage resources—whether reusing and

TABLE 1-1 Shift in perspective on resources, opportunities, and value creation

	1960s–early 1980s	Late 1980s–early 1990s	1990s	2000+
Unit of analysis	Standalone business units	Corporation as a portfolio of competencies	Corporation as an extended network of suppliers and partners	Corporation as a global, competence base, including customers and talent from anywhere in the world
View of value creation in strategy	Fit: Aspirations = resources	Stretch: Aspirations > resources		Co-creation: Joint aspirations > joint resources
View of resources	Resource allocation	Resource leverage →		Access to competence (resources on demand)
View of opportunities	Product space	Solutions and services space →		Individual experience space
Value creation process	Unilaterally by the enterprise →			Jointly by the enterprise and stakeholding individuals

redeploying core competencies in new applications across businesses or changing industry norms.

These premises broke the prevailing mental model for senior managers. The view of their role as one of resource allocation was challenged. They had to be concerned about corporate resource leverage.[35] Further, it became obvious that core competence was as important a resource as cash and physical assets—maybe even more so. Leveraging internal competence across competing opportunities, especially in identifying and developing new businesses, became a yardstick of managerial capability.[36]

The notion of resources, however, still remained confined to the firm. It focused on seamless movement of competencies across what used to be standalone business units. This view demanded that learning and internalizing new knowledge from alliances and partners become a critical component of the conception of resources and value creation. Most important, it reintroduced the concept of entrepreneurship into the large, diversified firm. The essence of strategy (and entrepreneurship) was about doing more with less. Value creation in strategy shifted to *Aspirations > Resources*. Why internalize competencies into the firm when one could have access to competencies through a well-developed global resource base?[37] Thus, value creation evolved from resource allocation to resource leverage:

- internally across business units, thereby reducing capital intensity, speeding up new business development, reducing risks and costs; and

- externally across suppliers on a global basis to reduce investment intensity and costs, enhance quality, and facilitate rapid response time. This expanded the notion of the firm as a locus of resources (competencies and investment capacity) to the extended enterprise (a key network of global suppliers).

In the first decade of the new millennium, *customers* emerged as a source of competence.[38] Consider the case of the LEGO enterprise. As Jørgen Vig Knudstorp, CEO of the LEGO Group, commented, "At LEGO, we stumbled across the phenomenon of customer co-creation, which is now becoming a major innovation practice."[39] LEGO's Mindstorms robotics line allows individuals to create robots using the familiar LEGO bricks. Mindstorms 1.0 was released in 1998, featuring a microcomputer and snap-on infrared sensors. Using their PCs as a sandbox, users could write computer code and snap together blocks of code to build their robot—just like they would do with the studded LEGO bricks. To LEGO's surprise, Mindstorms rekindled the child in thousands of adults, who made up over half of Mindstorms users. Independent websites sprang up, allowing enthusiasts to share instructions on how to build robots ranging from sorting machines to intruder alarms to land rovers. Over time, Mindstorms fans began to experiment with advanced programming design software made available by other firms such as National Semiconductor (NSC). To sustain the interest of these enthusiasts using its software, NSC then reciprocated by showcasing its work at robotics leagues. An entire ecosystem of capabilities was born.

Further opening up its design, LEGO invited enthusiasts to take part in the programming of the user interface of Mindstorms. In the fall of 2006, LEGO introduced Mindstorms 2.0 NXT, which features programmable "intelligent bricks" and new capabilities for motion and touch, as well as a range of new sensors such as gyroscopes and accelerometers. NXT includes a programming interface called LabView, which was co-developed with a select group of LEGO enthusiasts, some of whom have advanced degrees in robotics. For the launch, LEGO selected several robotics buffs from a large pool of applicants (many of whom already had their own blogs dedicated to Mindstorms), gave them access to inside information, and encouraged them to write about their impressions of NXT. LEGO also set up a message board allowing users to discuss their experiences with the new product generation and encouraged them to share pictures of their creative inventions. At that point, LEGO was no longer solely engaging a community of fans in designing, developing, and marketing Mindstorms NXT. It was now encouraging the community to evolve beyond the firm's control, doing much more than act as an extension of the firm's development resources: the Mindstorms community represented a whole new competence base, in creative conjunction with employees of LEGO.[40]

The traditional LEGO brick has benefited from digitization to enable customers to unleash their own creative imagination in expanded ways through joint value creation based on individualized experiences.

Using LEGO Digital Designer software, customers can now design and build any model they can imagine. They simply download the software, free of charge, and can then start designing from scratch or choose one of a number of starter models. Then they can upload their designs to the LEGO Factory Gallery, where designs can be stored and shared with other users. Designers could choose to have their own products manufactured for a fee. Customer-designed products featured the customer designer's picture on the box, and LEGO could also choose a few of the most popular customer designs for mass production.[41] The company also works closely with individual retail stores and develops unique offerings with them.

Within the LEGO Factory, the company turbocharged an online community that attempts to engage individuals from its player base (of over 400 million people) through message boards and a website called My LEGO Network. The dialogue created through these forums allows enthusiasts to exchange ideas. The company's core audience is children, but a large group of adult "super-users" (known as AFOL, Adult Fans of LEGO) also participate in the generation of product ideas, or downright invention of new products, such as LEGO Architecture, a good example of a fan-created enterprise on the LEGO platform that is also transforming the souvenir industry.[42] LEGO has become the supply chain for super-fans turned architects, manufacturing the bricks for the products they make, which they, along with the community, and supported by LEGO, distribute globally.[43] Thus, LEGO's strategy spans product-service offerings themselves as engagement platforms, as well as engagement platforms involving traditional building kits and customized products with retailers. Throughout, as Jørgen Vig Knudstorp, CEO of the LEGO Group, notes, "We gained a better appreciation of technique and touch, and a mindset that is crucial for successful co-creation. As we have learned, co-creation is not about just 'following rules,' but personal engagement is essential."

While every major shift in connecting value creation resources and opportunities has come with a new set of managerial requirements and social and technical infrastructure challenges, the role of the firm and the customer (and other nontraditional stakeholders like consumer communities) remained distinct until the turn of the millennium. The relationship between the consumer and the firm, which used to be bilateral (a standalone consumer has been the dominant organizing principle in both management and economic theory), has given way to firms having to deal with consumer communities that are well organized. The relationship can be bilateral and multilateral at the same time. Consumers, and individuals at large, want to influence how they will be served and therefore want to be involved in the activities typically thought of as internal to the firm. These entail qualitative differences in access to resources and the value creation process. The process of value creation shifts away from a firm and product-centric approach to a stakeholding individual and experience-based perspective. Global resource leverage using engagement platforms is enabling the transformation to this new value creation perspective, oriented toward co-creation of experience-based value—value that is unique to individuals, both personally and collectively.

The sources of competence available to managers have expanded yet again to include the *collective intelligence in the whole global system*—with the ability to rapidly source and access talent, expertise, knowledge, and skills from anywhere and anytime in the world, as we saw through the Local Motors and Nike examples. In this new view, strategy has become *Joint Aspirations > Joint Resources*. The managerial changes from this shift toward embracing all stakeholding individuals as co-creators of value are summarized in Table 1-2.

THE CO-CREATION PARADIGM OF VALUE CREATION

As shown in Figure 1-3, co-creation expands value creation as a paradigm in three fundamental ways:[44]

- how we conceive the *intensive* construction of value—value as enactment of agency through creative, intentional, integrative, and transformative engagement platforms;

- how we frame the *actual* nature of value—value as being embodied in dialogic, transparent, accessible, and reflexive domains of stakeholder experiences; and

- how we deepen the *virtual* sources of value—value as emerging from inclusive, generative, linkable, and evolvable ecosystems of capabilities.

TABLE 1-2 Strategic need and managerial manifestation of co-creation thinking

Strategic need	Managerial manifestation
Accelerating value creation opportunities and growth	Using interactions as the locus of value creation Accumulation of environment, individual, and interaction data, experiential learning, real-time insights, rapid knowledge New strategic capital and rapid discovery of new value creation opportunities Deeper collaboration with multiple enterprises and stakeholders
Reducing investment and capital intensity	Access to competence and capabilities in community-based ecosystems Using network resources to scale up and down quickly Convert fixed costs to variable ones
Reducing resource and skill intensity	Leveraging open and social resources, as well as multienterprise network resources
Reducing risks and operating costs	Involvement of multiple stakeholders in execution and formulation of enterprise initiatives Focus on efficiency in interactions and experience-based value creation Increase speed to actualization of value

As we will see in Chapter 2 in more detail, it is the purposeful innovation and engagement design of assemblages of persons, processes, interfaces, and artifacts that make for an effective co-creation engagement platform. The early movement of co-creation emphasized those individuals who were typically not included in the process of value creation, such as consumers. For instance, there were clearly delineated roles of producer and consumer. The former's role was to produce products that embodied value and enter into a process of exchange with consumers whose role was to consume products. Supply versus demand, with distinct roles of producers and consumers, was the bedrock of how markets, and by implication economies, were conceived. But, letting go of fixed roles, treating every individual as someone with a say in value creation, and recognizing that others' perspectives on interactions, outcomes, and value may not necessarily coincide with one's own, are critical. In this sense, co-creation is not only about intensifying engagements with those that are already included but also engagements that are multisided and designing systems of engagements purposefully by recognizing the creativity, intentionality, integrativity, and transformativity of interactions in creating value together.

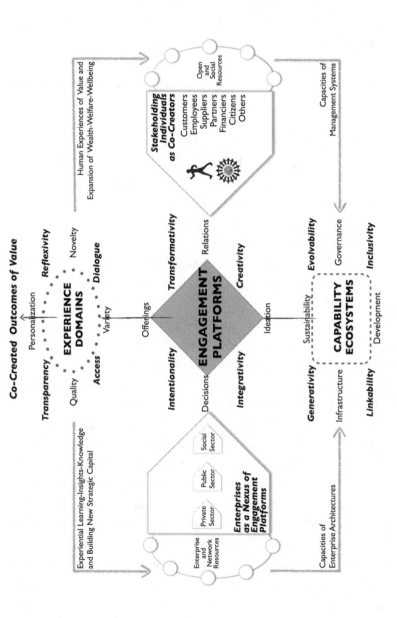

FIGURE 1-3   The co-creation paradigm of value creation

Note: Co-creation is joint creation and evolution of value *with stakeholding individuals*, intensified and enacted through *platforms of engagements,* virtualized and emergent from *ecosystems of capabilities,* and actualized and embodied in *domains of experiences,* expanding *wealth-welfare-wellbeing.*

As individuals jointly create and cultivate outcomes of change through engagement platforms, the domains of stakeholder experiences are where value is actualized and embodied. Therefore, as we discuss in Chapter 3, enterprises must pay attention to the configuration of co-creation experiences. We elaborate on how experiential learning, insights, and knowledge must be plowed back into the (re)design of engagement platforms. Chapter 4 discusses and illustrates how enterprises can go about building ecosystems of capabilities in the social, business, civic, and natural communities in which stakeholders exist and enterprise operations are enveloped. In the co-creation view, customers and all other stakeholders are seen as expanding the firm's competence base (resources and skills) in a process of joint value creation together. Co-creation can occur inside enterprises with employees as stakeholders; externally with customers, suppliers, partners, and other external stakeholders; and within and across the private, public, and social sectors.

Chapter 5 discusses the building of co-creative management systems across all the various value creating functional activities of enterprises. These range from customer-facing activities to channel and brand-building activities, to supplier and logistical activities, to new product-service development activities, to internal operational activities, to talent and project management activities, and all the way to strategy, performance, and enterprise risk management activities, all of which must undergo the appropriate enterprise transformation to migrate to co-creation. Chapter 6 discusses how co-creative enterprises must build and evolve the technical, social, and organizational architectures of co-creation platforms. Chapter 7 discusses how to achieve transformational change to build co-creative enterprises from the inside out. Any enterprise seeking to migrate to co-creation with its customers, partners, and other external stakeholders needs to begin with the nature of engagement between management and all co-creators inside the enterprise in a process of co-creative enterprise transformation. Building co-creative enterprises calls for innovating and designing co-creation platforms of engagements for creating the organizational change together with stakeholding individuals.

Chapter 8 discusses the evolution of economies and societies through the paradigm of co-creation, one where the convergence of private-public-social sector enterprise ecosystems on the experiences of stakeholding individuals expands value creation in economy and society in new ways. Such a convergence can build human capabilities and unleash human potential in new value creation in the world, in ways we are only just beginning to grasp. In the co-creation-based view, it is not necessary to make a distinction between value creation and appropriation as such. Co-creatively leveraging all stakeholder capabilities in meshworks of social, business, civic, and natural communities can lead to better states of governance, infrastructure, development, and sustainability, with "win more–win more" outcomes and expansion of wealth-welfare-wellbeing all around. Chapter 9 discusses this in more detail. Chapter 10 concludes the book with a summary of key perspectives in how co-creation transforms value creation and challenges in embracing the co-creation paradigm in enterprises, economies, and societies.

2 INNOVATING CO-CREATION PLATFORMS OF ENGAGEMENTS

Enterprise, as organizing agency, connects value creation opportunities with resources through platforms of engagements, as we saw in Chapter 1. Engagement platforms can be innovated anywhere in the value creation system and can be purposefully designed to engage different stakeholders around their individual domains of experiences. Value is a function of the co-creation experiences of individuals, both their experiences in interacting through the platform and the experiences of outcomes that result.

In this chapter, we delve into the innovation of co-creation platforms of engagements in more detail. Using an illustrative example of the Apple enterprise, we discuss how assemblages of Persons, Processes, Interfaces, and Artifacts (or APPI for short, as a handy mnemonic) must come together to constitute distinct "systems of engagements" that expand enterprise value creation in new ways.

We then elaborate on the co-creative engagement design principles of Creativity, Intentionality, Integrativity, and Transformativity (or CITI for short, as a handy mnemonic) and illustrate how they intensify co-creating actions among individuals and instantiate desirable and powerful states of engagement platforms through the interaction environments they afford.

We then return to the Apple enterprise example and conclude by motivating how enterprises must build a strategic architecture of multiple co-creation platforms of engagements everywhere in the ecosystem. This strategic architecture must enable and connect with stakeholder experiences to actualize value (see the top half of Figure 1-3 from Chapter 1 and the elaborative discussion in Chapter 3), while harnessing ecosystems of capabilities in the social, business, civic, and natural communities in which the enterprises operate (see the bottom half of Figure 1-3 and the elaborative discussion in Chapter 4).

ENGAGEMENT PLATFORMS AND INTENSIVE VALUE CREATION

An engagement platform affords environments of interactions, as shown in Figure 2-1. Consider Apple's Retail Stores. From the moment one walks into an Apple Store, the aesthetics of its layout draw you in. You can play with Apple products as if you already owned them. In many traditional stores, the product layout feels like an extension of the inventory room in the back. Not so at the Apple Store. Comparatively few products are spaciously arranged on large wooden tables, which avoids the traditional display cacophony in most retail stores.

The store environment is the stratum through which assemblages come to life for individuals experiencing the store. The physical layout and its implied aesthetic entail a "territorialization" of any assemblage: a physical arrangement of human/nonhuman objects and aesthetics, with all attendant meanings customers may accord them. All the components in the store have both content and expressive roles.[45] The store layout has a typical museum aesthetic where objects are supposed to be engaged with "intrinsically." In other words, the objects disclose something about themselves, the world, and ourselves (i.e., as entities being-in-the-world). This particular arrangement is not simply about physical coordination of content but expression of certain aesthetic values and imperatives.

To see the store as an engagement platform, we can pick any of the four APPI components of assemblages and bring in the other three components to instantiate an engagement platform. Let us start with *artifacts*. Customers can interact with an iPad, iPhone, iPod, or Apple TV; listen to a song or watch a video; or browse the Web. With the Apple laptops or iMac, they can experience various accessories in use. Apple employees are

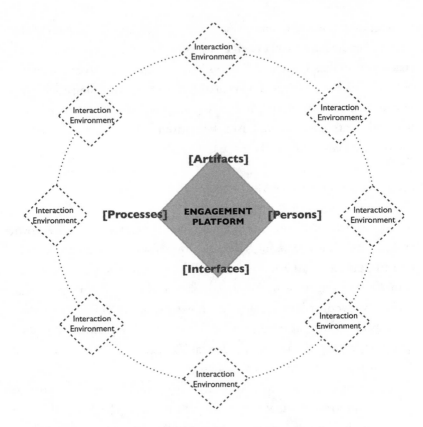

FIGURE 2-1   Engagement platforms

Note: An engagement platform is an assemblage of persons, processes, interfaces, and artifacts, whose engagement design affords environments of interactions that intensify agential actions in value creation.

nearby if you need them without any overt sales pressure. The customer gains from the interactions in terms of learning about the products and how to use them and testing the value of interactions with the products before purchase. Apple, through its employees, can rapidly gain insights into how people actually use the products, the kinds of questions they have, and how to help customers in the context of their value generation through Apple's products, sharing their learning from one customer to the next, and learning from each customer's past experiences and future intentions.

Hence, Apple employees are networked with everything else in the store in relations of exteriority, and any assemblage component can be flexibly reconnected. Employees function as catalysts for the consistency of experiences with the Apple product ecosystem's heterogeneous components. For customers, assemblages of the moment constitute a system of engagements: cognitive, emotional, and behavioral attachments. In many traditional stores, one's engagements fail to emerge into a coherent valuable unity—that is, platforms can also fail to constitute a system of valuable engagements.

In the case of Apple, the store also intends to afford a learning environment over and beyond a classic sales environment. The store is designed as a gateway for ordinary people to combat "feature-itis"—technology companies' tendency to overemphasize their products' features. At Apple Stores, both potential and past buyers (particularly nonteens) who think RAM is a goat, megahertz is a car rental company, and iCloud is a fluffy white thing in the sky can get plain answers to confounding questions like "How do I get a movie into my iPad and watch it on my TV?" or "How can I create a photo album and share it with Grandma?" In other words, Apple Stores enable agential action entailing various material, semiotic, and social flows across its assemblage systems—"deterritorializations"—creating new ways for all its assemblage elements to function and thereby generating new outcomes and experiences of value as a result.

Now consider another environment starting with *persons* that work for Apple. The famous Genius Bar environment is where knowledgeable Apple employees address any issues customers have with Apple's offerings and encourage them to ask questions and try out products and services with their help. The Genius Bar creates a uniquely original interaction between the Apple employee and the customer. Instead of offering a faceless call center interaction that prevents customers from demonstrating their struggles with the actual product-service at hand, the Genius Bar allows the customer to make an appointment by phone or online or with an in-store concierge at the entrance to the store and, for no additional cost, talk with a designated Genius employee who can answer questions and diagnose the repair or service issue. Yes, the employee in this case is a customer service staff member like many enterprises have, but this one is also "supposedly a genius." To be successful, the activated interaction environment that includes the "genius" must constitute a system of valuable engagements through creative, intentional, integrative, and transformative design. (We discuss these four elements of engagement platform design in more detail in the next section.) For now, note that the environments from the enterprise side have been designed decidedly for "two-sided" engagement of individuals that is more down-to-earth, encouraging "dumb questions" with more emphasis on "Bar" than on "Genius." This "collective assemblage of enunciation" conjures up a whole system of meanings and practices one typically associates with bars. But it is not your typical bar, since instead of a witty "bartender," it has a geeky "genius" who is bending conventions around the signifier "bar." Indeed, the Genius Bar itself is a carefully designed physical environment, typically located in the rear of the store (or another floor), with clear signage and a display of the appointment schedule on overhead TVs. Customers sit shoulder-to-shoulder on high stools, leaning over a long lightwood bar, speaking with employees wearing the obligatory black or blue T-shirt of the Apple creative set. There is clear "territoriality" achieved through location, signage, and appointment scheduling. Further, the artifacts in this assemblage have both content and expression that signify a bar aesthetic and mentality.

Another interaction environment afforded by the Apple Store as an engagement platform is a personal training environment for $99 a year. In these one-to-one sessions, a customer can engage with a personal trainer on whatever the customer wants to learn: how to get a new laptop ready for use, how to migrate from a previous laptop, how to edit photos, or any other "how-to" questions. While the customer learns, the upside for the company is in cultivating deeper and more authentic relations with the company; often the customer may buy additional products (Apple also sells approved non-Apple products in its stores) once he or she sees how they might be useful. For example, once a customer has become proficient at taking photographs, she might want to explore advanced photo-editing software.

Now consider *processes* of engagement in the Apple Store. A concierge orients entering customers, directing them to appropriate parts of the store, arranging an appointment at the Genius Bar for walk-ins, or even ordering online from the Apple Store (all using Apple devices). Note that earlier we had artifacts and persons acting as content and expression. Now we can see how processes can play the same dual role. A concierge not only dispatches a set of various processes but also signifies a "hospitality" atmosphere—and an upscale one at that. You expect to get pampered, taken care of, or whatever your needs might be, putting you at ease. There is a conspicuous absence of "checkout" counters in Apple Stores (especially smaller store formats), with precious retail space being used for the Genius Bar. Instead, roving Apple employees perform checkouts with Apple devices with compact paper receipt printers hidden underneath the very tables that display Apple products. With no "check-in" turnstiles and no "checkout" counters to negotiate with, the Apple Store is a much more accessible extension of the street or mall in which it is embedded, affording more fluid encounters. Note how this also adds to the already hybrid nature of the Apple Store environment. It is like a museum, a plaza, and a jeweler all rolled into one, but all these different meanings are signified by different APPI components of the assemblage. Of course, there are pure business implications as well (efficiency, higher margins, and so on), but the customers and the staff also have completely different "affects" triggered, and multiple other semiotic/social flows are enabled.

While most retail environments focus on the moment of the purchase transaction (e.g., getting the customer to buy as quickly and as much as possible through the exasperating "cross-sell"), the Apple Store design enables customer interaction environments that come long before the purchase (browsing, touching, and evaluating) and long after it (Genius Bar, one-on-one trainer). These before-and-after customer interaction environments have modest economic value in and of themselves, but they are what drive the actual purchase of Apple's offerings—through a timing and relationship that are controlled by the customer but are heavily influenced by Apple.

Finally, consider the various *interfaces* in/with the store and through the Apple Store app. You can make an appointment with the Genius Bar or personal trainer, place a product order online and track your deliveries, or pick up an item you ordered at a nearby store (personal pickup customers are given priority over those who have the item delivered to their home). With EasyPay, customers can scan the barcodes of accessories in the store; get reviews, ratings, and product specs; and pay for them within the app in self-checkout fashion. Of course, Apple's (mobile) devices are themselves interfaces to a larger world of play, exploration, and discovery of entertainment, productivity, and lifestyle media. Consider, for instance, the ease with which one can string together photos on an Apple device and send the photo album to a widescreen TV through AirPlay for a family room experience, replete with a music playlist to accompany the slideshow. These interactive assemblage configurations must be experienced to fully understand their virtual personal and social value. Note that all the activities that might result in learning bits and pieces of Apple "specs" (e.g., technical features of Apple products) would not necessarily amount to a system of "valuable" engagements. The assemblage systems constitute designed systems of engagements that *attempt* to connect with human experiences. It is important to constantly keep this in mind. In other words, *value is enacted in designed platform engagements but embodied in actual co-creation experiences.* We return to this crucial point in more detail in the next chapter.

CO-CREATIVE ENGAGEMENT DESIGN

The principles of creativity, intentionality, integrativity, and transformativity are key to the co-creative engagement design of platforms. Briefly, enterprises need to understand how all participants can unleash their creative energy through platform engagements. Individuals must have access to tools to express their creativity. The co-creative design of engagements must also consider the intentions of participating stakeholders.[46] Different individuals may have different intentionalities, given varying expectations and goals. What individuals want to do and accomplish on a platform, and how, must be understood. Then, engagement processes must be integrated into enterprise business processes and decision-making routines and activities. Finally, the assemblage must facilitate the transformation of interactions to valuable outcomes, through better risk-reward relationships, meaningful stakeholder experiences, and further enhancement of stakeholders' creative capacities.

Now let us examine these principles in more detail. Co-creative engagement design starts with a default position of everyday *creativity* as capacity and motive for ongoing growth and development, applicable to any domain of human endeavor. The way we perceive and intend things is "as further opportunities for action." In other words, all agencies are fundamentally creative, and creativity is immanent to action. Creativity in engagement is about expression, where some dominant initial form is transformed and reorganized to communicate a new meaning or insight.[47] It is about generating a solution to a problem through a new possibility that cannot be obtained deductively or causally from some known or habitual data. It is also about production in relation to the objective world of matter, energy, and life as conditions and means of action, with labor manifesting agential powers as object-related activity and as *pro*-duction, creating novelty.[48]

Creativity as historical disclosing entails sensing and holding on to inconsistencies in one's current disclosive engagements, intensive practical involvement, and experimentation in history-making practices of articulation, cross-appropriation, and reconfiguration.[49] Creativity in engagement, then, is about "difference" as a positive power to differentiate, producing intensities from virtual capacities and tendencies, with each actualization of difference unfolding new potentialities.[50] In other words, creative engagement enhances the possibility of transformation of outcomes (and individual capacities) in value creation. *Markets in the co-creation view arise from a nexus of differences*, understood in the particular sense we just introduced, over and beyond a nexus of exchanges.

The *intentionality* principle is about more than just paying attention to intentions. It includes beliefs, hopes, and judgments in a more pervasive feature of agency as pointing toward or attending to. Values are embedded in the general background in all our intentional relations.[51] Derived from the Latin word *intentio*, meaning "being directed toward some goal or thing," intentionality entails a bodily intertwining of individual perception and the perceived world as a range of possibilities teleologically ordered in terms of fulfilling purposes.[52] Agents project themselves into the present and the future by taking up practical projects and purposes—that is, culturally available possibilities. Intentionality at any point—awareness—is directed toward the current task and its implications for the larger project. Intentionality is not anterior to actual action but an ongoing accomplishment of reflection on prereflective desires and tendencies coursing through bodies in their engagements with their environments.[53]

Through engagement platforms, individual agents can mesh subplans and reasons and take others' plans and reasons as normative constraints. They can openly express readiness to be jointly committed to others. Participatory intentions can be interrelated through an engagement structure to coordinate planning, negotiation, and action across participants. Shared agency entails "we-intentions" as a distinct feature and not a mere summation of individual acts. Collective agency entails joint intentions to shared goals, interdependence, and common awareness in addition to individual contributions.[54] The establishment of engagement structures of interrelated intentions implies paying attention to how individuals relate to what the group will do, how individuals relate to the whole activity, and how individuals relate only to their part. In "we-mode" joint action, the engagement structure must enable processes that the group has conceptually constructed for itself to express collective intentionality and how individuals want to act as a group from being a private person in a group context to acting as a group member.

The *integrativity* of engagement design is concerned with facilitating information, control, and material flows across organizational boundaries by connecting all the necessary functions and heterogeneous functional entities (information systems, devices, applications, and people) in order to improve communication, cooperation, and coordination within the system so that it behaves as an integrated whole, therefore enhancing its overall productivity, flexibility, and capacity for management of change (or reactivity).[55] Integrativity arises from the grasping together as a system, the yet unrelated potentials in heterogeneous multiplicities.[56] Integrativity is a function of protocols. If networks are the structures that connect organisms and machines (the actors), then protocols are the rules that make sure the connections actually work (the actions). Protocols emerge through the complex relationships between autonomous, interconnected agents.

Transformativity means enabling the possibility of change in the form of value and, ultimately, states of agency (with respect to stakeholder relations, decisions, ideation, and offerings), which results in "win more–win more" outcomes. At a basic level, transformative engagement entails enhancing risk-reward outcomes in existing value creation relationships (recall the Nike example in Chapter 1) or in radically new co-creative designs of business concepts and operating models (recall the Local Motors example in Chapter 1). At a more intensive level, going back to the metaphor of "color mixing" in co-creative engagement (see Chapter 1), stakeholders as individuals (yellow) transform value together with enterprises (blue) in co-creative engagement. The magic that emerges (green) is a result of the transformation, but both yellow and blue are embedded in it. Symbiotic becoming in an assemblage implies the emergence of new properties for the whole that go above and beyond a simple aggregation of heterogeneous parts. In other words, it is not like a yellow LEGO piece and a blue LEGO piece coming together, where each of the individual pieces remains intact. Rather, it is like "color mixing"—a power of *becoming*. Transformativity is about differentiating and connecting forces, spatially and temporally, as a source of creation of meaning and value and manifested as new affectivity.[57]

The design of engagements in platforms must enable the transformation of stakeholder experiences to create valuable outcomes together. Individual agents affect the environments of engagement platforms and are affected by it. Agencies and states of an engagement platform are products of becoming; they are not transitions initiated or steered by something else. As individuals immerse themselves in the flow of co-creative engagement, they become more than themselves—using the human power of imagination to overcome the human body, as it were.[58]

In sum, *a co-creation platform of engagements is only as good as the creative, intentional, integrative, and transformative design of the assemblage system of engagements it instantiates.* We now return to the Apple enterprise example to illustrate and motivate this dictum, this time from the perspective of software developers as stakeholding individuals, in addition to end customers. Consider Apple's online App Store. This is where customers of Apple's mobile devices such as the iPhone, iPod Touch, and iPad have made over 50 billion downloads from over 775,000 apps as of June 2013, just five years after its launch and still counting. These apps are available thanks to over 275,000 registered software developers (who pay $99 per year each). The prices of the applications are set by the developers themselves (after basic screening by Apple) and range from "free" to "fee," with most priced under $5. Apple splits the revenue with developers on a 30 to 70 percent basis. In the first five years, Apple paid out over $5 billion.

Apple is designing for creativity in its co-creation platform of engagements. Through its SDK (Software Development Kit) assemblage system, Apple makes it easy for anybody with software development talent to engage in creating apps that engender new types of mobile end-user experiences. Software developers as app designers, entrepreneurs, and partnering enterprises can play together in a giant sandbox organized by Apple. The SDK system consists of applications programming interfaces, development tools, and resources such as programming frameworks, code templates, and tutorials that help developers better understand Apple's iOS platform that powers its mobile devices. Yet, the core layers of the technology behind SDK and its integration through iOS are proprietary to Apple, allowing it to enable a smooth, integrative environment of interactions for users of apps on Apple's devices, with over 700 million iOS devices having been sold to date.

What's key here are the Apple device simulators that allow developers to experience apps exactly as users would experience them. This is one way for Apple to ensure that intentionalities of developers can be brought into joint alignment with that of users. The same goes for the intentionalities among developers themselves and the Apple designers and engineers. At Apple's annual World Wide Developers Conference, developers engage both online with Apple and the developer community at large and "live" with over 1,000 participating Apple engineers. In addition to keynotes and demos, the conference has skills competitions, app design awards, and user interface design labs and workshops. For the developer set, the conference offers extensive code fixing and learning "Genius Bars" of sorts, with the "geniuses" here being over 1,000 participating skilled Apple engineers. Through its experience-based application development frameworks, Apple brings consistency to the quality of both applications development and applications use environments, while simultaneously giving enormous flexibility to developers in providing a wide variety of offerings and user experiences.

The Apple enterprise example also illustrates a process of integrative engagement through the use of live meetings and a dedicated SDK website as a complementary engagement platform, so Apple can build it *with* them. For instance, Apple has encouraged developers to share their development experiences both with Apple and with the community of other developers. By giving developers the ability to "visually compare" the performance of different parts of the mobile application and sharing this information with Apple's internal teams, Apple rapidly learned about the performance of applications early on. It also generated insights with selected business customers such as Johnson & Johnson (J&J) into how they wanted to use the iOS devices to create offerings in their own platform co-creation with consumers. For instance, J&J has integrated the iPhone into its LifeScan Glucose Monitor System. Imagine a young teenage girl who is a diabetic. She has to track her glucose and give herself insulin injections. Using the new J&J system, she does not have to figure out how much insulin she has to take before her meal. She can instead go into the meal builder app on her iPhone, pick the type of food she wants to eat, and use the app to estimate how many carbohydrates she will be taking in. The app then calculates the insulin dose that she needs. She can also view all of her previous readings and thus track her condition. In addition, she can communicate with parents, caretakers, doctors, and other diabetics and send both her glucose numbers and a message on the iPhone.

Apple distributes certified applications through its App Store, where Apple has over 400 million accounts (with credit cards on file). For many small developers, paying 30 percent of revenues for such wide access to a distribution and billing infrastructure is attractive. At the same time, Apple also provides tools for users to give reviews and ratings on the App Store, providing feedback to developers as well. This is where transformativity of the co-creation platform kicks in. Apps that show growth trends are advertised and promoted for free by Apple both in the App Store and in commercials. Consider the free application Tap Tap Revenge that Apple reports was one of the most popular free iPhone games in the first year of the App Store, with over 3 million downloads that year. This application challenges players to keep up with catchy tunes by tapping in the right spots on the phone's screen. It has evolved into a Web-age mobile stage for musicians and consumers. As noted by one of its founders who helped create a social Web browser called Flock, "It took two years and north of $5 million to bring Flock to market. In this case, the longest you spend building an iPhone application is three months, and it takes four or five people. There's less risk in terms of betting millions and years on something that might not work." Notwithstanding a better risk-reward relationship for Tapulous, the start-up that was created behind this application, music companies and artists interested in promoting their tracks flocked to this app. It also increased music sales inspired by the songs; for instance, in October 2008, players of this application bought over 50,000 copies of the feature track "Hot N Cold" by the pop singer Katy Perry. Tapulous now has paid versions for under $5 aimed at fans of specific genres of music or artists (e.g., the Dave Matthews Band) being released periodically. Apple of course benefits from each song sold (through its iTunes music store) as well as application sales. After Apple's 30 percent cut for the paid application, artists and music labels get paid for licensing their songs, and Tapulous keeps the rest, in addition to the revenues from those advertisements that appear alongside the games. In this fashion, the App Store continues to expand the value creation pie in "win more–win more" fashion, across the thousands of applications that generate a variety of new experiences through the iOS platform.

These examples also imply paying attention to stakeholder co-creation experiences in actualizing value on the one hand (as we elaborate on further in Chapter 3) and successfully leveraging co-creative enterprise ecosystems of capabilities on the other (as we elaborate on further in Chapter 4). Thus, Apple is bridging:

- "developer think" about user experiences, with
- "user think" about user experiences, with
- Apple's own "company think" about designing for developer experiences, with
- Apple's own "company think" about user experiences.

More broadly, the Apple enterprise example suggests that enterprises using upstream innovation methods to tap into talent outside the enterprise, such as crowdsourcing, mass collaboration, and open innovation, must incorporate the co-creation experiences of stakeholding entities to be successful. Further, enterprises have to connect, as Apple has done, "downstream co-creation" (e.g., the iOS mobile device as an engagement platform for you and I as end-users) with "upstream co-creation" (e.g., the iOS SDK as an engagement platform with developers and Apple's partners).

CRAFTING A STRATEGIC ARCHITECTURE OF CO-CREATION PLATFORMS

The instantiation of assemblages as engagement platforms requires not only purposefully designing interaction environments afforded by the assemblage but also strategically architecting a portfolio of multiple co-creation platforms of engagements, seamlessly networked as depicted in Figure 2-2.

The strategic architecture of the Apple iTunes store (with its assortment of music, movies, books, and more), within which the App Store itself is ensconced, entails multiple engagement platforms affording multiple, linked interaction environments. Customers' experiences of apps (like Apple's products in the Apple Retail Store) go all the way from the searching and browsing environments of apps to the actual purchase and download of apps. The iTunes store is a software platform that resides on devices bridging Apple's entertainment store on the Web. A "Genius" recommendation software is built into iTunes. These "geniuses," unlike those in the physical Apple Retail Store, are software agents that peek at your music collection—with your permission—and suggest tunes you might like given what you already have and mixes from your collection. Apple's Genius software is a creative combination of the tunes you like based on your own ratings, tunes you have compiled in your playlists, tunes others have in their playlists, and tunes others buy. Customers enjoy the freedom of continuously discovering new music and are creatively engaged in assembling tunes for specific contexts (e.g., a workout with NikePlus, or dining alfresco, or dancing at a wedding reception, or simply by genres or artists for different moods) or sharing those playlists with others. Radio stations in iTunes, to radio apps in the AppStore from Pandora to TuneIn, also extend the assemblage system, allowing new entities to "plug into" Apple's ecosystem. These "intra-actions"—that is, assemblages of other interactions translated to the site by mediators among agencies—entail connected assemblage systems, distinct only in relation to their mutual

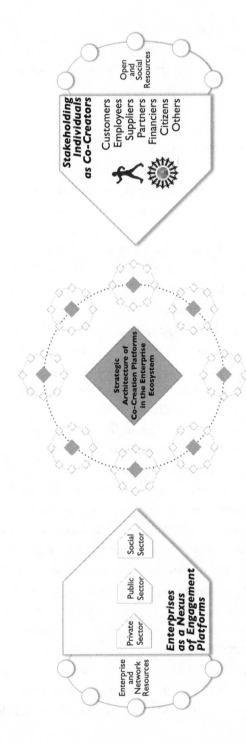

FIGURE 2-2   Crafting a strategic architecture of co-creation platforms

entanglement. Such agency is a local and partially connected event-site of production, mediation, and transformation, embedded and circulating in meshworks of communities, whose capabilities are leveraged by Apple inclusively into its enterprise ecosystem. Over time, this also allows for the coevolution of Apple's ecosystem offerings. For instance, Apple's iOS 7 launched in late 2013 included a built-in personalized radio station, and its new iPhone 5s came with a new motion co-processor M7 chip with contextual awareness capabilities (knowing whether the individual is stationary, walking, running, driving, etc., in addition to location), and Core Motion software interface, which in turn enabled Nike to augment its NikeFuel offering with a new fitness app, Nike+Move. As Phil Schiller, Apple's marketing chief, remarked during the launch of iPhone 5s, "With new software and applications, you're going to get a whole new level of health and fitness solutions never before possible on a mobile phone." It also paves the way for new wearable technology-enabled offerings and for Apple to start learning about the wearable device market and what consumers want, starting with the Nike partnership.[59]

Thus, crafting a strategic architecture of co-creation platforms not only entails the innovation of systems of engagements that afford interaction environments for creating value together with individuals but also innovation of the *platforms themselves*, together with platform-building enterprise partners (e.g., technology leveraging companies), as well as meshworks of communities. In the case of the Apple enterprise, it has tapped into the value of its global network of developers, business partners, customers, and fans, all of whom contribute to the strategic architecture and evolution of Apple's engagement platforms on the one hand—thereby spawning new sources of value creation—while facilitating co-creation experiences and outcomes of value on the other. Apple's strategic architecture of engagement platforms as offerings spans multiple assemblage systems. These systems range from the iTunes store (with the App store built into it) to its iPods, iPhones, and iPads; to its Macbooks and iMacs; to the Apple TV platform, all of which are anchored around its mobile iOS and desktop OS X operating systems. It also includes the Retail Apple Store platform "on the ground" and the iCloud platform that provides a unified framework for synchronizing multiple devices and their contents and expression "in the cloud." Apple's strategic architecture of its enterprise ecosystem also entails "external stakeholder engagement platforms"—from the iOS SDK as a platform with developers and Apple's partners; to platforms that involve its global supply chain, operational resource network, channel partners, and Apple user communities; to platforms for communicating with the financial investment community and other external stakeholder entities. It also includes the "internal stakeholder engagement platforms" that involve employees in Apple's internal and stakeholder-facing value creating activities.

Like any enterprise attempting to practice co-creation, Apple must constantly keep in mind that platform engagements are embedded in domains of individual co-creation experiences as the ultimate embodiment of value. The "jailbreak communities" of Apple's iOS devices can be leading indicators of feasible features desired by users, which is not surprising considering that these power users are driven by experience-based needs. This is not to legitimize all their activities, but the reality is that there are many desired features that are often already feasible or that exist in competing offerings (a case in point is the new mobile dashboard of frequently used settings in iOS 7). The key point is that Apple, like any other enterprise, must strive to afford interaction environments that enable *a variety of novel, personalized co-creation experiences*. At the same time, it must also connect with the *actual, lived quality of co-creation experiences*.

Leaders of the future must be orchestrators of co-creative engagement everywhere in the ecosystem in which the enterprise is enveloped. This implies leveraging network and stakeholder resources and accessing competencies in the ecosystem to support a strategic architecture of co-creation platforms. Most important, leaders must put the domain of stakeholder experiences at the center of the enterprise's strategic architecture of co-creation platforms, such that enterprises and stakeholders can engage in more effective joint value creation, where individuals can shape their own co-creation experiences. In the next chapter, we discuss how co-creative enterprises can successfully enable and connect with the co-creation experiences of individuals.

3   ENABLING AND CONNECTING WITH CO-CREATION EXPERIENCES

Innovating and designing co-creation platforms of engagements (and not just products-services) have become the basis of value creation in an increasingly commoditized world where informed, connected, socially networked, and empowered individuals seek to construct valuable experiences. As we saw in the previous chapter, strategic co-creation platform architectures afford multiple engagement platforms and interaction environments that must be designed through the lens of individual (stakeholder) experiences.

We begin this chapter with a look at engagement platforms from the view of individuation of co-creation experiences. Using the example of OnStar, we motivate:

- how platforms of engagements are embedded in co-creation domains of stakeholder experiences and must be enabled by experience-centric capabilities;[60] and

- how enterprises must enable the individuation of co-creation experiences through experience-based value creation networks that entail multiple partners, services, and collaborative communities.

We then discuss the configuration of co-creation experiences through the principles of Dialogue, Transparency, Access, and Reflexivity (or DART for short, as a handy mnemonic). Subsequently, we use the example of the Starbucks enterprise to elaborate:

- how interaction environments must connect with the actual, lived co-creation experiences of individuals; and

- how experiential learning, insights, and knowledge can be used to re-design engagement platforms and the interaction environments they afford.

We then use the examples of La Poste and Orange to illustrate:

- how enterprises must connect as much with the co-creation experiences of employees and managers inside the organization as with customers and external stakeholders; and

- how the personal and collective intelligence of stakeholders internal to the organization (and especially those that are responsible for en-gaging with external stakeholders) can be successfully harnessed by connecting with their co-creation experiences.

We conclude the chapter by using the examples of Buckman Labs and Mozilla to discuss:

- how enterprises must facilitate the flow of experiential learning, in-sights, and knowledge rather than manage it; and

- how collaborative, peer-to-peer, co-construction of new knowledge can harmonize multiple streams of knowledge and unlock imagina-tion and ideas from a diverse experience base of individuals.

INDIVIDUATION OF CO-CREATION EXPERIENCES

In the typical value creation process, enterprises and stakeholders had distinct roles. Stakeholders had a stake in value creation, but enterprises viewed stakeholders as being largely passive and docile recipients of value creation. In the co-creation view, stakeholders have a more active role, contributing through their differences in views of value and their agency in creating value. Individuals as stakeholders, whether inside the enterprise network or outside as part of the enterprise ecosystem, are integral to this differential process of jointly defining and creating value. Individuated co-creation experiences become the very basis of value creation.

Consider the field of telematics—the provision of mobile information and services to automobile drivers and passengers. As an example, let us look at OnStar, which was launched by General Motors (GM) as a way of providing safety and emergency services to their customers. Over time, OnStar has evolved as GM has learned more about the broader interests and needs of its more than 6 million customers as stakeholders in experience-based value creation. Instead of merely asking, "How can we use information technology to make driving safer and more secure?," OnStar now asks, "What do customers desire to experience through their cars? How can information technology improve the driving experience, whether during a long commute, a cross-country drive, or a round of neighborhood chores?" As the answers to these questions expand, OnStar is creating a new space within which customers can enjoy personalized co-creation experiences that make driving more entertaining, informative, convenient, and fun.[61]

Telematics is about providing connectivity to consumers in their vehicles, which demands wireless connections via satellite and telecommunication networks to common monitoring stations. The traditional OnStar interface is simple: the driver merely has to press a button on the dashboard, and a call center operator responds. Because OnStar can determine the precise location of the car at any point in time, it can provide a host of location-based services. Some of these are focused on safety. When an OnStar subscriber is in an accident, the OnStar service representative contacts the local emergency service and dispatches a police car or ambulance to the scene, guided by vehicle- and customer-specific data, as well as external data from the OnStar network.

Other OnStar services, however, are purely experience-extending amenities. For example, suppose an OnStar customer calls to ask, "Is there a Thai restaurant anywhere nearby?" The service rep can note the driver's location, tap a database to locate the nearest Thai restaurant, make reservations (if requested), and download the route to the vehicle's navigation system, all without compromising safety, as might be the case if the driver used a smartphone while driving.

Because the OnStar service is integrated with the vehicle, it has access to all the internal sensors and can continuously monitor vehicle functions and provide assistance when needed. For example, when a consumer locks herself out of her car, OnStar can open the door remotely. When a car's airbag is deployed, OnStar cannot only detect the accident, but it can also assess its severity. When a car is stolen, OnStar can help the police track it down, assuming the owner of the car has given permission to do so.

OnStar works because the system is configured so as to embed its platform of engagements within the experience domain of the driver, as depicted in Figure 3-1. It is focused on events—a Thai dinner, a locked-out driver, or a fender bender, and it is sensitive to the time and space context of events and the meaningful involvements of individuals. It allows individuals to engage with the interaction environments it affords through a flexible, yet simple, assemblage system.

OnStar's current capabilities are very impressive. But it's easy to imagine additional experiences that are well within OnStar's technological capabilities and that may already be available. Suppose I live in Pikes Peak, Colorado. The telematics service can communicate weather, traffic, or emergency alerts to me. Now, suppose I don't like the suggested route in its entirety. I may possess some specific knowledge that the system does not have, or I may want to alter the route to include certain points of interest. How can I interact with the system to co-create a route that is best for me?

The telematics systems must also adapt and evolve with me, the consumer, and learn about my preferences and offer new services as appropriate. When my telematics system discerns (from my past information requests) that I am interested in the performance of certain stocks or enjoy the music of certain artists or root for a specific sports teams, it can automatically offer me share prices, information on concert tours, and the latest game highlights. But it also must allow me to define and shape what it has given me so I can configure my desired experiences in the context of a particular moment in time. We will discuss the DART principles of experience configuration, which helps to do just this, shortly.

For now, note that OnStar can be seen as an engagement platform *embedded in an experience-based network of individualized value creation*, enabled by technological capabilities entailing wireless telephony, satellite

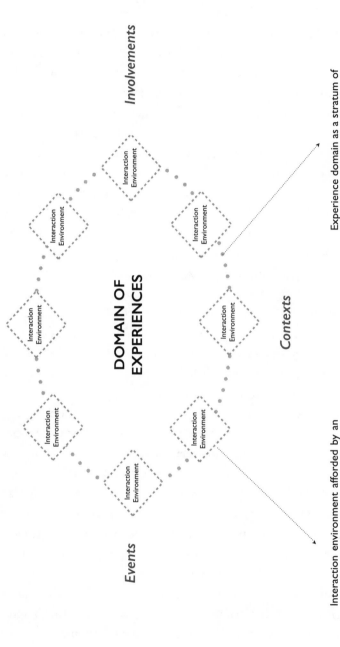

Meanings

Involvements

DOMAIN OF EXPERIENCES

Contexts

Events

Interaction Environment

Interaction environment afforded by an engagement platform

Experience domain as a stratum of involvements, events, contexts, and meanings

FIGURE 3-1 Domain of experiences

Note: An experience domain is a stratum of individual involvements, events, contexts, and meanings, whose configuration of experiences embodies actualized outcomes in value creation. Experience domains span environments of interactions afforded by engagement platforms.

communication, vehicle integration systems, and internal sensors, as well as the technologies needed to integrate the vehicle diagnostics into public networks, call center operations, and external services such as 911 emergency networks. The hardware and software requirements and the quality levels needed to deploy OnStar safely as a vehicle-based application are quite impressive, illustrating how technologies, creatively combined, can become enablers of valuable human experiences.

Now consider a few extensions of OnStar as an engagement platform. Since the Chevrolet Volt electric vehicle was launched in late 2010, drivers have been able to manage the charging of the vehicle, including the ability to charge during off-peak hours, through the OnStar RemoteLink mobile app. Suppose I am interested in knowing if I can reach my destination on a single charge. The RemoteLink app can not only answer this, but it can plot a route with recommended charging stations and even download it to the vehicle. The same RemoteLink app can also start a vehicle and its charging remotely, identify where it is parked, and even pay for the electric charging at accepting charge stations. Further, by linking the vehicle with smart power utility grids, the customer can direct the power utility to control when it charges, depending on the rates at different times of the day, when the power generated is coming from renewable energy sources. The win for a utility company, as stakeholding partner, is minimizing power spikes and maximizing grid efficiency.

GM has gone a step further by opening up the applications programming interface of its automotive cloud platform that enables OnStar-based services to developers. To illustrate its potential, consider a peer-to-peer car sharing service, RelayRides—a partner with GM—through which vehicle owners can rent out their idle cars and control the rates and the availability of the car. Through the OnStar applications programming interface, RelayRides allows renters to use remote features with their smartphones, such as unlocking vehicles remotely to access the reserved car. Thus, the owner need not meet the renter to pick up or drop off keys. Or consider medical equipment technicians as care providers for senior citizen patients in their homes. Using an OnStar-enabled application, medical equipment companies could verify whether technicians visited the homes. They could also generate new sources of value by linking with other network partners so patients could directly interact with support services, and technicians could respond more rapidly and schedule their visits to accommodate patient requests in real time.

Thus, the capabilities for individualized value creation through experience-based networks, in which engagement platforms are enveloped, require the efforts of a nodal enterprise that can connect together a variety of services, partners, and collaborative communities as part of the network. The enhanced competence base of such a network becomes an integral part of an individuated co-creation experience.

CO-CREATION EXPERIENCE CONFIGURATION

In reality, there isn't a "one-to-one" correspondence between interaction environments as conceived from the enterprise side and as actualized and experienced from the individual side. Rather, an enterprise's managerial tasks are to conceptualize and design engagement platforms that enable individualized experiences and to coevolve the design and the environments they afford with the individuals having these experiences. The DART principles are key to connecting better with *actualized differences* in co-creation experience configuration.

Dialogue is about shared communication and learning among equals. It entails empathic understanding built around experiencing and recognizing the emotional, social, and cultural background of experiences. It calls for a deep understanding of individual experience perspectives, which cannot be achieved without active conversation and sharing views around what is meaningful to individuals. Nurturing active dialogue is about engaging individuals on their terms and learning along with them as everyone evolves in their needs and experiences of value.[62]

Transparency implies visibility in the flow of information based on events underlying interactions in the engagement system. Information is the crucial component of transparency.[63] Interactions must be transparent in order to better access information and knowledge, engage in meaningful conversations, and assess risks and rewards. Transparency implies openness and communication that build trust. Without trust, individuals are reluctant to reveal vital information and will keep their opinions to themselves. When enterprises, customers, partners, and other external stakeholders establish collective transparency across the entire ecosystem, they begin to make mutually beneficial decisions and unlock new sources of value.

Access is about gaining information about others' experiences, contextual data, tools, expertise, skills, and the creativity of other agents in the assemblage system.[64] It enables individuals to guide their own experiences and to experience value through means other than ownership. Access has been made possible by a new generation of highly effective enabling technologies, which allow individuals to jointly create experiences of value like never before.

Reflexivity is the movement that enables the transformation of outcomes of value, and reflections on these outcomes, so it becomes part of the assemblage system and the value it generates.[65] Assemblages as platform constituents, stakeholders as value and experience co-creators, and enterprises as platform and ecosystem co-creators all play a role in reflexively feeding back into engagement platforms and making them better. This involves tools, information, insights, recommendations, meanings, lived experiences, and valuable creations of others. The key here is to tap into an agency that actively mediates between our structurally shaped circumstances and what individuals deliberately make of them. In the OnStar example, while the individual has access to many enablers of experiences, the individual must be able to interact, refine, and define value in the context of the individual's involvement in events in space and time and to co-shape meaningful experiences.

Through co-creation platforms that are DART enabled, enterprises can incorporate a broader view of value into their operations—one based on experiences that are meaningful to individuals, (re)design environments from the perspective of interactions that generate meaningful experiences, focus on what stakeholders truly value, and better manage stakeholder risk-reward relationships by tapping into the knowledge and skills of all stakeholders, both individually and as communities.

To illustrate the need for co-creation experience configuration, consider Starbucks, which began as a coffee roaster back in 1971 and then went on to build a global chain of coffee shops. As of 2013, Starbucks was worth over $13 billion. Starbucks affords multiple environments through assemblages that constitute its store. From a Starbucks enterprise perspective, consider a classic service process involving its baristas. There's a "transaction environment" in which the customer places a prepared drink to order, which is then given to the barista, who makes it. Once the order is ready, the customer picks it up and goes to the "finishing environment" and then either leaves the store or consumes the order in the "consumption environment" inside the store. If the latter, the customer becomes part of the tables and chairs, music, lighting, artwork, other customers, and employees in the store. The transaction environment itself involves an assemblage entailing a point-of-sale system, credit cards, cell phones, the barista preparing the order, the customer placing the order, and so on. The finishing environment involves an assemblage that includes condiments, lids, sleeves, napkins, trash and recycling bins, and so on. The "pre" transaction environment also involves an assemblage that includes menu boards, a showcase of food items, samples on a table, and so on. Throughout, the customer is an integral part of a given assemblage that is activated.

It is important to distinguish between the multiple interaction environments afforded by a particular engagement platform (e.g., parking, greeting, merchandising, menu, ordering, payment, pickup, finishing, consumption, doing other things in the store like using your laptop) and individuals' experience domains as contextualized through different experience scenarios. Consider just a few illustrative scenarios of experiences playing out every day in Starbucks stores:

- A customer enters the store and notices that the line is long. He sees that the person at the front of the line is involved in a conversation with the barista. He then sees a couple of tables that appear unoccupied toward the back of the store. He wishes he could simply place an order without physically waiting in line, especially as he knows what he wants on that occasion. Instead of waiting in line, he could just sit at one of the tables and start the work he was planning to get done on his mobile device. He is also happy that Starbucks offers free Wi-Fi, which is one reason he frequents this particular store, in addition to it being open 24 hours a day and having a train station and parking garage close by.

- The woman at the front of the line is aware that she is holding up the customers behind her. However, she just started a diet and exercise regimen and has been counting calories. Her doctor has also advised her to go easy on sugar. The barista has been patiently speaking with her, answering her questions and helping her to make good choices. The barista mentions that none of the Starbucks food items contain artificial ingredients. The woman is also a vegetarian and is pleased to hear about the new veggie options. As the transaction is being processed, the barista points to a nutritional information pamphlet at the finishing station.

- The man who is second in line notices the display of Starbucks cards that can be purchased in any amount and used either personally or as gifts. He wonders if they are also rewards cards, like the punch cards at other coffee shops. He then notices some free Apple iTunes redemption cards offering a free travel guide app from Apple's App Store. Apparently, there is a new iTunes app/book/song offered every Tuesday. He overhears the woman in front of him talking about nutrition and wonders what is taking so long. He is looking forward to having a piece of that coffee cake in the showcase.

- Another person in the line has pulled out his Apple iPhone and is exploring the Starbucks app that he had downloaded. He is pleased to see that it shows the balance on his plastic Starbucks card that he has been using. He notices that the card can be reloaded using his credit card. He wonders what else he can do with the app and starts interacting with its interface further.

- At the end of the line are a man, his wife, his teenage daughter, and his 9-month-old son. The man sees two small tables toward the back of the store, tells his wife to order a vanilla latte the way he likes it (nonfat milk, no foam, extra hot, with one extra pump of vanilla), and proceeds to push the two tables together so there will be more room for his family. He is also glad to see a restroom in the rear with a diaper changing sign and a plug point nearby for charging his mobile device. Meanwhile, his wife notices a wristband with "Indivisible" printed on it in a display with information about how Starbucks, in partnership with Opportunity Finance Network, creates jobs and announcing the new "Indivisible Blend" coffee on its menu. Being a social entrepreneur, she asks her teenage daughter to take one of the pamphlets. The pamphlet explains that for each purchase from the Indivisible collection, Starbucks will make a donation to the Create Jobs for USA program. As she makes a mental note to learn more about the program, her teenage daughter pulls out her iPhone and scans the quick response code on the display that takes her to the program information on Starbucks's website. Impressed, she decides to get the $5 wristband but not to purchase the Indivisible Blend (which costs $15) because she is not sure how the coffee tastes. She prefers the lighter blends that Starbucks has just introduced. As she waits, her thoughts wander to the time she spent working with a nongovernmental organization (NGO) in Africa and a coffee plantation she had visited. She wonders whether Starbucks is involved in any initiatives with coffee farmers. Her daughter asks how Starbucks recycles its cups, an issue she was exposed to in her high school as part of an environmental awareness program.

• Meanwhile, several customers are huddled by the espresso machine, glancing at the Starbucks cups on the fulfillment counter. One woman wonders if her order got lost in translation between the order taking and the fulfillment. She tries to see if her order is being prepared. A man is trying to figure out what to do about getting the hot sandwich that is being heated behind the counter and the espresso that will be brought to the fulfillment counter. Another man didn't know his drink came with whipped cream on top and decides to approach an already overloaded barista with his query.

As all these scenarios suggest, from the vantage point of the enterprise, the challenge is to better connect their engagement platforms with the actual experience domains of its stakeholding individuals as co-creators. The various interaction environments afforded by the enterprise (e.g., order, payment, pickup, etc.) imply the surroundings of individuals in assemblage systems.[66] Interaction environments normally manifest some things that persist and some that do not. An interaction environment is better described in terms of a medium, substances, and the surfaces that separate them. In this sense the environment surrounds all individuals in the same way that it surrounds a single individual.

Individuals activate multiple platform components for each afforded environment—for example, using the physical Starbucks card versus using a smartphone app in the payment environment. The difference between an interaction environment and an activated platform component is mediated exclusively by stratum-constituted boundaries of individual human experiences, with the function of separating the assemblage system and the interaction environment on the one hand and connecting the two on the other by letting causal effects pass through. Contexts, events, meanings, and involvements compose stratified environments that constitute systems of human experiences—sets of experiences related to one another by certain operations with a particular structure and functional unity. In the widest sense, all human experiences of any given individual make up that individual's narrative self.[67]

Starbucks definitely manages a variety of experience elements through store location, interior design, lighting, music, product options, lower-height Mastrena espresso machines so baristas are visible to customers, and so on. It recognizes that the creative combination of products, employees, and consumer communities shapes customers' experiences. While it affords broad environments through its designed engagement platforms, there is also the scope for individuals to define their own contexts in light of their experience domains and to enjoy different kinds of Starbucks experiences. Customers and other stakeholders must be able to bring their own contexts to an experience and shape their personal experiences accordingly. This means that the enterprises must have the foresight and capabilities to generate insights into the heterogeneity of individual experience domains and build the technical, social, and organizational capabilities that enable a variety of individualized experiences accordingly. At the same time, they must hone in on experience-based ideas that enhance value from the perspective of managerial agents. For instance, enabling customers to embed their favorite personalized drink through the Starbucks card—for example, "a tall, nonfat, no-foam, extra-hot caramel macchiato with light caramel and a dash of vanilla"—is a capability that speeds up the personalized transaction for an individual customer, while enabling Starbucks to simultaneously serve more customers faster, generating a "win-win" for both sides. The Starbucks mobile phone app is convenient for customers and makes their purchase go faster, including not having to wait for a card balance or printed receipt, and it also enables Starbucks to engage with customers outside the store and provide information like store hours, store amenities, and number of reward points, engendering store loyalty. While most money storage cards offer that service, and it is not necessarily individualized, with the Starbucks card, a customer can access its history online, so it is both a receipt tracker and a way to add funds via credit card or PayPal. It is also integrated with the mobile Starbucks app that allows for a much more seamless, meaningful experience.

Starbucks also has designed barista engagement processes that afford enhanced experience domains that benefit Starbucks, its employees, and its customers. Currently, Starbucks has a process of capturing the customer's name and the drink specification on the cup itself. This adds a personal touch for the customer, although in cases where the name is very long or has an unusual spelling, it can slows things down and be embarrassing to the customer as well. (With smartphone orders, perhaps the barista can simply read it off the screen and write it down, helping both sides.) Starbucks also affords a more meaningful experience for the barista who has to juggle many customer orders at the same time, as all the barista has to do is look at the cup. However, bringing transparency into the order-tracking experience for the customer without disrupting operations is an ongoing challenge.

Starbucks uses various means to gain insights into how others come to understand and engage with its designed platforms. It utilizes a variety of approaches, including observing how stakeholders interact with different components of engagement platforms; interfacing with them according to the meanings they bring; and ultimately participating in their contexts, anticipating contexts of experiences from the activated platform components, and engaging stakeholders in a dialogue about their experiences. Perhaps most interesting here is the platform that Starbucks provides where customers all over the world can use a registered Starbucks card to share their own ideas on how Starbucks can improve their experiences and make them more rewarding. This program, MyStarbucksIdea (MSI), is an online platform where customers are invited to submit ideas and co-create the Starbucks experience together. Starbucks management takes the feedback seriously, as evidenced from the more than 275 ideas that Starbucks has implemented in five years since the platform's launch in 2008. Some of the suggestions were improvements in the ordering, payment, and pickup processes; better atmosphere; more convenient locations; and ways to improve the quality of the drinks, merchandise, and Starbucks card. Some of the implemented ideas include the ability to send in orders by phone or Web, gift drinks, and "splash sticks" that plug the hole in lids to prevent sloshing (an idea that originated in Japan). MSI allows Starbucks to have an ongoing conversation with its customers around their experienced environments, as customers reflect on them, with Starbucks sparking some of the conversations around their internally generated ideas, new product launches, and new initiatives.

According to Chris Bruzzo, Starbucks's CTO, the purpose of MSI was to "open up a dialogue with customers and build up this muscle inside our company." By the end of 2008, there were nearly 50 Idea Partners active on the site—specially trained employees who act as hosts of the discussions, take specific ideas to internal teams, and advocate for customers' suggestions so "customers would have a seat at the table when product decisions are being made," as Bruzzo puts it, and "close the loop in an authentic way." The goal was to truly adopt customer ideas into Starbucks's business processes, including product development, store design, and customer experience.[68] In the first year alone, over 65,000 ideas were submitted and 658,000 votes were cast. In late 2009, the company announced that 50 ideas drawn from the site had been approved, including healthy food options as a major initiative for the company. This is no small feat for an organization the size of Starbucks. For instance, after Schultz returned as CEO, Starbucks announced that breakfast sandwiches would be discontinued in order to return the stores to a more coffeehouse-style experience. Through MSI, however, customers asked Starbucks to retain the sandwiches but requested more nutritious and healthier options (more whole grain, more fiber and protein, smaller portions, etc.). Starbucks Idea Partner Katie Thomson, a registered dietician and senior nutritionist at Starbucks, engaged in dialogue with the community, with Starbucks internally, and with the company's supply chain, finally implementing a new range of nutritious but tasty sandwiches in late 2008, with small ingredient changes that would reduce aromas so as not to interfere with the smell of coffee. Not only did the community vote (up and down) and decide, but members also discussed the ideas with Starbucks Idea Partners and helped make them even better. Says Bruzzo, "There are advantages to having that kind of transparency because it creates more engagement, and we actually get to iterate on our solutions while we're building them."[69] Ultimately, the MSI community cannot only see which ideas were the most popular but also engage with the company in dialogue as it reviews ideas, watch as the company takes action, and provide real feedback based on actual experiences.

Following the success of MSI, the company expanded its presence in social media. Starbucks overtook Coca-Cola as the most popular brand in Facebook in 2009 with over 5 million fans, where it uploads videos and alerts people to events. As of 2013, it had more than 34 million Facebook likes and more than 3.6 million Twitter followers, up from about 700,000 in 2009. On its YouTube channel, subscribers not only receive advertisements and informational videos on the company and the coffee, but Starbucks allows people to embed its videos anywhere on the Web, in contrast to many companies concerned that their videos might end up in places they don't want to be associated with.

This kind of continuous, iterative engagement among Starbucks, its customers, and its customer-facing employees (whom Starbucks refers to as "partners" and who have also chipped into the conversation)—together with its supply chain and external stakeholders—enables the brand to be co-created and managed in ways that challenge traditional brand management orthodoxies. Companies that engage customers in co-creating brands through their stakeholder experiences can create a "seeing culture," as Schultz puts it. It is important to drive co-creation thinking into the management of human capital and the (re)design of business processes and then back to points of interactions with stakeholders.

In June 2009, Starbucks raised the bar on its food even further. Sandra Stark, vice president of Food Category, said, "Starbucks customers have been telling us that they want better-tasting and healthier food options when they visit our stores. We answered their call with a delicious new menu of food made with real ingredients and more wholesome options." The company removed the artificial trans fats, artificial flavors, artificial dyes, and high-fructose corn syrup in all its food items. Some of the healthy food items rose to the top of the company's food sales chart within just a few weeks.[70]

Although MSI enables Starbucks to collect ideas, it also needs to engage in an ideation *about* experience configuration to discover experience-based insights and continuously redesign engagement platforms. It is only in so doing that better states of co-created experience outcomes are ultimately achieved, actualizing new sources of stakeholder and enterprise value. Further, MSI *itself* must be configured based on the engagement experiences of its users. Consider the nature of dialogue on the platform. For instance, when Starbucks announced that breakfast sandwiches would be discontinued in order to return the stores to a more coffeehouse-style experience, customers, through MSI, asked that Starbucks retain the sandwiches but requested more nutritious and healthier options (more whole grain, more fiber and protein, smaller portions, and so on), as well as hot sandwiches. The product marketing function initiated a discussion, along with in-house nutritionists, registered dieticians, and occasionally potential suppliers, to research this further. They played back to the community what they were hearing periodically to validate their interpretations. During this process, senior managers expressed concern that the smell of hot food might interfere with the aroma of coffee in the store, thereby undermining "the coffeehouse experience." Starbucks made this issue transparent to customers and explained it was exploring ways to solve the problem; it even invited MSI participants to contribute their solutions. In the end, the dialogue around various aspects of the new product lines involved a great deal of back-and-forth among Starbucks and its stakeholders. The platform also exhibits reflexivity considerations in that all recent ideas are automatically visible on the front page, so users can see what ideas have been freshly posted, which were the most popular, which are under review by Starbucks, and which are undergoing implementation. They can also observe the process as the company takes action and provide personal feedback based on actual experiences. Finally, everybody has access to the posted ideas on the site, although submitting ideas and responding to others' ideas through the MSI community does require acquiring and registering a Starbucks card that, on the enterprise side, enables it to generate further experiential learning, insights, and knowledge rapidly.

In addition to external stakeholder experiences, enterprises must connect with the human experiences of employees and managers inside the organization. Successfully connecting with external stakeholder experiences mandates co-creation with internal stakeholders. Starbucks, for instance, also connects with the human experiences of its employees and managers, all the way from its internal training to community support activities to strategy execution, through its internal Partner Café engagement platform. As Adam Brotman, Starbucks chief digital officer, remarked, "Baristas and store partners are on the front line and are the most important communication vehicle for both espousing and explaining what it is we are up to digitally." Brotman goes on to note that Starbucks is working on doing a better job of giving them tools and bringing them along around its digital programs. Further, Starbucks has also sought to "relocalize" its stores by engaging employees, in addition to community designers, in changing the look and feel of its stores from that of a cookie-cutter corporate giant to the local neighborhood coffee shop. It allowed store managers and employees to change the look of individual branches to appeal to local sensibilities, and it began to offer different types of beans in different regions, rather than insisting on batches large enough to distribute across all of its stores. While Starbucks uses classic lean thinking principles to shave precious seconds in filling each order or making it easier to ring transactions and decrease the time it takes to do an electronic transaction, every store also has its own customer-traffic patterns, and employees and store managers are encouraged to come up with their own adjustments and solutions rather than just apply a single solution sent from headquarters.[71]

Starbucks recognizes how all interactions with customers, employees, and other stakeholders can be made co-creative: by redesigning relationships with people and the physical environments of interactions as engagement platforms, as well as by using Web-based environments. Curt Garner, CIO of Starbucks, notes that there are about 100 IT projects ongoing as of 2013, with about 35 of them being customer or partner facing. While enterprises still need to carefully design internal processes to deliver consistently high-quality experiences, rooting out all internal variations in the delivery system, at the same time they must paradoxically "free up" how they approach the design and specifications of types of experiences. It is not either consistency in the delivery system or flexibility in what is delivered but consistency *and* flexibility.

CONNECTING WITH EMPLOYEE AND MANAGERIAL CO-CREATION EXPERIENCES

It is hard to co-create with customers and other stakeholders if managers do not do so inside the organization with their customer- and stakeholder-facing employees. Employees often have a sense of where and how the customer/stakeholder experience is broken and what experiences they might value. Moreover, employees often have ideas about how an organization's business processes can be improved to enhance the customer experience. How do enterprises connect with employees and their managers' co-creation experiences? Consider the case of La Poste Retail, the division of the French Postal Service that manages its 17,000 post offices and distributes the products of its Mail, Express Package, and Postal Bank Divisions.[72] Toward the end of 2007, the senior sales and marketing officer of the French Postal Network, Marc Zemmour, and a key member of his team, chief strategy officer Fabien Monsallier—a manager who loved to experiment with new approaches—decided to launch an exploratory effort in co-creation after being impressed with its rejuvenating potential. They had reached the conclusion that engaging employees more actively in improving services was vital. La Poste Retail had been steadily losing sales because of the rapidly decreasing volume of mail, about 5 percent annually, brought on by the rise of online communication; this sales decrease had been only marginally offset by growth in the package business. In spite of great efforts to develop additional services, the Distribution Division had also continued to lose sales, and post offices were frequently being closed.

Like many postal services, La Poste Retail had been the butt of many jokes about the patience required to endure long lines and the lack of motivation of its employees. Zemmour and Monsallier believed that the absence of a customer orientation at La Poste Retail was central to its problems. The history of La Poste Retail was one of top-down, command-and-control management. It still used the term "brigade" to describe teams of tellers and was organized into seven hierarchical levels. Zemmour and Monsallier made a pitch for a new managerial approach based on co-creation. In order to test whether a co-creative approach would work at La Poste Retail, they approached the Center-East region, one of the six large regional areas of La Poste Retail, headquartered in Lyon. The region comprises a network of 4,000 branches and employs close to 7,000 people. Julien Tétu, who manages the region, volunteered to pilot the project.

The team quickly settled on three locations for the pilot co-creation effort: the heart of downtown Lyon, the suburbs, and a small countryside town. These were chosen to tap into the experiences of three primary groups of customers: mass market individuals, professional individuals—such as those working in a small or home office—and low-income individuals, such as immigrants living in tough urban neighborhoods. The team reasoned that the three locations would give them a representative sample of customers.

In each of the three locations, the group followed the same sequence of three workshops. Day one involved a co-creation workshop where teller employees discussed their interactions both with customers and within the postal hierarchy itself. In the first part of day two, customers joined teller employees to share their respective experiences in the post office. In the second part, the co-creation team conducted working sessions with the post office managers to debrief what they had learned with the employees of the post office and their customers. Tétu had invited Jacques Rapoport, the new CEO of La Poste, to come to Lyon and learn about the co-creation project. This project fitted nicely with the early steps Rapoport had in mind to transform the retail network of La Poste: establish some basic service standards for big post offices and begin to transform the traditionally partitioned post office building by creating open spaces with individual service islands that "explode" its waiting line. The service standards that were defined included, among others, a maximum allowable wait time for simple operations (less than 5 minutes); an average allowable time required to claim a package or a registered letter (less than 8 minutes); a maximum time allowed to respond to a complaint (48 hours); and the guarantee that all tellers will be open if the wait time exceeds 10 minutes to demonstrate the "all hands on deck" readiness of each local team. As Tétu noted:

Our network is not a technical or mechanical network. It is 100 percent human. The quality of our service depends entirely on the men and women who welcome and serve our customers. Our service quality is directly proportional to the competencies, the intelligence, and the daily motivation of these men and women. To change the physical nature of these post offices or simply apply new service standards won't change a thing, unless teller employees personally participate in this adventure from the start. We need them to co-create this change with us.

The co-creation approach was meant to engage post office employees in improving four customer experience areas: access, customer care, service, and advice. The problem had been stated clearly, and the ambition was linked to each topic set, thereby challenging each individual to generate a personal response. It turned out, however, that employees were more interested in their own work experiences than in customers' experiences. It became evident that the key to co-creating the customer experience with tellers was to first co-create the teller experience with tellers. And this wasn't about the teller's experience of serving the customer but about the teller's experience of being served by management. For instance, one popular initiative was the creation of a simple wall spreadsheet on which employees could schedule themselves according to the demands of each post office, allowing, for example, young mothers to adjust their working hours to fit the needs of their children. Employees were willing to come in early or work late, provided they could flexibly schedule their hours. As the power of "self-organization" dawned on management, and the co-creation of tellers' work experiences together with tellers was under way, the momentum began to build as some of the tellers became passionate about co-creation and began volunteering to engage in conversations with customers about customers' co-creation experiences. It became apparent to them that customers would, for example, love to see the post office open to match the hours of the open-air market in each village, town, or city block. Shopping for fresh food and other basic necessities of life at open-air markets is a staple of French social life. Because these markets open as early as 7:00 a.m. two or three times a week, some customers wanted the local post office to open at 7:00 a.m. as well on those days so they could shop and do their post office business at the same time. In the traditional design, La Poste could not afford to allow co-created opening hours at the local level, since it could not physically keep track of the specifics of every open-air market days in each village, small town, or city block. By default, by conducting multiple surveys on customer preferences on opening hours, it had defined a standard schedule that best matched what it perceived to be the needs of customers and the constraints set by regulation and union negotiations pertaining to its workforce. The schedule it had come up with was the best countrywide compromise it could devise and "sell" to the nationalized unions.

The most remarkable achievement of the transformation that ensued was that many new post office schedules resulted in a net extension of opening hours at the constant manpower level, something the management of La Poste had wanted to do for years but had never dared include as a negotiation item with the unions. Because teller employees and customers had established this need for longer opening hours together, it was now happening all over Paris, with many post offices open from 7:00 a.m. to 7:00 p.m. on weekdays and 10:00 a.m. to 3:00 p.m. on Saturdays. Customers could now go to the post office before and after work. By letting employees and customers determine their own opening hours at the local level through self-organization, La Poste had again unleashed the powerful forces of co-creation. The customers' experience has improved because they are now able to better fit in their postal business with other activities. Employees and managers of the local post office also enjoy a better experience, since they now have a better relationship with customers and benefit from a better anchoring in the community. The customers' cost of doing business has decreased because they no longer have to make needless trips just to accommodate the post office's hours. Post office employees and managers are less likely to have to deal with frustrated customers. La Poste also wins in the new setup. Its cost is reduced because the new system shifts some of the peak demand traditionally found during lunch hours, at the end of the day, and on Saturdays to the new early-morning open-air market hours. This results in a more effective matching of customer demand with employee presence, resulting in fewer overtime hours. La Poste not only learns more about customer preferences in real time but now has an engagement platform that endears the local post office to its community, paving the way for a stronger presence in the neighborhood.

By the summer of 2008, more than 1,200 people had taken part in the co-creation transformation. Based on this early success, CEO Jacques Rapoport challenged five other regions to introduce a similar participative process in their region. The method developed by the Center-East region was "suggested, but not imposed." Michel Garnier, head of the Paris region, decided to co-create the deployment of the approach, borrowing the tools developed by the Center-East region but granting everyone a license to modify them in order to encourage appropriation at all levels. On May 2, 2008, at the Institute of the Arabic World in Paris, Michel Garnier launched the first wave of the new "Welcome to La Poste of the greater Paris region" in the presence of 100 post office managers. He immediately stated his ambition to reorganize the 571 districts of the region through co-creation in two years. To do so, in addition to his management team and his area managers, he mobilized his sales managers, the project managers of the regional support teams, the organization specialists, the internal consultants that had been earmarked for the program, human resources personnel, and many others. Through this program, the management of the region also designed and implemented a new retail format in the Paris post offices by adapting to the region the main features of the proposed nationwide program. But, compared to the human, cultural, and social transformation, the real estate component is only a small part of the story. While the live co-creation platforms evolved, the management of La Poste Retail resolved that some problems could not be properly addressed at the local level because they involved nationwide processes or issues. To address these issues, management decided to develop a Web-based platform for post office employees. The idea was to give all employees the opportunity to report problems they felt needed to be solved or make suggestions for improvements in the four customer experience areas. They hoped to offer employees a network vision of all co-creation initiatives underway and to invite them to participate in them through the site. Six months after its launch, 1,578 suggestions had been published, unleashing a participative wave where the employees discussed each suggestion at length. During that time, 12,873 comments had been posted, with 9,772 votes on suggestions!

In November 2009, Jacques Rapoport proudly reported that the Paris region had reduced its average wait time by 60 percent over a year, while at the national level the 1,000 largest post offices had reduced theirs by 50 percent. In September 2008, only 42 percent of people were able to mail a registered letter in less than 5 minutes but by October 2009, 74 percent were able to do so. For the 1,000 largest post offices in France, this number was as high as 84 percent (86 percent in all of Paris). For more complex operations such as depositing or wiring money, in September 2008, only 65 percent of customers were able to do so in less than 10 minutes, but by October 2009, the number had gone up to 82 percent.

The most spectacular customer service results have been achieved in the regions that have embraced co-creation. The Center-East region, while it was historically a strong commercial performer, was dead last among regions in terms of quality: only about 40 percent of its post offices met the national quality standards. A year and a half after launching the co-creation effort, the region is now tied for first place. The other two regions that also embraced co-creation—the greater Parisian region and the southern region—have also made spectacular progress. Regions that stayed away from co-creation have not exhibited any noticeable progress. In offices that were renovated, 95 percent of customers claimed to be satisfied with La Poste Retail's services. No comparable benchmark from a year ago is available, but La Poste was a notorious laggard in all comparative benchmarking studies involving retail places or banks. Now, 92 percent are comfortable with the new layout, and 93 percent are pleased with the new level of service. La Poste does not publish the results of its employee surveys, but the engagement of its employees is also rising rapidly, particularly in all post offices that have embarked on the co-creation journey. The correlation between employee and customer satisfaction is intuitively evident to all who have participated in the effort. As Julien Tétu put it:

You can change the standards and the decoration, but if the employees don't also change, you will get nowhere. And the best way to have people accept changes is to co-create them. For me, the real power of co-creation is that it releases "collective intelligence." But co-creation releases it in a structured way and not as a random process. We structure how the employees can express themselves so we remain within the strategic objectives of the company. And this form of expression is amazing!

In the co-creative enterprise, every employee who interacts with customers—the call center operator, the service representative, the sales associate, the logistics manager, the engineer, the product developer, the supply chain partner, and the community manager—is responsible for making the interactions more co-creative, making the human experiences more meaningful, and generating additional mutual value. In most established enterprises, while there is an immediate opportunity to connect with employee co-creation experiences on a local basis, leveraging the value creation ideas of employees on a large scale requires an enterprise-wide Internetworked engagement platform for managing a diversity of ideas. Consider the example of Orange, the operating brand of France Telecom.[73] Orange's "intrapreneurial" engagement platform, idClic, has totally changed the way the company innovates by supercharging the employee suggestion box. All employees are encouraged to come up with ideas—for instance, on process improvement, facility optimization, or product revamping—promote an idea through a blog, and gain visibility by acquiring points for comments on other employees' ideas. Orange received more than 21,000 ideas in just one month in 2007, a total that practically doubled in the same month in 2008. By early 2011, four years after Orange had rolled out the site, over 110,000 ideas had been posted on it. Over 40 percent of all employees had contributed or commented on an idea, and more than 10,000 projects had been implemented. Collectively, the projects had produced more than €1.1 billion in earnings or savings. Its success lies in ensuring that employees (innovators as they are called) have full transparency from the submission of an idea, and if it is accepted by a network of over 6,000 experts (who interact with both employee innovators and line managers whose functional activities are affected by the idea), its movement in almost real time through the idea management process all the way through to deployment. Throughout, attention is paid to the experiences of employees, experts, and managers and of a core team inside the organization that supports the platform on a daily basis. By promoting internal entrepreneurship, Orange unleashed its virtual innovation capacity that did not find expression in its traditional hierarchical organization.

EXPERIENTIAL LEARNING, INSIGHTS, AND KNOWLEDGE

In large enterprises, it is equally important for every individual who is inside the organization as a co-creator to be able to rapidly access and harness others' experiential learning, insights, and knowledge, whether for decision making, solving a complex problem, or addressing emerging opportunities. Peter Drucker and Alvin Toffler have long recognized the increasing critical role of the "knowledge worker" in the process of enterprise value creation—and seeing enterprises as living systems rather than machines—leading to a view of organizations as "knowledge creating" rather than mere processors of knowledge. Employees learn through opportunities for problem solving and tackling unusual and unanticipated tasks in a process of "double-loop" learning with stakeholders.[74] Because the co-creation process presents an evolving and continuously changing milieu, managers must continuously rethink their actions. More important, they have to act and react in real time.

Enterprises have been going beyond knowledge management to building dedicated knowledge co-creation platforms designed around individual employees' co-creation experiences, especially those on the front lines. When heterogeneous customers interact with the firm, they will make demands that cannot be predicted. When a customer says to a frontline employee, "Help me solve this problem," the question is posed not just to that employee but to the entire organization. How can that employee access the knowledge base of his peers around the world to help that customer as quickly as possible? How can the organization combine the experiences and skills of its employees to create new knowledge rapidly? The capacity to create new knowledge in real time has two critical dimensions: the ability of the individual to identify new insights rapidly and the ability to share these insights with others rapidly so that consensual decisions can be made on how to act. An interactive and a collaborative environment that enhances the capacity of managers to access competence on demand is a key for agility. Further, because competence is widely distributed in the system, the direction and intensity of flows of knowledge and information cannot be predetermined. Patterns will emerge over time, subject to continual change. Thus, it is prudent for management to think in terms of facilitating the flow rather than just managing it, and to provide managers with open access to competence on demand rather than developing predetermined structures for access.

Consider Buckman Laboratories, a $500 million specialty chemicals company based in Memphis, Tennessee, with around 1,500 employees in over 100 countries.[75] Buckman produces more than a thousand different specialty chemicals and competes in a variety of businesses, from pulp and paper processing and water treatments to leather, agriculture, and personal care. It enjoys a competitive edge due to its ability to apply the power of *all* its employees to every customer experience. And central to this capability is its global knowledge network called K'Netix, which is integral to Buckman's information infrastructure. We can look at a classic Buckman story illustrating a typical application of K'Netix. A managing director for Buckman Labs in Singapore—let's call her Mary—has been asked to propose a pitch-control program to an Indonesian pulp mill. Pitch is a chemical released from wood in the pulping and refining processes, whose composition depends on the characteristics of the tree from which the wood is obtained and other environmental factors. If pitch is not separated from the pulp, it affects paper quality and can cause problems in paper mill operations. Thus, developing an effective pitch-control program is an important and complex aspect of paper mill management.

Mary logs into K'Netix and asks for an update on recent pitch-control approaches around the world. Three hours later, she gets a response from Memphis that refers to a master's thesis by an Indonesian student in the United States on pitch control of tropical hardwoods, and she suggests some Buckman chemicals that might be appropriate for this application. About an hour later, a Canadian manager sends a note about his experience in solving the pitch problem in British Columbia. Later, Mary receives data from Sweden, New Zealand, Spain, and France, followed by an offer of technical expertise and scientific advice from the company's central R&D group. In all, Mary receives 11 postings from six countries, forming several conversational threads that enable each participant to learn something new. The net result: the contextual knowledge created helps Mary secure a $6 million order from the Indonesian mill.

This would be interesting enough if the Buckman network included only the firm's technical experts. But everyone at the company has access to the same system, right down to frontline employees. Consider another legendary Buckman story. One of Buckman's paper customers in Michigan realized that the peroxide it was adding to remove ink from old magazines was no longer working. A Buckman sales manager presented this problem to the knowledge network. Within two days, salespeople from Belgium and Finland identified a likely cause: bacteria in the paper slurry were producing an enzyme that broke down the peroxide. The sales manager recommended a chemical to control the bacteria, and the problem was solved. Now imagine how that customer feels about doing business with Buckman. With the company and the customer co-creating knowledge, a new level of trust and value through satisfying co-creation experiences can emerge.

Knowledge co-creation platforms must be woven into the culture of the organization. As Bob Buckman, ex-CEO of Buckman Labs, noted, "[Our focus has been] 90 percent culture change and 10 percent technology change. Technology is the easy part. . . . The focus needs to be on culture change and how to shift to a networked communication model." Just as knowledge is associated with individuals, at Buckman, the platform is identified with the organization. Knowledge, by its very nature, is tacit. Despite the popular term *knowledge management*, knowledge cannot be "managed" as such. Rather, knowledge emerges from the virtual through intensification in engagement platforms like K'Netix and is embodied in the experience domains of individuals. What can be managed, therefore, is the explicit information that results from continuously generating knowledge in the context of specific problems. But change the context, and new recontextualized knowledge often needs to be regenerated.

As knowledge is regenerated continuously, the information associated with a person's knowledge can certainly be codified into new, explicit information (for instance, writing down the influence of enzymes in peroxide breakdown in paper slurry), as in the Buckman example. For most managers, the challenge is how to creatively balance the codification of tacit knowledge into explicit information. The focus has to be as much on enabling individual employees to come together to co-construct new knowledge in the context of a particular situation as on gaining efficiencies through codification to develop new organizational routines.

Further, with the convergence of industries and technologies, the ability to harmonize multiple streams of knowledge is becoming more and more critical. For example, the personal care products industry today needs to work with the pharmaceutical industry, as creams, shampoos, and soaps take on a pharmaceutical function, such as antiwrinkle products, hair growth, or healthy living. Biotech increasingly needs large-scale computing, and the automotive industry realizes that a car is increasingly "software on wheels" with remote engagement capabilities, as we saw in the OnStar example. From a knowledge co-creation standpoint, this means that intellectual diversity (for example, managing chemical, software, and electronics engineers in a single team) is as great a management challenge as race, gender, and age diversity. To be effective, a knowledge co-creation platform must engage the total organization, including multiple levels, functions, and geographies, and must promote an absence of boundaries.

Obviously, Buckman Labs has had to spend a respectable amount of money to create and support its K'Netix platform. Is it possible to calculate the return on this investment? Bob Buckman, seeing K'Netix as part of the central nervous system of the company and, as such, inseparable from its soul, dismissed this question as such, albeit acknowledging that about 4 percent of company revenues were spent on the network initially, with about a 93 percent increase in operating costs per associate. Since then, there have been tangible benefits that have been quantified: improved speed of response to customer inquiries (down from as much as three weeks to six hours); an over 50 percent rise in sales from new products, indicating a sharp rise in profitability from innovation; about a 50 percent increase in sales per associate; and a decrease in the cost of training with the learning center from $1,000 per hour to $25 to $40 per hour. Other benefits are harder to measure, though; for example, some customers say that Buckman's knowledge co-creation platform is a critical factor in selecting it as a supplier. In the strictest sense, it may not be possible to precisely measure the total benefits and total costs of the

Buckman system. But it's clear that few of Buckman's employees, managers, customers, and suppliers who have experienced its power would want to go back to operating without it.

Note, too, that Buckman's experiment was launched pre-Internet. The lesson here is that technology per se is only important insofar as it affects the ability of a manager or employee to get work done. More important than the technology of knowledge co-creation is the social commitment that the company makes to the underlying concept and a corporate culture that supports it. Having said that, Buckman Labs continues to coevolve its now Web-enabled K'Netix system but with a clear focus on enhancing customer, employee, and stakeholder experiences of value and coevolutionary (re)design of its platform purposefully over time.

K'Netix now combines e-mail, bulletin boards, computer-simulated conference rooms, libraries, and electronic forums. Each forum uses a common structure featuring "knowledge catalysts" to facilitate co-construction of new knowledge—for example, threaded conversations—as seen from the employee's perspective. The threaded discussions are indexed by topic, author, and date and contain questions, responses, and field observations. A forum specialist and a group of subject experts take the lead in guiding discussions and ensuring the integrity and quality of advice. Subject experts also serve as section leaders, answering requests and preparing weekly summaries. They extract the threads, edit, summarize, assign keywords, consolidate the insights, and then organize, validate, and verify the information before transferring it to an evolving repository of interconnected "knowledge bases" supplemented by external information sources.

The knowledge bases have multiple forms, ranging from relatively loosely organized expertise possessed by knowledge workers to highly organized and more structured knowledge bases. The system is experience-centric, semistructured, and dynamic, yet flexible, interconnected, and evolving continuously. The evolution is both organic and guided. There is a rapid exchange of knowledge among individuals separated by time and space. The key is that it enables individuals to bring their contexts of space and time while drawing on the collective knowledge and insights gleaned on a global basis. They also have regional forums that continue to evolve as they work on building local language capabilities (including European, Latin American, and Asian languages).

Today, it's possible to create a technical conversation in real time focused around the problems and needs of a particular customer—an unusual and important capability. The platform also fosters internal dialogue by way of online discussions on issues such as compensation. Conducting transparent debates about topics like these among company employees would not be possible without a culture in which implicit trust is strong—an indication of the importance of the social architecture in the creation of a powerful knowledge co-creation platform.

Thus, thanks to an evolving K'Netix, Buckman employees have unfettered access to competence, resources, and experiences from a hundred countries around the world. Frontline employees can spend their time serving customers, while specialized groups are devoted to capturing and codifying useful knowledge. Buckman's IT group is responsible for the technical architecture, while the social architecture is overseen by personnel from the knowledge transfer group, associates, product development managers, research librarians, and many others. Too often, initiatives are user hostile and counterintuitive, making it hard for employees to interact with the system. The knowledge sharing and creation culture has become deeply embedded at Buckman. Compliance becomes the norm rather than the exception. The Buckman example suggests that collaborative, peer-to-peer, co-construction of knowledge can unlock imagination and ideas on a scale and scope like never before. Employees have skills and capabilities that cannot be captured in vitas and databases. To tap those hidden resources, knowledge co-creation platforms are needed that enable thematic knowledge co-creation communities to flourish.

The Buckman example illustrates organizing for learning *in* doing in an experimental and discovery-based manner, based on the social dynamics of knowledge co-creation emergent in communities and enacted in routines to revirtualize competence. In the sociology of interpersonal and collective relations, knowledge is harnessed in an organizational culture, influenced by reciprocal learning, trust, enterprise narratives, and languages of communication.[76] In the co-creation view, experiential learning takes place in the process of interactions and from experience outcomes, and it contributes to unexpressed knowledge in the virtual as the basis of unique competencies. This latter tacit knowledge has to be intensified and actualized to generate unique enterprise value. Individuals know about the world and become an integral part of it when their creative, intentional, and transformative engagements become a way to change their human experiences and revirtualize and reactualize learning in a virtuous cycle. The co-creation view thus reconciles traditional theories of individual learning and organizational learning.[77] It also recognizes that every individual in an organization is an active learner and potential co-creator of value.

Mozilla and the Firefox browser provide a good illustration of the precision required in establishing the right employee engagement platform from the inside out. Mozilla recognized early on the need to strike the balance between maintaining control and letting motivated people run with their passions. Mozilla had more than 120 employees, without whom Firefox would have remained a good open source project but nothing like the force that it has been on the Internet. Mozilla's decision-making process is highly distributed through a crowdsourcing volunteer community platform for product development, software coding, distribution, and promotion. Touching code that goes into Firefox is a very disciplined process. But there are lots of areas for participation—whether it's building an extension or localizing the product or building new products—that don't need that degree of discipline. If Mozilla is the heart of the system, its community is the arms and legs. For example, Firefox couldn't be distributed to its more than 300 million users without its community. Mozilla provides the platform—a form of "scaffolding" for people to work from—so anyone in the community can innovate. Some of the people who make decisions about code, however, are not employees. Some people with a high degree of expertise and specialization just cannot be hired. As long as Firefox provides co-creation experiences that are meaningful to these rare individuals, it increases its chances of success amidst evolving competition from the likes of Apple Safari, Google Chrome, and Microsoft Explorer.

The Buckman and Mozilla examples are also suggestive of how the engagement design principles discussed in the previous chapter can be gainfully utilized in innovating employee engagement platforms to generate and manage ideas, share contextual knowledge and best practices, and co-create value in the process. More generally, they suggest how engagement platforms can enable employee participation that encompasses a range of mechanisms in involving the workforce in decisions at all levels of the enterprise, whether undertaken directly with employees and/or indirectly through their representatives, and with different roles and contributions (e.g., employees as experts in the Orange example). Employee engagement can be deconstructed according to its nature (from information sharing and communication, to problem solving consultation, to co-shaping decisions, to co–decision making), its degree (the extent to which employees have a say in influencing decisions about their work and organizational management), its level (organizational unit and function), its form (indirect/direct, nonfinancial/financial), and its participatory content (nature of issues).[78] For instance, information sharing entails the provision of data about the enterprise, from workplace matters to more strategic issues, and engagement with employees or their representatives that allows employees to participate in a dialogue with employers. Consultation is about the exchange of views, but final responsibility for decision making may reside with management. Engagement between line managers and their staff and teams is the glue that holds together more formal practices and makes them work. Increasingly, however, the workplace is undergoing more democratization toward bottom-up ideation and problem solving and more influence and control over decision making without ceding efficiency in the process. In the co-creation view, management starts with the potential of democracy, heterarchy, collaboration, and self-managing teams, with appropriate emergent constraints structuring the organization. In contrast, autocracy, hierarchy, bureaucracy, and command-and-control teams[79] have been predominant in traditional management following the treatment of employment relationship in a contractual framework in which workers agree to let managers direct their work within certain limits in exchange for income.[80] Note that even in the latter case, engagement platforms can help enhance the "right to manage the relationship" with a say in job design, work assignments, and activity co-ordination. While managers and workers grapple with modes of engagement (and forms of responsible autonomy versus control), the remolding of participation in enterprises continues. We return to a discussion of management systems, enterprise architectures, and achieving transformational change in organizing agency, in Chapters 5, 6, and 7.

As organizations recognize the immediacy of enabling and connecting with co-creation experiences of stakeholders, they must also connect with the communities in which they operate and are enveloped in and mesh together the joint network resources of community-enabled enterprise ecosystems. How enterprises can build capabilities in meshworked social, business, civic, and natural communities and leverage co-creation ecosystems of capabilities is the subject of the next chapter.

4   LEVERAGING CO-CREATION ECOSYSTEMS OF CAPABILITIES

In the previous chapter, we discussed how engagement platforms are embedded in the domain of people's human experiences. Enterprises, as a nexus of engagement platforms, are enveloped in both the communities they serve and in communities whose resources they depend on, as shown in Figure 4-1. Every enterprise must engage community stakeholders to build capability ecosystems along with them. To do so, as we will discuss in this chapter, enterprises must mesh together value creation resources in social, business, civic, and natural communities—by finding common denominators, similarities and overlaps—and connecting them with value creation opportunities. Using the Starbucks example in the previous chapter, we explain how enterprises can do just this.

We then use the detailed example of the ITC enterprise to illustrate how to build and leverage co-creation ecosystems of capabilities using the principles of Inclusivity, Generativity, Linkability, and Evolvability (or GELI for short, as a handy mnemonic).[81] The ITC example also motivates how multiple enterprises can work together to jointly expand the capacities of private, public, and social sector ecosystems in economy and society as a whole, a subject we discuss in more detail in Chapters 8 and 9.

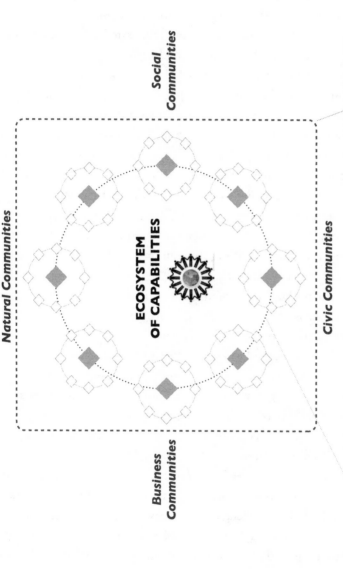

Natural Communities

Social Communities

Business Communities

Civic Communities

ECOSYSTEM OF CAPABILITIES

Strategic Architecture of Enterprises as a Nexus of Engagement Platforms

Private-Public-Social Sector Ecosystem as a Meshwork of Social, Business, Civic, and Natural Communities

FIGURE 4-1   Ecosystem of capabilities

Note: A capability ecosystem is a meshwork of social, business, civic, and natural communities, whose leveraging of capabilities virtualizes agential capacities in value creation. Capability ecosystems envelop engagement platforms.

COMMUNITIES AS ENVELOPING ENGAGEMENT PLATFORMS

Consider the coffee supply ecosystem in which Starbucks participates. It is composed of innumerable supply agencies spread across various natural communities (e.g., local ecologies of coffee growing regions), social communities (e.g., Rwandan artisans and their families), civic communities (e.g., Conservation International and Fairtrade Foundation), and business communities (e.g., farmers, wholesalers, Starbucks, and other buyers). Similarly, on the demand side, human experiences with coffee stores are embodied in consumer communities and local neighborhood citizen communities. Each type of agency within those communities can be described as a *multiplicity of potential capacities* that can be intensified through engagement platforms and can actualize new sources of experience-based value. These ecosystem capacities are critical in constituting ecosystems of enterprise capabilities, since all agents in the system possess an indefinite number of affects that can be converted into capabilities in co-dependencies with other agencies in an enterprise's strategic architecture of multiple engagement platforms.

In the case of the Starbucks enterprise, enhancing co-creative capacities in its capability ecosystem means having to overhaul its organizational design to allow engagements with all these various stakeholders at different stages of the supply-demand chain. This means initiating the recruitment and training of experts and managers to develop resident capabilities, adapting and practicing new ways of decision making and governance mechanisms to accommodate new goals, and constantly negotiating and experimenting with these capabilities to co-evolve sustainable outcomes of value for all stakeholders.

For instance, Starbucks needs to ensure a consistent and sustainable supply of coffee beans to support its retail sales growth. In the past, Starbucks has found itself in challenging situations with its coffee bean suppliers over fair trade issues and the branding of coffees based on their origins. Starbucks has attempted to tackle the issue more directly by collaborating with partners such as Conservation International to buy responsibly grown, ethically traded coffee, while at the same time integrating farmers more deeply into the Starbucks value chain by participating in the farmers' value chain. The goal is to enhance inclusivity of farmers in the Starbucks ecosystem by helping to create a better future for farmers. For instance, Starbucks is mitigating climate change effects with farmers as part of yield-enhancing solutions through farmer incentives ranging from preventing deforestation to providing capacity-building resources, including loan programs through social investment organizations. There is also a particular focus on small farmers: in 2009, about 85 percent of Starbucks coffee was grown on small-scale family farms with less than 12 hectares of land. Through its Small Farmer Support Initiative, a joint engagement platform with the Fairtrade Foundation (part of a global network of "fair trade" labeling organizations), Starbucks is now more actively engaged in dialogue with farmers in east Africa and Latin America. As a result, since the opening of the company's Farmer Support Center in Costa Rica, Starbucks has seen improvements from participating growers in quality evaluation scores, a 20 percent increase in yields per hectare, an 80 percent reduction in the use of pesticides, and a 5 percent increase in suppliers' performance scores for sustainable practices. Starbucks is also giving its customers the opportunity to connect with entrepreneurial artisans from local communities in its supply-side regions who are creating a better life for themselves and their families through its "Shared Planet" engagement platform online and through sales of merchandise in its stores, such as fabric tumblers and hand-sewn totes created by Rwandan artisans.

The Starbucks Shared Planet platform was created in 2008 and has evolved with an increased commitment to environmental and social responsibility. On this platform, the company makes a commitment to do good to its community and the planet from the way it buys coffee to minimizing its environmental footprint to being involved in local communities. Starbucks engages directly with its customers and other stakeholders on the interactive Shared Planet platform. The company encourages individuals to interact with its Global Responsibility annual reports in key focus areas, inviting them to create their own custom reports of portions that matter to them, share and discuss aspects with friends via social media, and submit ideas through the MSI platform discussed in the previous chapter.

Starbucks Shared Planet has three key areas of focus: ethical sourcing, environmental stewardship, and community involvement. The main goals, supporting goals, and KPIs (Key Performance Indicators) in each focus area are publicly stated, and progress is reported with full transparency. Take environmental stewardship. Starbucks customers have the opportunity to bring in a reusable cup for their beverages, reducing their drink price by 10 cents (in North America) and reducing their environmental footprint. For its part, Starbucks has taken steps in using renewable energy, conserving energy and water usage in its stores, and undertaking "green construction" of its stores. Most important, these pledges provide transparency and access, inviting customers to engage in a dialogue around company activities. Further, in a bid to connect better with the local neighborhood communities in which Starbucks stores are embedded, Starbucks engages a community of store designers who emphasize local materials and craftsmanship, reused and recycled elements, use of renewable energy, conservation of energy and water usage, and "green construction" of its stores, with motifs entailing storytelling and sensory engagement with the Starbucks coffee heritage, its ethical sourcing, and its socially and environmentally responsible activities. Starbucks Shared Planet is in keeping with the company's revitalized mission statement: "to inspire and nurture the human spirit—one person, one cup, and one neighborhood at a time." As part of Shared Planet, Starbucks promises to "reinvigorat[e] the in-store experience for its customers by focusing on the aspects of stores that make each one unique." As Arthur Rubinfeld, president of Starbucks Global Development, said, "We recognize the importance of continuously evolving with our customers' interests, lifestyles, and values in order to stay relevant over the long term. Ultimately, we hope customers will feel an enhanced sense of community, a deeper connection to our coffee heritage, and a greater level of commitment to environmental consciousness."[82]

Starbucks continues to find ways to connect with NGOs and other partners to build joint engagement platforms that harness the collective reach of community involvement in the neighborhoods of Starbucks stores. For instance, Starbucks partnered with V2V, an online platform that connects volunteers to service organizations. The connection with V2V was originally made by a Starbucks employee in the United States and was soon extended to a Starbucks V2V platform that sought to be a catalyst for conversation and connection, inspiring people to contribute to a cause greater than themselves. Starbucks set a public global goal of facilitating more than 1 million hours of community service every year.

Online at MSI, Starbucks shares its corporate goals, describes what it has achieved, and invites ideas on underachieved goals and where it has challenges. Authentic engagement breeds trust over time. We believe there is no other way in an openly networked society to build the trust that many institutions have lost. Starbucks is connecting with the experiences of customers in the social communities in which their stores are embedded, as well as civic communities at large. Starbucks is also connecting with employee and managerial experiences throughout its value chain, as well as extending and deepening external stakeholder engagement in the ecosystem in which it operates. Through its multiple engagement platforms, Starbucks emphasizes that "You" as an individual are an integrative part of its enterprise ecosystem—from the farmers and communities on its supply-side, to its employees inside, to the in-store experience and local neighborhood communities on its demand-side, and beyond to the larger fabric of human experiences in society at large.

CO-CREATIVE CAPABILITY BUILDING

The crafting of a strategic architecture of the co-creative enterprise ecosystem is in reality a morphogenetic process of experimentation and discovery. On the one hand, co-creation platforms are embedded in stakeholder experience domains in the communities served by enterprises. The enterprise as a platform orchestrator must evolve the interaction environments afforded by assemblage systems based on stakeholder value of co-created experience outcomes. On the other hand, the domains of individual experiences are, in turn, embodied in the communities to which they belong, with their social, business, civic, and natural facets. The enterprise, as ecosystem innovator, must *virtualize co-creative capacities* in meshworks of communities that constitute the enterprise ecosystem. We now discuss the GELI principles of co-creative capability building to do just this. In applying these principles, enterprises have to start with the common denominators, similarities, and overlaps of communities, corresponding to the strategic architecture of co-creation platforms being crafted.

Inclusivity stands for the social ethic of including all stakeholding individuals who can make relevant and sincere contributions and granting them equal opportunities to do so, free from external or internal coercion.[83] This moral compact builds on the principle of having respect for everybody and joining in solidarity and responsibility of each for all. It is important to note that inclusivity does not entail universally binding norms of action but instead only an unrestricted access to platforms of engagement and participation therein. Inclusivity is all about *being sensitive to difference*, which is a signature trait of co-creation platform architectures.[84] A capability ecosystem is deemed democratic, and legitimately so, to the extent that those affected by it are included and provided the opportunities to influence outcomes.[85] At the macro-level, such inclusive capability leverage facilitates deliberative democracy that can promote justice. At the community-level, collective problem-solving efforts gain legitimacy and effectiveness when they include all expressions and criticisms of a multiplicity of stakeholders. More specifically, inclusivity can deliver fair solutions to collective problems exactly and only when individuals engage one another from their situated positions in acknowledgment of others' situated positions. Recognizing differences and making them consistent—that is, preserving the heterogeneity of individuals through complementarities and imbrications of material and semiotic elements—is a foundational logic of the strategic architecture of co-creative enterprise ecosystems.[86]

The *generativity* of a capability ecosystem is a function of technical, social, and organizational capacities of interactions in the environments that the architecture of engagement platforms afford to facilitate the generation of potential outcomes of value to individuals. Generative mechanisms are the ways that entities act and that exist as their causal powers.[87] A generative mechanism endures, and, under the appropriate circumstances, it is exercised as long as the properties that account for it persist, with undischarged potential energy for new transformations.

The *linkability* of the capability ecosystem is a function of networked capacities across the interaction environments of engagement platforms within the enterprise, as well as across multiple enterprises in the ecosystem of social, business, civic, and natural communities in which enterprises operate. As new information and communication technologies connect the world more deeply in global networks of instrumentality, linkability is about establishing new connections that can create new capacities in the system.[88] The components of linkages are both autonomous and dependent vis-à-vis the network, and they may be a part of other networks and thus of other systems of means aimed at other goals. The performance of a given network depends on its connectedness—that is, its structural ability to facilitate interactions among its components—and its consistency—that is, the extent to which there is sharing of interests between the network's goals and its components' goals.

The *evolvability* of a capability ecosystem is a function of the capacities of individual components to form assemblages whose emergent properties refer to a component's "inside"—that is, to the interactions among the lower-scale components that compose it—retaining its heterogeneity. As such, assemblage systems have to be designed not for "final use" (however defined) but based on the evolvability of capabilities in a manner that enables future modifications and extensions based on stakeholders' changing interactions and the enterprise ecosystem's changing capabilities. That's why an assemblage's capacity to respond to a selective challenge by producing the right kind of variation is called its evolvability.[89] Evolvability is about change—especially change that deals with new complexities—and the new, more complex whole systems becoming greater than the sums of their parts.[90]

To illustrate how enterprises can build and leverage co-creative enterprise ecosystems of capabilities, consider the example of ITC, an Indian conglomerate with businesses in agriculture, food sales, and other industries. Its Agri Business Division (ABD) was originally a trader of agricultural commodities procured from public markets and cooperatives where farmers came to sell their crops. In 2000, the company faced two challenges: improving its position in the global commodities-export market, particularly in soybeans, and sourcing high-quality agricultural commodities for the company's newly launched packaged/branded foods business. The problem was that the quality of Indian farmers' crops was below the level ITC believed was needed to compete in international markets, and Indian farms' productivity was both too low and not rising fast enough to support ITC's growth. The root cause of the problems was the plethora of small, inefficient farms that dominated the country's agricultural sector and state-run markets that were opaque and corrupt.

ITC concluded that the best way to improve the firm's position was to lift the economic performance of the entire ecosystem by designing new engagement platforms between the company and the Indian farmers to co-create mutual value. This meant building a new ecosystem of capabilities. As a company with an Indian soul, its leaders empathized with the small farmers' hardships and their fierce desire to stay independent, and they personally wanted to help lift as many of them out of poverty as possible. ITC recognized that farmers were frequently cheated on weight and price and often were not paid in full for their crops on the day of the sale, which violated government regulations. ITC reasoned that the best way to raise small farms' productivity and quality was to help growers improve their methods, and the best way to do that was to teach them what "efficient" farming means. Enhancing the individual farmer's experience was a primary goal at the outset. However, to be successful, ITC has also had to engage multiple stakeholders, including the social and natural communities in which the farmers lived and operated, and civic communities and NGOs that had cultivated rural relationships with farmers. It was also important to involve the Indian government entities responsible for the state-run marketplaces, or "mandis," as they are called. At the national level, there was impetus to improve the efficiency of the mandis on the one hand and pressure from the business community on the other, such as multinational packaged foods companies looking to source vegetables and crops through contract farming following the liberalization and general opening up of India's markets.

The first engagement platforms ITC built entailed an assemblage system called e-Choupal (*choupal* means "meeting place"), which consisted of village-level information and communications technology) kiosks with Internet access managed by an ITC-trained local farmer (called a *sanchalak*). These kiosks are typically located within five kilometers of the farms in the sanchalak's village, with about four or five villages being served by a single kiosk. Farmers gather around and interact with the sanchalak and other farmers in the village and sometimes with ITC personnel. The e-Choupals provide information in the local language on the daily weather forecast, prices of various crops, and other agricultural news. Farmers can learn about the weather conditions and farming methods specific to each crop and region, agricultural extension services, and agriculture universities in ITC's enterprise network that offer expert advice. ITC also provides an e-mail service through which farmers (via the sanchalak) can interact with technical people at ITC, specific agricultural scientists, and fellow farmers in other villages who may have dealt with similar challenges.

The choice of a farmer as sanchalak for the human assemblage component of the e-Choupal platform was not obvious to ITC. Indeed, it was originally the least obvious choice, as ITC explored the village postman and other village-level candidates such as civic community leaders. On the other hand, choosing a farmer as sanchalak meant honing the profile and selection process to identify those individuals with credibility in each village who would be seen as trustworthy agents of change, among other criteria, such as the layout and location of the farmer's dwelling, his or her education, and his or her ability to physically support the information and communications technology digital infrastructure. Every sanchalak, once chosen by ITC through its due diligence, must take an oath before the community that he or she will serve the community's best interests without discrimination. The sanchalak also agrees to a social contract that he or she will spend part of his or her income on community welfare. Hence, the creative capacity of the engagement platform is a morphogenetic process, whose design emerges from continuous enterprise experimentation in building its components together with the communities in which the platform is embedded. Note that the co-shaping of the e-Choupal platform itself involves another platform of engagements to actualize the very elements of the capability ecosystem supporting the focal e-Choupal platform.

The second e-Choupal engagement platform consists of hub facilities located 25 to 30 kilometers from the villages, where farmers bring their grain. Each of these hubs serves about 40 to 50 Choupals. ITC's hubs not only give farmers an alternative option to going to the mandis, but they also provide electronic weighing, conduct objective quality testing, ensure spot payment, and provide rest-stop services. ITC began to employ intermediaries from the mandis (called *samyojaks*) at its processing centers who handle much of the hub logistics.

In 2004, ITC expanded its hub facilities to include distribution capabilities and began building a third engagement platform called Choupal Saagar, which sells fertilizer, seeds, pesticides, farm equipment, and other goods and services. This platform enhances value by using insights generated from ITC's ongoing dialogue with farmers to shape the mix of merchandise sold at Saagar outlets. The dialogue happens both when farmers transact at e-Choupal (through the sanchalak at the kiosk and when farmers are at the hub facility) and particularly in dedicated "live forums" facilitated by ITC personnel on a rotating basis across villages. Through such dialogue, ITC has gained a more granular understanding of the interactions among soil types, seeds, and fertilizers, which it has used to promote new hybrid seeds, fertilizers, and tilling techniques that help farmers save money in seed, land preparation, plowing time, and water usage, while helping them maximize crop yield. As a result, ITC has also improved its soil-testing services at its labs and built a data warehouse of soil properties in the villages where it operates. This data is now used by agricultural input entities in ITC's partner network to, in turn, generate better products and services for farmers. Further, by aggregating the demand of the villages, the company creates the scale to obtain much better prices from manufacturers than the villages could on their own. Sales and service personnel for the fertilizers, seeds, pesticides, and equipment companies also now have a platform through which they can engage with the rural market, both making their job more exciting and generating new sales for their enterprises. Choupal Saagars also act as a major outlet for ITC's own branded products, while continuing to strengthen relations with its farmer suppliers. The Saagar platform continues to evolve its growing network of companies eager to tap into India's rural markets. ITC acts as a nodal company—pulling together the resources, products, and services of many different suppliers of "farmer input" and buyers of "farmer output" and injecting into the system a lot of agricultural expertise from its own enterprise network resources as it continues to evolve.

In the case of ITC, its capability ecosystem had to evolve in accordance with new tiers of its strategic co-creation architecture that enabled it to also become a "reverse distribution channel" of not only farming goods and services but rural market offerings in general. ITC began to evolve the role of samyojaks to serve as a link between ITC headquarters and rural retailers (which include people in villages as retail agents generating additional incomes for themselves). Originally, sanchalaks were asked to introduce rural retailers to the samyojaks where needed and to help in partnering banks within ITC's business network to assess the credit risk for each retailer. However, sanchalaks with predominantly farming and agricultural skills, as opposed to inventory management or distribution skills, were increasingly ill-suited to retail goods and services on a growing scale. In fact, many sanchalaks themselves began to express reluctance to being seen in their villages as mercantile people selling products and collecting money. The sanchalaks are now reserved for a more consultative role, acting as facilitators without experiencing social alienation in their villages.

Thus, the building of various co-creative capabilities in the ecosystem is the means through which singular capacities emerge. In the case of ITC, while the sanchalaks had become an institution in and of themselves, attention had to be paid to the evolution of platform components. The sanchalak's and samyojak's roles have continued to evolve through differentials in capability building, including ongoing experimentation with new forms of community-based models. This will presumably result in new singular capacities that will take its co-creative ecosystem to new levels by linking downstream co-creation with upstream co-creation and transforming value creation on both demand and supply sides in "win more–win more" fashion. Through continuous engagement, experiential learning, and real-time insight generation, via dialogic and transparent interactions with the various stakeholders in its ecosystem, ITC has identified several new potential value creation opportunities, including an employment exchange for rural youth, employability skill building, rural tourism, and biomass-based energy.

Profits have multiplied five times since the launch of e-Choupal, now reaching $20 million. On the cost side, ITC has dramatically improved its procurement efficiency. It has reduced its transactions costs by 25 to 30 percent on average by eliminating some of the handling cost involved in the mandi system (including transportation, labor, bagging, and commissions). There are also revenue gains from partner companies that pay commissions on all products and services sold through its Saagar retail platform, offering new services such as "Choupal Haat"—a physical platform for enterprises to engage more creatively with rural consumers, and augmenting commodity-selling revenue from providing its downstream commodity customers a flexible menu of paid service options, including packing, storage, option to cancel, quality segregation, credit terms, and so on. The bulk of ITC ABD's revenues, however, come from internally supporting its food businesses. Out of ITC's agribusiness division revenues of Rs 5,695 crore (approximately $1.3 billion) in 2011–2012, internal sales for supplying commodities to the FMCG business were Rs 2,282 crore (or about $500 million). ITC e-Choupal is seen by senior management as a strategic source of competitive advantage, a core capability that supports ITC's food businesses, which has been able to produce higher-quality products without higher costs, thereby driving more sales. A case in point is the Aashirvaad brand, which became one of India's largest-selling wheat flours within just two years of its launch. In other cases, ITC has been able to create a new market where there was none. For example, ITC was able to launch ready-to-cook instant pasta at the very low price of Rs 15 for an 83-gram packet, when the only other similar product was an import priced at Rs 85.

Building co-creative capability ecosystems requires a focus on the experiences of all stakeholders (individuals)—paying as much attention to the engagement process through which a stakeholder identifies and becomes included in and involved with the organization. Indian farmers who use ITC's e-Choupals and hubs are deeply excited about being part of ITC's capability ecosystem and not just because it is helping them grow higher-quality crops and raise their incomes. They are also happy about being able to participate in the transformation of their own wealth-welfare-wellbeing and that of their communities at large. ITC employees—who believe they are improving the lives of both farmers and rural Indian citizens—share in that excitement and are equally engaged. Becoming a co-creative enterprise implies continuously enhancing the wealth-welfare-wellbeing of all stakeholders while building new strategic capital (i.e., new sources of innovation, value creation, and competitive advantage). This requires not only continuously meshing capabilities and revirtualizing creative capacities in the capability ecosystem but also reactualizing more valuable co-created experience outcomes through continuously evolving engagement platform architectures that intensify value creation in new expansive ways while managing risk-reward relationships together with stakeholders.[91]

ITC's co-creative capability ecosystem continues to become more tightly woven into the social, business, civic, and natural communities in which it operates as it expands the virtual space of potential ecosystem value creation opportunities. When stakeholders engage as co-creators, the interaction environments afforded by the platform must actually realize meaningful outcomes of value to individuals. "Virtualizing" value creative capacities is about designing for "real" outcomes that have not been "actualized" yet. After outcomes are actualized, co-creative enterprises must respond to insights originating from the actual co-creation experiences of people, continuously designing and redesigning what is of value, as discussed in the previous chapter. For instance, ITC has gained a more granular understanding of the interactions among soil types, seeds, and fertilizers, which it has used to promote new hybrid seeds, fertilizers, and tilling techniques that help farmers save money in seed, land preparation, plowing time, and water usage, while helping them maximize crop yield. The knowledge gained from farmers has also allowed ITC to provide soil-testing services at its labs and build a data warehouse of soil properties in the villages where it operates. Agricultural input companies can use this data to develop better products and services for farmers. ITC has driven the design of new weather insurance products for farmers, with new pricing structures reflecting more accurately the impact of rainfall and temperature changes on individual crop yields. This deeper personalization involves a more granular and direct level of communication and interaction with individual farmers—augmenting their interactions through sanchalaks that enhance e-Choupal scalability through its partnership network. ITC is growing its network of global resource partners from seed companies such as Nunhems, which offers hybrid seeds; Bayer, which has expertise in crop science and the use of fertilizers and pesticides; International Development Enterprises India, which provides drip irrigation technologies; the Central Institute for Medicinal and Aromatic Plants and agricultural universities, which provide information on best farming practices; and Well Grow, which is an internal ITC unit that supplies neem-based fertilizers. Through a new engagement platform, demonstration farms, ITC has showcased production and harvesting techniques (e.g., irrigation, plant beds, intercropping, etc.) and new crop varieties to increase the quantity and improve the quality of crops, to diversify crops, and to improve efficiency. By digging deeper into what new farming experiences farmers truly value, ITC is moving farmers from subsistence farming to profit earning and improving their standard of living, which in turn benefits ITC's enhanced partnership network to sell valuable products and services. ITC now understands that every village, every sanchalak, and every farmer is different, with unique needs, motivations, and desires for growth. The services and solutions had to be what the village actually needed rather than what ITC believed would be good for the village.

To enable all of the above, ITC had to create an IT-enabled enterprise architecture that supported a wide variety of engagement platforms, from supporting both the procurement of crops, to selling a variety of product-service offerings to farmers, to incorporating the various partners using ITC's network. Given the heterogeneity of individuals and offerings to be supported, the system had to be intuitive, easy to use, and flexible to support a variety of applications and business processes. The interfaces had to be in multiple languages and intuitive for farmers to use. Further, the technical architecture had to accommodate changes easily due to continuous changes in regulations and tax laws, especially as the concept of futures and options in the Indian commodities market was evolving. ITC also had to integrate the rural distribution platform with its enterprise financial systems so management could improve decision making through real-time visibility of end-to-end financial implications of enterprise actions in its value chain.[92]

Thus, ITC has built an inclusive, generative, linked, and evolvable enterprise capability ecosystem that engages vendors and partners on the one hand and end customers and users on the other. Value creative capacities engendered by ITC's strategic architecture of multiple co-creation platforms ultimately entail infrastructure, sustainability, governance, and developmental capacities from whose virtual states actual value emerges through intensive co-creative engagements of stakeholders. Co-creative capability building has spread from the ITC e-Choupal initiative to ITC's other businesses, including the company's paperboards business. For instance, ITC chairman Deveshwar spearheaded a farm forestry initiative to mobilize subsistence farmers and tribal people to plant trees in local wastelands—a strategy requiring substantial investment, a longer gestation than is typical, and considerable senior management attention to manage market uncertainty and business risks. In an innovative model, the natural resource ecosystem is regenerated every four years. ITC has also invested extensively in R&D to create clonal tree saplings that are disease resistant and grow faster in harsh conditions, which makes the growing of pulpwood species on degraded wasteland sustainable and offers a continuous source of income for growers. These buyers are free to sell to other buyers besides ITC, similar to the e-Choupal model. In the process of changing the lumber supply chain in this manner, ITC has also transformed its paper business into a significant producer of environmentally friendly, chlorine-free paper and paperboard.

As social responsibility in business gains momentum, private sector enterprises are playing a more active role in tackling economic development, environmental protection, and other social issues. This movement has required many enterprises to work more closely with governmental organizations, nonprofits, civic groups, and consumers. In ITC's ever-expanding capability ecosystem, farmers also have access to land records, health and education services, NGOs working for cattle breed improvement and water harvesting, and self-help groups. Its effectiveness, however, depends on making participants' engagement experiences more meaningful and plowing back insights gained into deepening capabilities, making them more sustainable. Ultimately, co-creative enterprises must better manage the triple bottom line as well—balancing economic success, environmental stewardship, and social progress—to achieve sustainable social legitimacy. ITC's commitment in this regard has resulted in a more holistic view of the linkages between the decline in agricultural productivity and the deterioration of the natural resource base. For instance, its Mission Sunehra Kal initiative, a rural capacity-building program, is active in as many as ten Indian states, empowering rural communities to adopt sustainable changes that make them economically competitive and socially secure. It aims to accomplish this not only by helping farmers with new farming practice solutions to achieve higher income, but also by enabling communities to develop and manage water, soil, and forest resources for long-term ecological security, empowering rural men and women by creating new nonfarm livelihoods and facilitating the development of primary education, health, and sanitation infrastructures. Further, ITC has contributed to augmenting forest cover and water harvesting work in tandem with its internal practices of energy efficiency and conservation. ITC has been water positive for nine years running, creating more than twice as much water-harvesting capacity as consumption, and has been carbon positive for six continuous years, sequestering twice the amount of carbon dioxide emitted by its operations. ITC is so far the only company in the world that continues to be carbon positive, water positive, and solid waste recycling positive.

The ability to manage co-creative enterprises organization-wide and in the ecosystem in which they participate is a direct function of the *co-creative capacities of management systems*, the subject of the next chapter.

5   BUILDING CO-CREATIVE
MANAGEMENT SYSTEMS

The co-creation-based view of enterprises involves a profound democratization and decentralization of value creating management systems toward the locus of interactions among individuals inside the enterprise and between the enterprise and its customers, suppliers, partners, and other stakeholders. Individuals in organizations need to think in terms of engagement platforms, experience-based offerings, and capability-based ecosystem innovation opportunities and connect then with value creating resources through the co-creation experiences of the individuals they serve. Further, the development of compelling co-creation experiences with stakeholding individuals requires that they be allowed to engage in styles of interaction of their own choosing and not only those dictated by the enterprise.[93]

In this chapter, we illustrate how co-creative enterprises must develop management systems that let individuals participate in designing the value of product-service offerings through their co-creation experiences and together with other stakeholders. These include customer-facing activities, brand-building and channel management activities, supplier and logistical activities, new product-service development and internal operations, strategy formulation and execution, talent and project management activities, and performance and risk management activities, all of which must undergo the appropriate transformation to migrate to co-creation.

CUSTOMER EXPERIENCES, SERVICE, AND RELATIONSHIP MANAGEMENT

Despite decades of sincere efforts by companies to understand customers and become customer-focused, managers and customers remain deeply disconnected. Managers in large organizations do not have the opportunity to understand and viscerally experience the business as their customers do. Infrequent and planned visits to key customers do not provide a meaningful perspective on how customers experience the business. The irritations all of us have felt as customers in using call centers are a good example. Customer experiences have been a distant reality for most managers—especially senior managers—as customer experiences have typically not been seen as sources of value creation. Further, like customers, managers are a heterogeneous lot. Though IT systems have traditionally assumed that all managers at a given level need similar information, the reality is that every manager has a unique approach to managing. This can contribute to significant variance in "feel" for the customer experience among managers. Further, because frontline employees are closest to the customers, they are most likely to understand customer concerns. In an airline, a hotel, a retail store, a financial services firm, a utility, or a government agency, the people closest to the customer experience are the call center operators, the salespeople, and the service representatives. How can enterprises engage them through co-creation?

One of the authors witnessed an innovative use of a call center in Kobe where Nestlé was experimenting with one of its four "captive" call centers in Japan—call centers staffed with company employees rather than contractors.[94] The head of Customer Relationships, Junpei Fujisaki, was spearheading a new initiative dubbed "CRM as Dialogue" that was vividly emphasized all around the call center. Agents seemed more relaxed than in a conventional outsourced call center. Fujisaki explained that his focus was on ensuring that employees were happy because if they were not, they would not be able to engage customers in a meaningful dialogue. Most important, he said, was the quality of the conversations and the "active listening and probing mindset" of employees. These employ-ees had undergone a qualitatively different kind of training. The call cen-ter overlooked the beautiful Kobe Bay, and employees had the best view. These customer-facing employees were referred to as "line managers" rather than just "staff" to reflect their disproportionate influence on the customer experience.

Every so often, one of the call center employees would get up, go to the center of the room, and write on a board some insights she had gleaned (all the employees were women) with her name after the statement. Oc-casionally, someone from the product development group or the interac-tive marketing group on the other side of the floor (without a direct view of Kobe Bay) would stop by and read the comments. If anything caught their attention, they would arrange for that particular issue to be explored further. In this way, call center employees were actively engaged in the new product development process and in fine-tuning the marketing of new products along with customers. Each month, an award was given for "best co-created insight," as judged by departmental managers. Now, contrast the sense of self-worth generated for the Nestlé Japan's call center employees with the experience of typical call center employees measured on "average handle time." The same jump in experience quality of em-ployees applies to the over 1.5 million customers who called the Nestlé center and were encouraged to share their experiences.

In emerging markets, customer call centers can be a rich place for cus-tomer experimentation and generating insights through customer experi-ences. Consider the Customer Care Center at Nokia India, which handles customer service and repair of Nokia's cell phones. Every year, Nokia used to launch a large number of new cell phone models, producing a service challenge of major proportions. India was one of Nokia's fastest-growing markets, and in 2006, the company had a commanding 70 percent market share there. Sanjeev Sharma, then CEO of Nokia India, told one author that market leadership wasn't good enough for Nokia if the firm wanted to become "invincible." This meant focusing on customer retention as much as customer acquisition.

Given the fast pace of new product introductions into the market, Nokia had to contend with several issues involving malfunctioning handsets. In a high-growth market like India, where over 70 million cell phones were sold annually at that time, it was hard to keep up with the never-ending flow of customer service calls coming through the call center and retail care centers. Shivakumar (Shiv), then head of Service Operations at Nokia India, was working relentlessly to reduce turnaround time (TAT) and provide an excellent service experience at every touchpoint. Shiv's group had previously launched several TAT-related initiatives to reduce response time and improve service by improving process quality, and Nokia had run several successful quality management, Six Sigma, and continuous process improvement programs. In 2006, Sharma got together with Shiv to explore how co-creative thinking could enhance their approach to customer care.[95]

After a series of workshops discussing co-creation opportunities, call center employees started listening to customer calls with a "different ear," as Shiv put it. By focusing on customer experience in addition to call productivity, customer care managers began to see new co-creation opportunities. They got ideas for new experiments. For example, what would happen if the call center sought out customers rather than waiting for customers to call them? By contacting previous callers for a dialogue, they discovered that many customers would pay to have their phone picked up from home or from their workplaces. If the phone could not be repaired, they would be happy with a substitute handset as long as the individual's contacts and content were transferred over to the new phone and it was fully charged. This retrospectively simple insight triggered the implementation of more creative ideas, such as the development of a "floating mobile van" that stops at selected Nokia dealers, makes simple repairs on site, takes phones to a central repair center, and returns them on the next round a few days later. Many dealers got very excited about the van and started competing with one another to have it parked outside their stores, even offering to share in the cost of mobile van operations. In this fashion, Nokia dealers became involved, as a community, in the redesign of the new repair process between customers and Nokia.

The Nokia co-creation team also began imagining what would happen if the repair process at the centers was made transparent to customers. Several customers had expressed the desire to know what was happening to their expensive phones as they were being repaired. As Nokia listened to conversations with customers in the call centers, it became evident that much of the "soft" contextual information about service problems was not being captured in the database—for example, the fact that the handset had been dropped into water or that the same problem had occurred several times before. The Nokia co-creation team realized the best way to guarantee that the description of the problem was accurate was to open the call center database to customers—in other words, let customers add the information themselves. This move eliminated multiple calls to ensure that all the information was accurate, thereby reducing Nokia's costs while creating a better customer co-creation experience.

Nokia also began recognizing the potential role the call center could play in channeling customer insights to the teams that were developing new cell phone software tailored to the Indian market. For example, a New Delhi disc jockey called the Nokia service number to suggest a change in mailing list software. In the conversation that ensued, the team discovered he had redesigned the software for big mailing lists. They invited him to the Gurgaon headquarters of Nokia India, where he showed the team how he had tinkered with the software. All they had to do was import his fix into the software, and a new application was born. With that, the team realized the call center was more than a repository for problems; it could also be an engagement platform for co-creating insights with millions of Nokia users, some of them even acting as augmented developers.

Many stories of the dawn of co-creation thinking in enterprises start with a corporate crisis. In June 2005, Jeff Jarvis, a Dell customer (and a professor of journalism), posted a blog entry called "Dell Hell." He had recently purchased a new laptop, paying a high price for a four-year, in-home customer service warranty. He experienced many problems with it, from overheating and network connectivity problems to CPU usage issues and machine malfunctions. The service representative who came to Jarvis's house couldn't fix the problems because he did not have the necessary parts, so Jarvis was ultimately forced to send the laptop back. It turned out that the replacement machine did not work properly either. Only after e-mailing Dell's chief marketing officer did Jarvis get someone to resolve the issue and receive a full refund. Jarvis ended up buying an Apple computer, and in August 2005, he blogged an open letter to Michael Dell, suggesting

that Dell management read blogs, ask customers for guidance, and participate in the conversation that customers were having *without* Dell.

Dell already had active programs in place for customer satisfaction,
service quality, and market research. In fact, the company at that time was
considered by many to be highly customer-oriented. After all, Dell had
largely invented the "direct model," in which the company interacts directly with its customers. It relied on excellent phone and online customer
support to connect with them. The problem was that Dell's customer-
oriented activities were largely Dell's view of the customer experience, not
the customer's. In other words, Dell's customer orientation was largely
product-centric and service process–centric and, thus, firm-centric. Dell
treated its customers as passive recipients of its offerings and processes,
disproportionately influencing the nature of customer value and staging
rather than co-creating, the customer experience. The focus at Dell was on
connecting the company's offerings to the customer, not on allowing customers to interact with Dell's products and processes on their own terms.

The "Dell Hell" blog post gave a voice to thousands of frustrated
customers who had been experiencing poor customer service from Dell
and unleashed a raging customer storm that had been simmering in the
market.[96] The blog discussion was a leading indicator of Dell's problems.
Once a stalwart on *Fortune* magazine's list of "America's Most Admired
Companies," Dell saw its customer satisfaction metrics plummet, and
Dell's stock price began a sharp decline. In the fall of 2005, Dell had to
issue a profit warning.

In April 2006, Dell finally joined the conversation. The company began
tracking blog posts, and it launched a "blog resolution team" to offer customer service and technical support, dispatching technicians to complain-
ing bloggers and earnestly trying to solve their problems. In July 2006,
Dell launched its Direct2Dell blog, with Dell's Lionel Menchaca giving
the company a human face and a no-nonsense voice. The company took a
while to find its stride. Bloggers, including Jarvis, blasted Dell's first blog
posts as classic corporate communications gobbledygook. Deeply etched
ways of "enterprise-think" limited Dell's ability to exhibit authenticity and
shift to co-creation mode. To its credit, the firm became more humble. It
acknowledged that Jarvis and other bloggers "were kind enough to tell us

what we're doing wrong" and that it would "keep working to get it right." The company asked for patience: "Give us some time and we'll prove it."[97]

For starters, Michael Dell made a point of personally meeting with Jarvis. Dell later remarked:

These conversations are going to occur whether you like it or not, okay? Well, do you want to be part of that or not? My argument is you absolutely do. You can learn from that. You can improve your reaction time. And you can be a better company by listening and being involved in that conversation.[98]

Dell began to see co-creating insights with customers as the linchpin of his strategy for "Dell 2.0," saying, "We need to think differently about the market and engage our customers in almost everything we do. It's a key to regaining momentum as a technology industry leader."[99]

Dell retrained its staff to take on more problems and more responsibilities—for example, higher-end techs could scrap their phone scripts, and techs in some countries were trained in empathy. Dell stopped counting the "handle time" per call that rushed conversations by motivating reps to transfer customers promptly, pushing them to become someone else's problem. The transfer rate fell from 45 percent to 18 percent. At Dell's worst, more than 7,000 of the 400,000 customers calling each week suffered transfers more than seven times. "In order to become very efficient, I think we became ineffective," said Dick Hunter, the former head of Manufacturing turned head of Customer Service.[100] The minutes per resolution of problems came down to the forties.

Dell trained a squad of 42 employees to spend their workdays engaging with customer communities on Facebook, Twitter, and other social media. The percentage of negative blog posts about Dell dropped from 49 percent to 22 percent. A key bit of information from the company's social media crew was that potential customers spent 99 percent of their time on the Web doing research and just 1 percent actually buying.[101] As a result, Dell dialed down the hard sell, helping customers make more informed choices, and focused on generating real-time insights usable for new products and markets.

With Michael Dell returning as CEO of Dell in 2008, the company further expanded its engagement with customers. As he stated, "I'm sure there's a lot of things that I can't even imagine but our customers can imagine. A company this size is not going to be about a couple of people coming up with ideas. It's going to be about millions of people and harnessing the power of those ideas."[102] Although Dell's sales fell in the Great Recession of 2008–2009, one of the few bright spots came from its embrace of the social media website Twitter. Dell had attracted 1.5 million followers on Twitter by late 2009, and its Twitter feed led directly to sales of $6.5 million in PCs, accessories, and software. The company received kudos for the authenticity of its engagement with Twitter users and recognition for its efforts to engage with customers across a range of social media.[103] However, with the market shifting to mobile computing and PC demand declining, the company faced the daunting challenge of remaking itself, yet again, by focusing next on software and higher-margin corporate IT and services. In September 2013, Michael Dell took the company he had founded private—away from the public scrutiny of Wall Street financiers—in a bid to revitalize and reshape it for the longer term in the wake of tumultuous changes in its business landscape.

DISTRIBUTION CHANNELS AND RETAIL EXPERIENCES
While the Web has been a disruptive force in "dis"-intermediating entities in the value chain system, in a lot of industries, distributors and dealers still play a significant role in the value creation process, although some aspects of their roles need to be redefined through co-creation thinking. Brother Industries Ltd., which has been around for more than a hundred years in the sewing machine manufacturing business, provides an example of the latent opportunities that can be tapped into through co-creative engagement of the distribution and retail network.[104] In 2008, Brother was the leader for sewing machines on its home Japanese market, with a 33 percent share measured in units sold, and it was the runner-up globally to Singer, with a 20 percent share of the worldwide market. However, as a latecomer to the U.S. home sewing machine market, and without access to U.S. dealer channels to sell its high-end machines, Brother had to focus on low-end machines sold through mass-merchandise channels such as Walmart. This strategy allowed the company to enter the U.S. market successfully, but Brother discovered that the market was saturated and

offered little growth potential. With the beachhead established at the low end of the market, Brother started wondering how it could develop a more lucrative, higher-end business that would help it penetrate the specialty dealer channel. Brother's first step was to design embroidery sewing machines suitable for this dealer channel. These machines were priced from $1,000 to $2,000, with higher-end computerized models such as the Innov-is 4000D going for as much as $5,000. The embroidery machines were lightweight and portable, with variable speed control and a wide selection of built-in stitches. Sales of the 4000D model proved higher than Brother expected at first, but these early sales slowed down as competitors started offering their own high-end machines. Internet channel competition further eroded margins.

Brother sought a new approach to increase its sales. In 2006, designers and engineers from Japan traveled to the United States to visit "super-users" of the company's machines. Immersive market research with these enthusiasts revealed that the existing machines were too small—in particular, the arm was too short for big projects such as quilted tapestries. Most of the enthusiasts were older women who had difficulty seeing the detail of thread tensions and needle holes; some of them had to use magnifying glasses. Most revealing, they often went online to share their passion with fellow enthusiasts, showing off specific projects and learning from one another's sewing experiences. Furthermore, while Brother had been providing "amateur-style" patterns and "family-style" patterns such as Disney and Nickelodeon characters, the super-users were exchanging professional-style patterns and customizing their designs.

In 2007, Brother began developing a new high-end machine, code-named the X1, for these enthusiastic "crafters," with a price point higher than the $5,000 ceiling it had in the past. This machine had the world's longest arm at 10 inches, a built-in camera that captured the point of sewing, the world's biggest color touch control panel, digital connectivity through a USB port, and a Web-enabled library of embroidery patterns that could be downloaded directly into the machine. The company also launched a social networking website dedicated to sewing and quilting hobbyists, where customers could share their sewing experiences, including photos of their projects. In other words, the X1 had all the makings of a product as an engagement platform. However, Brother had to rely on the support of its retail network through which sewing machines were sold.

A core insight was that if Brother could help consumers learn more about sewing through its dealers and craft shops, it could develop the market for a product as expensive as the X1. The company began sending instructors to dealers to teach them how to make projects with crafter hobbyists and also began adding to the resources it offered craft shops. Until then, specialty stores had been viewed as a place where products could be displayed and an occasional craft magazine could be picked up, but not as a place for learning and exchange. Brother realized that craft shops are community and education centers for enthusiasts and their friends and that working with them was a great way to enhance offerings and reach new customers. For instance, the company learned together with these craft shops that many young homemakers wanted to learn about sewing but did not have enough time or know where to begin.

Customers could engage in meaningful conversations with knowledgeable and skillful dealers-salespeople about products and projects. They could also take training classes at the shops, regardless of the brand of machines they owned. Brother also experimented with the retail space as a communal network. Online customers now have access to design software that allows them to make custom designs, share their designs with the community, and engage in conversations with other enthusiasts about their designs. Brother also began enabling the community to bring their experiences offline, tapping into the power of live interactions.

Meanwhile, Brother also reoriented its sales organization to support its co-creative initiatives. Salespeople shifted from the mass channel to the dealer channel, and they devoted a significant amount of their efforts to finding capable local dealers who could accommodate the hobbyists. The new product could be sold only by Brother-certified dealers, who agreed to develop the ability to train customers and engage them through in-store quilting and sewing clubs. A very important element of the approach was that it was not a hard sell. Customers could bring their own sewing and quilting machines to the stores, whether or not they bought them there. Some dealers were reluctant to take part because the new activities were time-consuming and did not necessarily lead to direct sales. To overcome this short-term bias, Brother invited dealers to its training facility, where the focus was not only on the product but also on how to create sewing projects. With support from the educators who conducted in-shop seminars and demonstrations for customers, dealers were beginning to see the potential for sales growth. Brother also changed the content of its semi-annual dealer meetings, which used to be primarily focused on entertainment but were now training-oriented, featuring both product and project education and business education. Interestingly, dealers began to willingly pay a registration fee for the meetings because they could "see" their value. The Brother example underscores how essential it is for traditional enterprises to co-creatively think about, and follow through, in managing the distribution and retail network together with channel stakeholders from inside the network.

CUSTOMER COMMUNITIES, BRAND MANAGEMENT, AND NEW PRODUCT DEVELOPMENT

While the essence of social media is to build a network of like-minded individuals, personal engagement in community co-creation can place individuals at the center of market- and brand-building processes. Hindustan Unilever Ltd. (HUL), India's largest consumer goods company, scored a big success in using this approach to breathe new life into Sunsilk, one of its leading brands. India has one of the world's largest youth populations, and HUL needed to attract more female customers between the ages of 17 and 22 to its products. Sunsilk, a leading brand of shampoo in India for many years, was increasingly viewed as outdated, as "Mom's brand." To change that perception and rejuvenate the brand, the company decided to launch the Sunsilk Gang of Girls (GoG) online community in June 2006.[105]

HUL understood that girls enjoy the process of communication itself, not just its end result, and therefore the goal of establishing the community was to make Sunsilk GoG a place for them to express themselves. HUL first conducted some traditional market research, interviewing its target market and learning that young Indian girls wanted "dollops of fun," "a dose of advice," "lots of sharing," "personalization of beauty care," and "professional growth." The company then repurposed a previous website, sunsilknaturals.com, which had over 100,000 registered users and a popular message board feature. HUL observed that site visitors tended to go beyond discussions of hair care and talk about celebrities, their favorite films, and other life issues. Using its global marketing expertise and working with a conventional advertising agency, HUL launched a media campaign to draw consumers to the new site, including a classic media blitzkrieg campaign in print, on television, and online, supplemented with offline events involving product displays and activities at malls and cinemas. It also organized the site to enable interactions among Sunsilk GoG members, HUL, HUL's partners, and its extended network of hair care professionals and beautification experts.

GoG was designed to maximize the participants' engagement with one another—around any topic of their choosing, not just hair care—through group blogs for each "gang" and a "talent show," in which site members voted on contributors' uploads. HUL even partnered with Monster. com to post resumes of registered members. Mentions of HUL products were few on the site; instead, the site focused on general hair-related topics. One of the most popular features was the "hair makeovers" option, which provided icons that consumers could select from to test new looks for themselves, including changes to hairstyle, hair color, lipstick, lipliner, eyeshadow, eyeliner, blush, and even contact lenses. The site also allowed users to converse with hair stylists at HUL salons about their specific hair and makeover needs. This aspect was inspired by Apple's Genius Bar, and HUL called it the "Hair Care Bar." Users were also offered a chance to win a "tress-busting experience"—an invitation to a social event and an appointment with a renowned hair stylist—if they purchased a bottle of Sunsilk.

Gangs of girls flocked to the site. Eighteen months after the launch in June 2006, Sunsilk GoG had 614,000 registered users, forming 37,154 gangs (limited to 50 members per group). Sunsilk's sales growth rose from 2 percent annually to 17 percent, and its market decline reversed as Sunsilk's share in the Indian market rose from 18 percent in 2002 to 40 percent in 2006. Brand metrics, such as recognition and identity, also saw meaningful gains as the brand scored its highest-ever score on "modernity" (up by 27 percent). Sunsilk became more popular among teens and younger adults.

In 2009, Unilever opened up its innovation process to external talent, inviting seven well-known hairstylists to co-create new offerings for different hair concerns and then connecting these offerings with the global Sunsilk user community. The hair concerns included straight, curly, and damaged hair; shaping, volumizing, and coloring hair; and scalp care and hair loss—each addressed by hair professionals with relevant expertise. HUL rolled out the co-created products as the Sunsilk Co-Creations line.

When properly constructed and supported, online communities can expand mutual value even in business-to-business settings. For example, the German software maker SAP has fostered a series of online communities with over 1.3 million members in total, bringing together a wide range of parties, of which the company's internal experts are only a small fraction. The communities create a powerful center of gravity around SAP products, and they have taken over part of the role of the company's customer support function.

The largest of SAP's online communities is the SAP Developer Network (SDN). Established in 2003, this community for developers, analysts, consultants, integrators, and administrators centers on the use of SAP's offerings. More than 900,000 individual members across 195 countries share their experiences and insights on a range of forums, blogs, and a wiki, and have access to an e-learning catalog, technical articles, white papers, how-to guides, and software downloads. And the community is growing fast: in 2008, 5,500 members posted in forums compared to just 2,000 in 2007. A second online community that SAP supports is the Business Process Expert (BPX) network, which is the IT world's largest business process community, with over 300,000 members covering 15 industries. This community connects SAP customers, SAP internal experts, business analysts, application consultants, IT managers, and enterprise architects through a series of resources similar to those on SDN.

The great potential of this kind of community is illustrated by SAP's substantial savings in customer support. Prior to the establishment of SDN, queries from customers were forwarded to SAP's support organization, which was quite costly to maintain. Now, 10 to 15 percent of queries are resolved via SDN forums, translating into savings of over $10 million in

2007. Participation in this problem solving is boosted by a point system and public acclaim. Community members reward one another with points based on the quality of their answers to problems. They also offer points for blogs, code samples, wiki editing, white papers, and technical articles based on effort and quality. There is a public ranking of contributors, helping individuals make a name for themselves in front of the community and within their own organizations (e.g., Indian software integrators advertising themselves as top contributors on SDN).

In 2009, SAP announced the launch of additional communities, including one dedicated to understanding International Financial Reporting Standards (IFRS) and another supporting a partnership with PlaNet Finance to give new businesses access to microfinance and technology. The communities are linked into a single network: members can use the same identity across all the communities, and topical searches lead to a wealth of content and links. Members from over 200 countries make 6,000 posts per day, and there are a million topic threads in the communities. As Mark Yolton, senior vice president of SAP community network, noted, "The SAP community network provides a trusted and validated environment to exchange ideas, discuss needs, and identify solutions for co-innovation that leads to more revenue, growth, and value for customers."[106]

Established companies must also exhibit "openness" in co-creatively managing new product development processes with external talent and connect this external engagement all the way through its enterprise activity chain to sales and delivery. Consider Wacoal Corp., Japan's leading intimate apparel company.[107] Its operations include the planning, design, and manufacturing of lingerie, innerwear, and outerwear products. The company has a long tradition of focusing on customer experience in crafting its products. In its "Human Science Institute," thousands of women's figures, from teenagers to senior citizens, are measured each year. With its accumulated knowledge of body types, design possibilities, and product options and costs, the company has consistently pioneered new product concepts, such as the iBra, a stitchless, seamless, and tagless bra. But in the late 1990s, Wacoal saw a flattening in sales growth. In response, the company experimented with a semitailored product line, where customers' bodies were measured and lingerie was customized to fit. In developing this line, the Wacoal design team gained many "soft insights" from their inter-actions with customers, a precursor for the broader co-creation to come.

In May 2001, Yasuyuki Cho was tasked with developing Wacoal's busi-ness and innovating new product lines, with a focus on online and other emerging technologies. Cho had spotted a latent market opportunity that he dubbed "home fashion" for the style-conscious consumer. While many apparel manufacturers concentrated on fashion in the workplace and others on comfortable apparel for the home, there seemed to be a "white space" opportunity at the intersection of fashion and comfort. This led to the de-velopment of a "house wear" concept, known as *Ouchi wear* in Japanese.

Cho sought to use online technology to design the new line. As he told the first author, he wanted to find a way to engage young working women in Japan in a dialogue about the new Ouchi wear concept. To do so, he approached Cafeglobe.com, a popular Web community and social interaction platform for Japanese working women (akin to iVillage.com in the United States). Cafeglobe has over 60,000 members, mainly work-ing women in their twenties and thirties. The idea was to create a Cafe-globe subforum dedicated to intimate fashion. To generate traffic to the site, Cho hired a popular young fashion model to act as facilitator of the conversation with Cafeglobe members. As hundreds of women came to the site, the Wacoal design team introduced to the community what Cho called "joint collaboration with potential customers," inviting all to par-ticipate in the shaping of the new Ouchi wear line. Over 1,200 women ultimately joined as co-creators.

The Wacoal design team had already developed concept sketches for the line and presented those ideas, complete with detailed drawings and explanations about the concept behind the clothes. The initial goal was simply to collect feedback, but at the urging of several participants, the Ouchi team began encouraging the community to comment in more depth on the designs. At this point, Cho realized his team was not quite tapping into the potential of the rich conversations happening in the community. He saw that some women in the Cafeglobe community were discussing their own design ideas—some of which modified the original sketches and others that offered unique starting points. His first insight was triggered by the receipt of faxes from community members showing hand-drawn sketches for new garments and matching accessories. This meant having to convince his team that this was an opportunity rather than a problem. In a pilot experiment, Cho created a set of online tools inviting community members to make changes, submit original designs, and vote on the design, color, and material for the garments offered. The results amazed both Cho and his team: somehow the community was suddenly breathing new life and energy into an already exciting new line.

Perhaps the greatest surprise came from the fact that the women involved in the design were busy young professionals. Seventy-five percent of them were between age 25 and 35, and 80 percent of them worked. Most also had children and were employed full time. And yet they found the time to look at patterns, suggesting different shapes for a collar here, moving buttons and redesigning buttonholes there, or going through the trouble of changing shoulder fits or pockets. When Cho actually met some of these women later on, he realized he had offered them a new experience: the ability to channel their creative tendencies and become designers. Through the tools the team had designed, Wacoal had revealed the artist inside each of them, making it extraordinary fun and giving them a new sense of self-worth. For that, busy young professional women were finding the time.

For the internal team, this meant going back to the drawing board and revising the collection based on the new community ideas. The Ouchi wear team started developing prototypes of the new collection, and Cho sweet-talked Takashimaya, a leading department store in major cities in Japan, into showcasing the line in a live trial in one of its stores. He was directed to sales managers at the Shinjuku branch in downtown Tokyo, with whom he organized a visit by members of the Cafeglobe community to come and try out the new collection. The Wacoal design team, company planners, marketing personnel, store sales managers, and community members came together face-to-face at the event. Cho could see that the Takashimaya sales managers and salespeople were excited, which made him feel confident they would eventually want to adopt the new line because of their early involvement. The Cafeglobe community members were delighted to have a chance to meet one another in person and interact with the Wacoal design team. Cho saw that they shared a sense of pride and ownership in working together. Once this live connection was established, Wacoal managers and the customer community continued their interactions online, allowing the team to finalize the collection and move it into production and launch mode.

The resulting collection turned out to be a big hit for Wacoal, with sales exceeding $1 million the first year. The end-to-end process proved a lot faster than usual: while Wacoal's conventional product development process typically required 11 months from planning to sale, the Ouchi wear development took only three months. There have been over a dozen new launches since then, all considered highly successful. These launches have followed the model devised by Cho, involving a series of co-creative stages for each product launch—from concept planning, design proposal, voting and suggestions, and sample production to in-store trial, production, and sales.

In moving from trial to production, Wacoal's co-creative engagements have to extend all the way up and down the supply chain. One of the challenges has been in communicating and discussing the nuanced positioning of collections, both online and through more video-based communication approaches. Wacoal has also faced challenges in securing resources from the company side to manage the engagement with the community on an ongoing basis, keep them informed, and interact with them throughout the process. This is the classic challenge of scaling up a new approach amidst established global product development processes. On the other hand, there is an opportunity cost of not doing so, with increased competition from business models in the fashion industry at large.

The Wacoal example illustrates that product development in the co-creation view is not about meeting a different set of specifications but rather about developing unique ways to co-opt and co-create with customers by rallying internal teams. This is a very tough challenge, and it is especially hard for professional trained individuals who have been socialized inside the organization in "company-think"—whether as a designer, engineer, marketing manager, or service agent—to think and feel like a customer (individual). It takes keen insight to see life through the customer's eyes and truly share the customer's dreams, desires, and aspirations. Engaging the product development team in exploring how customer experiences evolve can have profound implications for how the process of product and service design is managed in co-creating individualized experiences.

BUSINESS-TO-BUSINESS SALES AND STRATEGIC ACCOUNT MANAGEMENT

Thanks to advances in communications and collaboration technologies, enterprises are building new technology-enabled management capabilities to make collaborative sales planning in strategic account management processes more co-creative, especially across multiple geographies and time zones, without the burden of travel. Instead of talking to disembodied voices over the phone or looking at thumb-sized video images at a videoconference, a new-generation 3D computer-simulated environment offers participants the feeling of being in the same room, which keeps them focused, engaged, and motivated.

Consider the case of Schneider Electric, a recognized global leader in helping business customers manage their energy use. In 2008, Schneider grossed $26.9 billion in revenues, employing over 120,000 employees and maintaining more than 25 R&D centers globally. On the sales side, it had over 60 Global Strategic Accounts in sectors such as IT, finance, utilities, and retail. One such account was IBM, with whom Schneider Electric has been pursuing a global strategic partnership, providing IBM data centers with power, cooling, and lighting control, as well as energy-saving and monitoring solutions. Schneider Electric engaged in a collaborative planning process with IBM to identify areas of improvement and growth, vet these ideas on both sides, and develop a joint action plan that generates solutions of mutual value. The idea was to bring the best minds around the world from both sides to co-create valuable solutions.[108]

In 2008, Schneider Electric began to think about a Web-enabled engagement platform that would reduce the cost and time of travel for such collaborative planning and also enhance its effectiveness. IBM (like other Schneider customers) was also focused on reducing its carbon footprint and energy expenditures, in both its offerings to customers (e.g., green data centers) and its work practices. Flying executives around the world was not the greenest method of selling green data center solutions. But phone calls and webinars were poor substitutes for live meetings in this collaborative context. Schneider worked with the Gronstedt Group to leverage technology tools around Second Life, a 3D computer-simulated world platform. Says Michael Sullivan, vice president of Strategic Accounts at Schneider Electric, "Our pilot in Second Life was to see if it was possible to have a collaborative meeting and customer co-creation workshop without the travel time and costs, and perhaps create a means for even more customer intimacy and interaction because we could collaborate much more often with key people." Anders Gronstedt, president of the Gronstedt Group, says, "Second Life enabled an immersive collaborative environment that kept participants completely focused on the tasks at hand. Such virtual worlds succeed where 'flatland' Web applications of webinars fail."

IBM already had 20,000 employees using Second Life and other computer-simulated worlds and some 50 Second Life islands for everything from recruiting and new hire orientations to mentoring and sales role playing. IBM had found the immersive environments offered by Second Life to be ideal for encouraging open discussions and generating new ideas. Consequently it wasn't hard for Schneider to convince IBM to participate in the Second Life session. According to Sullivan:

The Second Life environment created more of a sense of team than in previous meetings. Our customer, IBM, had seven senior managers present, and Schneider Electric had nine present (senior managers, the account team, and solution specialists). With everyone represented as an avatar, it was difficult to tell the IBM team from the Schneider Electric team. As we worked closely together to brainstorm and identify key value areas around IBM's business drivers, it created a sense of one common team.

A typical interaction on Second Life unfolded thusly: IBM and Schneider avatars gathered in an open-air setting along a computer-simulated tropical coastline hosted by the Gronstedt Group. The goal was to identify areas where IBM and Schneider Electric could work together to create the best value for IBM's Strategic Outsourcing business. As Gronstedt commented, "With the goal of growth, both sides came to the meeting prepared and armed with one vision: the co-creation of value for their work together." Steve Andersen, president and founder of Performance Methods Inc., which developed the collaborative meeting model used in the meetings, says, "Before you can even talk about the meeting, you have to look at the prework phase. Each side typically shows up with a few issues, and we insist that they clear the air before the collaborative planning meeting begins. This forum is an opportunity to grow the business relationship, and it just can't be done until both parties are ready to move forward together."

A typical meeting began with an update by IBM. "Unlike two-dimensional Web-conferencing presentations, the 3D Second Life environment gave participants the perception of being there—keeping them focused, engaged, and motivated," says Gronstedt. As team members brainstormed potential areas of value, their ideas appeared on a computer-simulated whiteboard. Then they voted on ideas by individually clicking on their three favorite entries. After the votes were tallied, the team worked to develop action plans for the top three ideas. At the conclusion of the meeting, participants were invited to teleport to IBM's Green Data center in Second Life to see computer-simulated representations of how Schneider and IBM were working together to achieve corporate energy efficiency.

Computer-simulated worlds provide a glimpse into the future of co-creation platforms. Second Life enables participation in multiple dimensions. Sullivan notes, "In a typical business meeting/customer workshop with 16 people, only a few people can speak at one time. Second Life offered the additional advantage of enabling people to type in their ideas concurrently and then ranking and voting on ideas concurrently." Imagine getting together to co-create projects. A 3D "wiki texture" tool allows groups of architects to create real-world buildings together. For Schneider Electric, the benefits accrue through the enhanced customer partnership, creating barriers to competitors and increasing its share of wallet. In addition, the co-created customer solutions can be leveraged globally across other sectors. The enhancement of team productivity and cost savings affects the bottom line directly. While Second Life, in particular, may not be a viable platform for most companies, a new emerging generation of browser-based simulated worlds makes access a lot easier. Another powerful trend—gamification—makes collaboration more engaging. A new generation of business leaders has grown up with online games. They thrive on the sense of engagement, storytelling, character identification, immersion, problem solving, and feeling of accomplishment offered by games. Game mechanics like experience points, badges, levels, quests, goals, achievement rewards, time pressure, and deleted scenes motivate more people to participate at a deeper, more engaged level. Says Gronstedt, "Most companies aren't clamoring for a place in virtual worlds yet, as the notion is still new and the co-creation platform benefits are still emerging. But dismissing the importance of Web 3D technologies and gamification that millions are already using in collaborative planning would be like dismissing the Internet in 1994."

Now consider large business to "small" business interactions. Large enterprises wishing to sell to smaller ones can build a business network if they're willing to engage with small businesses to fulfill the smaller organization's needs, such as infrastructure, access to capital, and market knowledge. GE Healthcare is one example. One of GE Healthcare's fastest-growing customer segments is small outpatient imaging centers (OICs) to which GE sells imaging machines and diagnostic pharmaceuticals. There are more than 6,000 OICs in the United States, which are owned by over 2,500 different parent companies—a very fragmented market of small businesses, but one that generated about 40 percent of GE's diagnostic imaging business. They were therefore considered to hold great promise for a co-creation effort.

GE Healthcare's then general manager for OIC Marketing, Rob Kulis, wanted to help develop a new business model through which the firm would have more dialogue with its customers and develop more collaboration. To get started, Kulis organized several co-creative workshops with OIC customers, from physicians to center managers. Rather than tell them what GE Healthcare planned to do, he began by inviting participants into an open dialogue, following a brief interactive presentation on the co-creation movement and on GE Healthcare's aspirations in co-creating value with them. Kulis engaged everyone in a candid discussion around several exploratory themes, including health insurance changes, improved imaging technology, and the increasing popularity of imaging for a range of medical uses. He also emphasized to participants that the dialogue need not revolve around GE-selected themes, as had been the case in the past.

OIC customers discussed their needs in securing legal, financial, staffing, and planning resources to support and expand their facilities and stay competitive. The OIC owners faced increasing costs, stiff competition, and legal changes such as the 2005 Deficit Reduction Act (DRA), which had reduced Medicare/Medicaid payouts for certain imaging procedures. The DRA affected the profitability of OICs, and in some cases, it meant that the companies would at best only break even on investments made in the latest imaging technology. The result was a consolidated marketplace, tighter capital markets, and a longer wait for revenue and return on investment. To survive, OICs faced restructuring in the core functions of their business.

Many people in the OIC business did not have any prior experience in running such a business, as they typically had worked as physicians in hospitals and had not been involved in business planning and financial operations or in the actual building of OIC facilities. So GE decided to offer assistance in business planning that would allow for financing facilities and equipment in ways that preserved capital and maximized cash flow. OICs also needed to select equipment to align better with market demographics and demand, train technical staff to use that equipment most efficiently, and make full use of IT tools. Further, OICs had to aggressively market their services by making referrals easy for physician practices and publicizing that their exams were quick, pleasant, and comfortable for patients. Finally, OICs had to streamline their workflow for maximum throughput and improve their cash flow by clearing up accounts receivable, collecting and processing payments quickly, managing reimbursements effectively, and applying strong purchasing discipline.

Kulis recognized that putting together a business network that would help OICs with these core functions would reap great rewards—for both them and GE. He and his team envisioned that such a network would provide advice, consulting, and solutions for the myriad business problems the OICs faced. In 2007, Kulis launched a Web-based platform consisting of a comprehensive network of product and service vendors in finance, legal services, information systems, imaging center design and building services, marketing and communications, and business services. GE Healthcare evaluated the vendor partners based on market needs matched with a vendor's specific capabilities, knowledge, presence in that market, and responsiveness. The vendors who joined the network were contractually obligated to meet certain levels of service and quality standards rather than receiving payment for affiliation. Kulis believed that creating customer value was more important to the long-term growth prospects of the network (and GE Healthcare) than any moderate royalty fees that might have been generated. GE Healthcare not only gave OICs access to this network but also provided educational content, access to industry conferences and webcasts, and a peer-to-peer network for sharing best practices.

After consulting with OICs, Kulis offered two levels of service. The first was the nonmembership level, which was open and free of charge to any OIC registering on the portal. The second service level was the membership level, which cost $20,000 annually and targeted the top 20 percent of GE Healthcare's OIC clients. For centers that committed to using a certain amount of content, participating in the best practice–sharing community and providing ongoing feedback through blogs, the membership fee was waived. The membership level provided everything in the nonmembership level plus access to an "Ask an Expert" platform, where clients could submit questions to any vendor partner in the network, gain access to vendor partner white papers and intellectual property, and get more extensive educational content. In addition, webcasts and tuition for special conferences were included in the fee.

During the first 15 months of the program, GE Healthcare invested about $2 million and reaped the reward of registering over 1,500 clients as nonmembers and 100 of the top 20 percent of clients as members. Ultimately the program improved customers' equipment purchasing and thereby strengthened GE Healthcare's business (revenue figures are not public). For example, if an OIC was expanding and needed to locate good properties, the faster it could solve that problem, the faster it would need equipment for the new locations. Additionally, by providing customers with objective advice through the vendor network, GE Healthcare enhanced its position in the minds of customers, which improved customer loyalty and ultimately led to less competitive buying situations for GE Healthcare's equipment, services, and solutions. Most important, GE's salespeople began seeing the synergy between the Web-based engagement platforms and extending their direct sales relationships with clients.

COLLABORATIVE PUBLIC SERVICE INNOVATION

We have so far discussed examples of co-creative management of stakeholder relationships mainly in the private sector. We now discuss an example of service innovation in the public education and professional training sector. This example also illustrates the potential for public-private partnerships in educational reform through co-creation thinking.

SENAI (short for SErviço Nacional de Aprendizagem Industrial) is among the oldest and most well-known entities in Brazil, with a mission of promoting professional education in technology and innovation and enhancing the competitiveness of Brazilian industries.[109] It is recognized for its strong technical training programs in mechanical, electrical, and product design. One of SENAI's primary goals is to fulfill the ongoing needs of the Brazilian industrial sector for skilled labor and technological capabilities.

In the late 1990s, SENAI faced three key challenges: (1) how to engage its clients to better understand their needs and expectations, (2) how to train and prepare its current students and keep former students "up to date" with the latest trends and requirements from the industrial sector, and (3) how to deal with the rapidly changing profiles and expectations of its students, particularly Generation Y.

To respond to these key challenges, in a pioneering initiative, the institution decided to embrace co-creation at the operational level of SENAI, encouraging local stakeholders—students and industry—to jointly participate in creating an integrated community, which would then facilitate the development of technology-enabled solutions and new engagement platforms. SENAI Santa Catarina's regional director, Sergio Roberto Arruda, said, "SENAI should not create products for their clients but *with* their clients." SENAI decided to first pursue a co-creation platform aimed at bringing together students facing two major challenges: deciding on a career and entering the job market.

To address the career decision, SENAI, with the support of Symnetics, a consulting organization in Latin America, piloted a platform called "Experiencing a Career," created to engage students around information and practical knowledge regarding the prospects of each course offered by the institution and to help them co-create an experience when deciding upon a career. By definition, the type of experience valued by each student was understood to be different, as each student has a different context and individual-specific aspirations. The early prototype of the platform was conceived as different interaction environments with specially designed places/spaces to allow students to clear doubts, discuss their concerns, and conduct lab practices, both with the faculty of SENAI and with other current students, alumni, and industry professionals.

In the past, SENAI did not interact much with potential students who faced one of their most important challenges: deciding on a career. Students often were not able to make informed choices due to lack of visibility into the experience of a career, lack of proper decision-making processes, lack of contextual information, and lack of easy access to "the right people." Quite often, after devoting much time, effort, and energy to a professional course, students realized it did not correspond to their talents and interests and eventually dropped out of the course. This unsatisfactory outcome also generated costs for SENAI, especially in technology courses, where the number of dropout students and lack of new classes tended to be higher.

Starting in 2008, the "Experiencing a Career" platform has enabled students to engage in productive dialogue with professionals and teachers about different technology careers, to read alumni reports about career changes and the improved economic outcomes brought about by specific courses, and to exchange information with other helpful parties. Students can browse through different teaching environments, access an electronic display with the best projects developed by students, and watch videos with testimonials from successful alumni about their experiences after finishing the course. Questions on different professional opportunities, required skills, job offers, and average pay are freely discussed, supported by a SENAI professional. The receptive atmosphere leads to an empathic understanding of needs and expectations. Another innovation by SENAI is experimental classes that give potential students hands-on experience with the course's main themes. At the end of the visit, SENAI promotes a wide-ranging debate, engaging technology experts, coordinators, and teachers and allowing for community participation with room for questions and answers.

To aid students in entering the job market, SENAI launched a second platform of Web-based environments dubbed Students in the Shop

Window, which was meant to give more exposure to students' projects developed during their studies. In this platform, students, alumni, and industry discuss problem-solving ideas and share their experiences while developing real projects, resulting in students' mutual development, greater exposure for skilled professionals, and more gains for industry.

To bring industry and students together, the Students in the Shop Window platform offers a broad space for sharing experiences, developing joint projects, and searching information so that students can develop and expose their talents co-creatively with other students and industries interested in developing similar technology-led solutions. SENAI has worked with industry to design the interactive tools, thereby bringing stakeholders into the planning process to accommodate their real needs and expectations.

The project-based environments are equipped with an automatic voting system for the best projects developed by students. SENAI supports students receiving the most votes by jointly producing a professional video showcasing the technological solution (developed together with an invited teacher), which becomes part of the online collection of projects, accessible to students and industry. In addition, SENAI facilitates co-creation in ongoing projects. Students developing projects can post pictures and/ or videos so that other students—or companies—can make suggestions to improve them. A continuous dialogue is guaranteed through interactive tools for online communication and supporting content exchange. There is also a complementary space for suggesting ideas for the development of new projects and solutions, viewed by both industry and students, so that they can share mutually interesting themes.

The level of interaction between SENAI students and industry is likely to increase as they develop solutions together that are more practical and adaptable to industry realities, while at the same time helping students improve their skills and gain a competitive edge in the job market. Consistent with SENAI's role as an institution that prepares industry-focused student competencies, the development of shared projects and solutions facilitates industry access to highly skilled professionals.

As noted by Hildegarde Schlupp, general director at SENAI-Joinville, who spearheaded the implementation of these core platforms, "The new environments contribute to the interaction among students and industry, with SENAI facilitating communication, the development of competencies, the generation of new ideas, and the sharing of new experiences. Each environment offers different interactions in different moments while students and companies interact with and through SENAI."

Through all these efforts, SENAI has generated benefits and economic gains for both students and industry. Students are now given the opportunity to choose a career that best meets their vocation, as well as to enter a professional environment where their competencies are duly recognized. Industries can be sure they are hiring a professional who is able to generate practical and value-driven solutions without requiring additional and costly training. From SENAI's perspective, the co-creation platforms help the school to understand the real motivations determining students' choices, thus reducing the possibility of launching courses that do not meet their expectations. SENAI can develop new teaching competencies for its faculty, which are more aligned with new, industry-suitable solutions.

After 12 months, SENAI increased its number of enrollments by 30 percent. Due to its success, this engagement platform model, now called Mundo SENAI (World SENAI), was rolled out to all 27 Brazil states, with some state-specific adjustments. Its problem-based educational approach (co-created with industries to match their expectations) and a set of purposefully designed tools have significantly improved SENAI's performance and reduced conventional brand building and marketing costs through positive word-of-mouth effects. But there is more to come. The philosophy of co-creation is starting to permeate the delivery of courses as younger students expect to co-shape their learning experiences to a greater degree than ever before. SENAI is urging and helping many of its faculty to experiment with interactive technologies that work. These experiences can occur before or after class, and they involve not just one-on-one teacher-student dialogues but also open discussions with many students in a full-fledged learning community.

SENAI is enabling learning communities that co-create knowledge around a framework of themes and conceptual threads. Participants include practicing professionals, engaged alumni, consultants, and authors. Past students can suggest and create new content based on their skills, knowledge, and personal learning experiences, while the role of the professor shifts to facilitating more participant-centric learning experiences. Furthermore, SENAI plans to link together the newly developed platforms into a broader set of environments where the projects co-creatively developed by students are presented as part of the institution's teaching-learning process.

According to Arruda, SENAI wants to expand its co-creation platform through various initiatives for continuous interaction with their stakeholders. SENAI believes its future will depend more and more on its capacity to promote learning and innovative initiatives together with students, industries, and partners, and increasing institutional learning and awareness through interactive dialogue.

In 2011, a major government program, PRONATEC (short for National Program of Access to Technical Education and Employment), approached SENAI with a big challenge: double the number of student enrollments until 2014. To accomplish this, SENAI is reshaping its usual class concept. Besides bringing students into their units, SENAI is broadening its operation, looking for a wider range of student profiles and reaching them where they are. As Arruda said, "The classroom can be anywhere." Co-creation has become a central part of SENAI's core principles as an enterprise with an ultimate mission to co-create economic development in Brazil.

DIVISIONAL COLLABORATION INSIDE
THE DIVERSIFIED ENTERPRISE

We now shift to building management systems through co-creation thinking *inside* large organizations. We begin with diversified enterprises, where co-creation cannot only increase the benefits of collaboration but also reduce the collaboration costs. Interaction of people from lower levels within enterprises can enable identification of solutions for day-to-day shared problems. Operational planning processes can be co-created in "win more–win more" ways. Consider the case of Ferrosur and Loma Negra, business units of the Camargo Corrêa holding company in Argentina. Loma Negra is the country's largest cement manufacturer, and Ferrosur is a cargo rail company operating in the southeast of the Buenos Aires province. It is also one of Loma Negra's main suppliers, transporting cement from Loma Negra's plants to the distribution center near Buenos

Aires, which is the largest market in the country. Loma Negra represents nearly 30 percent of the total volume transported by Ferrosur.

Although belonging to the same holding company, Ferrosur and Loma Negra had a typical supplier-customer relationship. The volume transported was in the past determined primarily by the rail market transport fee. Loma Negra relied heavily on trucks to transport the surplus production of cement, which resulted from market growth. This approach hid great sources of synergies and clearly was suboptimal for Camargo Corrêa.

Led by Ferrosur CEO Pablo Terradas and Loma Negra Supply Chain director Eduardo Blake, co-creation allowed the two companies to discover a new collaborative approach that unveiled hidden sources of value. Teams representing different levels in the business relationship, such as commercial and overall planning, were formed. By engaging in dialogue around these groups of interactions, the teams finally envisioned a singular new co-creative approach for their joint planning processes.

In the past, the outcome of the planning processes was a high-level plan that wasn't always accomplished, and neither business seemed to fulfill expectations around cost and efficiency. The new co-creation approach encouraged collaboration between the two sides to plan as a function of the total transportation cost and total value maximization. After mutual points of validation and consultation were established, the process resulted in a more reliable plan, with flexibility for emerging changes and opportunities. The first outcomes were significant cost reduction and profitable opportunities to increase transportation usage.

The two businesses ended up with a unified process characterized by mutual participation, whereas they had been separate and parallel processes before. In-depth knowledge of each other's needs also grew. Interactions based on document exchange shifted to face-to-face interactions in which operational conditions and decision-making patterns could be understood by both sides. Another important step was allowing the interaction of people from lower levels in the organizations, as they could more easily identify solutions for day-to-day shared problems. In the past, any dialogue had occurred mainly during the last stage of the planning process—basically, the exchange of documents on volumes and product mix—in order to validate the next year's plan. One basic problem was that this approach didn't encourage a thorough understanding of each other's operational realities and limitations, leading to difficulties when trying to realize the annual plan. The new management process encourages strong participation of both sides from the beginning, establishing new environments of interactions such as validation meetings and the unification of operational data as a pathway for a common and unique vision. Co-creation allowed the two sides to build a more reliable transportation plan while establishing a pathway to increased rail cargo by defining common opportunities and structuring shared investment projects. Moreover, this led to the analysis of new transport opportunities in areas in which Loma Negra relied solely on trucks. New strategic value for the group was co-created by accounting for new cargo volumes, optimizing transport and capital allocation, and streamlining business performance. Cost savings emerged from reduced plan-deviation risks and lower supply chain costs (i.e., better rail usage).

Although co-creation enabled maximization of value outcomes for both sides, sustaining it required establishing fair business rules and a clear communications process between the business units and between the business units and the holding company. This communications process had to explain how value was being co-created and then how revenues and cost savings were assigned following jointly defined business guidelines in a way that minimized conflict between the two units. The Ferrosur–Loma Negra example illustrates how co-creative planning systems can leverage collaborative interactions inside large, diversified enterprises. Focusing merely on the individual efficiencies within business units often failed to generate the maximum value for the holding company. Synergies would remain under the surface without real cooperation between the business units to maximize total performance. Setting up specific teams dedicated to proactively articulating the key interactions, identifying shared pain points from past engagement experiences, and using co-creation principles to make collaborative planning more co-creative have proved to be valuable pathways to success for Ferrosur and Loma Negra.

STRATEGY MANAGEMENT

The pace of co-creative enterprise transformation is a direct function of the extent to which the enterprise's own strategy management is influenced, if not shaped, by a process of co-creation. For strategy development and execution to become more effective, the strategy management process must become more democratized and decentered, where the process is as much bottom up as it is top down. Co-creating strategy requires that top management and senior managers in charge of the strategy process no longer view themselves as the sole experts in developing, evaluating, and implementing strategy. They must adopt a distributed view of strategy involving a process of engaging multiple constituencies in the interactive resolution of complex issues. They must also encourage the continuous coevolution of strategy across a wide spectrum of themes and supporting initiatives launched between themselves and the people who have the most at stake with the company—namely, the customers and employees of the firm, with creative inputs from partners and other stakeholders.

Consider Real Tokio Marine Vida e Previdência (RTMVP), created in Brazil in 2005 through the joint venture between two global financial conglomerates, the Dutch bank ABN Amro and the Japanese insurance company Tokio Marine and Nichido Fire Insurance, each with a 50 percent stake.[110] The joint venture had four business units: two life insurance units (one retail, one corporate) and two pension services units (one retail, one corporate), and a combined distribution network across Brazil entailing ABN's 2,000+ Real Bank branches and Tokio Marine's network of agents. In early 2006, RTMVP senior management undertook the challenge of articulating its joint venture strategy and fleshing out the corporate value proposition for the business that would tap into the synergy between the two partner companies and strengthen relationships with the distribution network in marketing its insurance and pension products. The challenge for the new venture was to develop a strategy that took into account the partners' strategic guidelines while keeping growth sustainable.

Zilea Santos, chief of operations, felt she had to take a fresh approach to strategy development, especially given the two very different corporate cultures involved. She knew that she had to somehow engage collectively the sales channel (bank relationship managers and insurance agents), RTMVP employees, and retail and corporate clients in a dialogue that would bring a sense of shared contribution to the organization's strategy development process. In each of the four business segments, this meant approaching the following stakeholders as co-creators:

- Retail life insurance and pension: bank relationship managers, pension clients, insurance clients, and agents
- Corporate pension clients: client company HR directors, client company finance directors, client company HR benefits managers, and selected client company employees (both retired and current workers)
- Corporate insurance: Real-ABN agents, Tokio Marine agents, and bank relationship managers

For starters, RTMVP ran several "live" co-creation workshops in each of the four segments involving all these co-creators. From RTMVP's side, there were a development team and a leadership validation team. The development team consisted of eight to ten people (area managers and coordinators) from the respective business segments. The leadership validation team was much larger and as intercompany and interdisciplinary as possible. It involved everyone from the president, finance directors, and actuarial directors to managers of business units, support areas, operations, and sales from both the ABN Bank and Tokio Marine channels. The development team was involved in the dialogue in the co-creation workshops, while the leadership validation team was involved in strategic conversations such as formulating the business value proposition and navigating implementation challenges. The call center coordinator was also present in every co-creation workshop.

One of the main themes that emerged from the workshops was the training experience of the sales channel. A training engagement platform, dubbed Treinamento Sob-Medida (tailor-made training) was designed to make the training a positive experience and strengthen the new partnership. This platform enabled the sales channels and the different operational areas to learn the operational system. It also enabled the company to learn rapidly about needs, opinions, and suggestions introduced by participants via an employee service team and the call center. RTMVP induced a highly flexible system for continuously adjusting the training platform throughout the team-building process, making it more attractive to participants because it addressed their expectations.

The engagement platform was designed to rely on a human network of about 595 qualified people across Brazil, viewed by the company as "resource multipliers" responsible for engaging 8,000 employees in a two-sided e-learning function. This platform was well received because of its emphasis on co-creative engagement in on-site training, including place and support teams, to e-learning. The training transformed the way sales teams are prepared and changed a "cold and discouraging" product offering into something attractive, compact, and complete. The joint venture also generated new strategic capital by ensuring the efficacy of the training and the assimilation of its content, incorporating new insights about the behavior of employees and sales channels, and learning about key success factors in designing future training programs.

RTMVP has also spearheaded the development of a Web-based engagement platform for ongoing generation of ideas. Dubbed Uma Idéia Puxa a Outra (one idea calls for another), this platform is focused on product development and products under construction. The platform seeks to make in-house employees and the bank an integral part of the process for creating products in such a way that products are designed based on the knowledge of the sales channel and aligned with the needs of the customers and the channels. Any employee can suggest ideas for new products, coverage, and/or services. These suggestions are put together in an exhibit to be shared with all system users, which facilitates the co-creation of ideas with new suggestions and inputs of third parties, all of whom can post reviews and vote for or against. The ideas selected by the RTMVP Selection Group are posted for follow-up. Uma Idéia Puxa a Outra also links to the Treinamento Sob-Medida (tailor-made training) platform.

In addition to co-creative idea generation, the Uma Idéia Puxa a Outra platform is being designed for "thematic community areas" that will engage individuals with common functional interests—for example, co-creating communications campaigns oriented toward certain products or services to promote customer education and continuous improvement of the quality of customer experiences. The ideas discussed on the platform can range from strategic innovation to product-service innovation to even simple high-impact operational ideas. One simple idea that emerged is a "transparency flyer." Intended for delivery to clients as they are purchasing insurance, it informs them in clear and concise terms about the key features of products, including what is *not* covered in their policy—thereby addressing the common uncertainties consumers have about the insurance they are about to buy. Co-creators of selected ideas were invited to participate in a Discussion Forum for Co-Created Ideas that validated the rationale and functional and financial feasibility of the ideas. Finally, the ideas selected for implementation were validated by the development teams, the RTMVP Executive Committee, and the end customer.

These engagement platforms helped co-shape RTMVP's customer and sales channel value propositions. RTMVP gained a co-created view of customer satisfaction and loyalty, rather than the conventional firm-centric approach used in the past. Moreover, once each business unit determined its own value propositions, RTMVP was able to consolidate them into a corporate-level value proposition. By analyzing all of the value outcomes in detail, the company identified seven common key attributes, three—channel support, joint product development, and channel education (on products)—related to the sales channel and four—client ease, transparency, access, and specialized consulting services (expertise in financial planning when selling products)—related to clients. RTMVP now had a corporate value proposition that was derived from actual customer experience and from all business units and that was shaped by customer input. It was a detailed value proposition that was then inserted into its strategy map whose goal was to associate the strategic intent of RTMVP with its strategic goals, target levels of performance and action, and plans for key initiatives. Overall, this strategy map was composed of 25 strategic objectives distributed across five perspectives of the business: financial, customer, channels, internal processes, and people and technology. These elements were now clearly anchored in the map around its new co-creative thrust with customers, and they served as an important tool for discussing strategy execution at meetings held every three months.

The RTMVP example illustrates how a co-creative strategy formulation process can serve as the glue that binds two very different corporate cultures—in this case, a Dutch financial services giant and a Japanese insurance company. Through the co-creation paradigm, RTMVP was able to engage clients, the sales channel, and employees collectively, bringing a sense of shared contribution to the organization's strategy. Armindo Pereira, a business unit manager of corporate life insurance at RTMVP, says, "The difference between participating in a co-creation initiative and other initiatives we participate in is that this kind of project changes our mind forever. After understanding the co-creation principles, I really go to my clients in a different way." Santos, the operations chief, says:

For me, being the leader of an initiative like this was a grateful surprise; we surely imagined that it would bring some new and insightful ideas, but we could never imagine the importance and the relevance that the initiative achieved. We never imagined when we started our co-creation project that we would finally co-create our value proposition—we would finally co-create our company's strategy!

Santos offers three tips for anyone thinking about an organizational strategy co-creation program:

• Start small and learn with the project before a big implementation.

• Be patient—it takes some time to internalize the principles and for people to think in a co-creative way.

• Don't be afraid of losing some control, as the process will be completely inspiring.

Strategy in the co-creative enterprise is an ongoing coevolutionary process of creative organization. Organizing to access resources from the extended network (from suppliers and partners to consumer communities)—including competencies, knowledge, infrastructure, and investment capacity—significantly expands the notion of available resources. A focus on control and ownership of resources gives way to the importance of accessing and leveraging global resources through engagement platforms for co-creating unique value with customers and all other stakeholders. The co-creation process also challenges the assumption that only the aspirations of the firm matter. Every participant in the ecosystem collaborates in value creation (and simultaneously competes in economic value extraction). This results in constant tension in the strategy development process, especially when the various stakeholding units and individuals in the ecosystem must collectively execute that strategy. In the new strategy framework, the distinction between strategy formulation and implementation disappears. There is no handing-over process between thinking and acting. It is no longer like conducting an orchestra playing a particular musical score but more like a jazz improvisation. In the co-creation view, strategy is about active adaptation within broad, long-term directions (strategic intent). The evolution of organizational routines is the driving force behind its adaptation. Variation, selection, and retention of organizational routines are a function of co-creative engagements with stakeholders and the value of co-created outcomes.

TALENT AND PROJECT MANAGEMENT

The human resources function has a big opportunity to co-create employee experiences that build high-quality engagement in the enterprise, eventually leading to growth and creating employee ambassadors for the enterprise. The importance of employee engagement is well known. For instance, Hewitt Associates found that employee engagement levels at high-growth companies exceeded those of low-growth companies by more than 20 percent. Watson Wyatt found that the stock price of companies with high employee trust levels outperformed stocks at companies with low trust levels by 186 percent. Towers Perrin found that the more highly engaged employees are, the more likely they are to put customers at the heart of what they do and how they think about their jobs, and the less likely they are to leave the company.

Yet, many enterprises struggle with engaging talent. They often fail to recognize that the employee's (recipient) view of the engagement experience can be quite different from the enterprise's (provider) view. Moreover, employee's overall expectations are continuously changing. Surveys show that if employees don't consider their jobs meaningful and challenging and aren't focused on their personal and professional growth and development, they won't stay with that company. Furthermore, an employer's intangible and emotional associations with work—for instance, "It's fun to work at this company," "We have a passionate and intelligent culture," "There is a strong team feeling here"—are just as important as "functional" employment benefits.

To look at a few examples, 24/7 Customer, a BPO call center company, has utilized a co-creative engagement model with its employees despite the conventional view of call center agents as interchangeable and dispens-able. Agents who will work for the same client are recruited together as a group through an audition-like process. 24/7 also encourages self-managed staffing of the call center, where the group decides autonomously who will cover what shifts. The company also urges employees to "adopt" one of the organizational values (respect, transparency, taking ownership, focus on results, and teamwork), with their business cards and cubicles rein-forcing the chosen value.

Google uses a co-creative approach in attracting talent to the firm. HR staff work with their peers in brand management to attract recruits through an "employment branding" strategy. Existing employees blog with potential recruits, while candidates can view videos of Google em-ployees describing their work experiences on YouTube (which is owned by Google). The Aditya Birla Group, a global diversified conglomerate, is exploring how to engage employees in co-creating the experiences of induction (i.e., new employee orientation), job design, and the ongoing work experience. Aditya Birla is fostering more co-creative interactions not only across Corporate HR and Business Unit HR, but also between HR and the IT function. As Santrupt Misra, head of Corporate HR and IT, puts it, "Co-creation is the key to superior success." His goal is to con-tinuously harness the company's co-creative potential by fusing HR and IT—perhaps one of the biggest organizational challenges in becoming a co-creative organization.

Enterprises must work on finding new approaches to managing talent that focus on the skills of individuals, their attitudes about learning, the competence of teams, and the organizational ability to continually recon-figure task-based teams with the best talent. At Industrial Light & Magic (ILM), work is hardly as robotic as in its *Star Wars* flicks. Its ever-changing teams form and reform rapidly around projects involving freelancers and full-time employees. It is "Free Agent Nation" exemplified.[111] ILM has a permanent staff of about 700, but that can swell by as much as a quarter during the winter and spring when effects work is being done on summer blockbuster movies. By using a common production platform to share techniques between films and video games, managers can oversee teams of hundreds of artists on big films. The key is open communication and dialogue that is visible to all. As with open-source systems, peer recognition reigns supreme. From ILM's perspective, a scalable workforce creates rapid IT training and HR orientation challenges, but also constant evaluation of talent against project requirements.

IBM needs to tap into skills from its employees around the world to compete effectively and provide superior service to customers. About one-seventh of its 375,000-plus employees are based in India. The company builds project teams that are multigeographic and multicultural. The composition of project teams varies according to the nature of global projects and work patterns and the access to talent that is required. Technology-based talent engagement platforms support the interactions among employees, their managers, and the HR department, with personalized learning plans that can be discussed with mentors and coaches. Managers have input into the leadership capability assessments, and employees can engage in direct dialogue via online chat and videoconferencing tools.

The focus of IBM's talent management efforts is on employees within their first five years at the company. As part of IBM's Fresh Blue program, new employees are immediately involved in a simulated project before they can work on real projects, including training programs and acculturation methods that use IBM's Second Life simulation tools. For instance, in its computer-simulated Rehearsal Studios, the company has experimented with avatars of IBMers who act as "tough sells" before avatars of IBM salespeople. Afterward, the participants discuss the interaction in transparent fashion. The Greater IBM Connection is an internal social network for current and former IBMers that taps the knowledge and know-how of older IBMers and retirees. For instance, for its World Development Initiative, IBM tapped the Greater IBM Connection to engage volunteers who agreed to carry additional responsibility for identifying and leveraging business opportunities for IBM at the "bottom of the pyramid" in India, Kenya, and China. This initiative has also morphed into a leadership development effort to help identify and develop globally astute leaders who are culturally aware and can bring global citizenship values to IBM. These leaders can link projects with IBM's strategic thrusts across the globe. The key here is designing collaborative work environments around IBMers and their personal views of meaning and effectiveness, as well as creating mechanisms for generating bottom-up views and opportunities to top management.

Thus, as these examples of talent and project management suggest, while organizations must engage in flexible and dynamic reconfiguration of talent and resources—often across time zones and cultures—they must also engage employees in the talent reconfiguration process rather than just use a typical assignment-centric view. Companies must not only find ways to engage employees in co-creative fashion in reconfiguring global network and community resources on demand, but they must also encourage co-creative leadership at all levels of the organization. When leaders engage employees and harness human energy, management processes become more co-creative. Both managers and employees win when each side understands the value of engaging the value co-creator on the other side, using internal platforms that facilitate active, explicit dialogue among them and allowing responses in real time to their changing needs and expectations.

STAKEHOLDER ENGAGEMENT AND RISK-RETURN MANAGEMENT

The economic crisis of 2008 and the challenges that persisted into 2009 revealed serious limitations and dangers of many of the traditional ways of risk management.[112] There appeared to be too much unbridled focus on "returns" (return on investment) and not enough attention paid to the "risk" underlying that ROI. Some critics argued that because returns on certain strategic initiatives were so great, risks that were present were either invisible or ignored.[113] Following the 2008–2009 financial crisis, numerous calls arose for drastic improvements in risk-return management, with a specific call for more formal risk considerations in managing an enterprise's deployment of specific strategic initiatives.

Sustainable value creation requires balanced risk taking by focusing on co-creation opportunities that can generate superior returns and rewards, while simultaneously reducing risks for both enterprises and their stakeholders. Besides customer and employee activism, increased shareholder/investor activism and governmental intervention are driving greater expectations for better management of risk-return relationships.

Consider the case of Harley-Davidson, which achieved consistent superior performance in terms of ROI, growth, and shareholder returns over a 20-year period beginning in 1986.[114] In the mid-1980s, Harley-Davidson began serving otherwise unmet needs (i.e., lifestyle, freedom, adventure, community, and a whole new culture), while pursuing a growing customer group (the baby boomer generation). Harley's innovation, delivery, and branding of its offerings were all centered on a unique Harley experience. Harley's brand has itself shifted from a youthful countercultural persona to middle-aged nostalgia. The company enabled owners to co-create their unique experience with other Harley fans by involving them as a community, in addition to personalized parts and paraphernalia. In 1983, Harley formed the Harley Owners Group (HOG) to encourage owners to become more actively involved in the sport of motorcycling and the Harley experience. Over 1 million Harley owners belong to HOG, and they regularly turn up to compare their bikes at rallies and shows. About half the company's sales were typically to new customers, while the other half were to committed and loyal Harley riders.

As ex-CEO of Harley, James Ziemer, said, "You're not going to change the bike you ride when you've got its name tattooed on your shoulder." What is even more amazing is that even some of the salespeople and Harley executives sport those same tattoos. Through its unique organizational design, Harley has engaged its own employees as much as it has its biker community over the years. The center of gravity of its return driven strategy was the supporting tenet of employee and stakeholder engagement.[115] In Harley's model, the company communicates holistically, since its own employees are involved in the process. This is in contrast to the typical disconnects between the brand promise, the customer experience, and the employee experience of many companies.

The employee conversations and discussions with Harley owners create shared contextual meaning, a basis for dialogue that generates unique experiences for individuals. Harley's employees and managers have immersed themselves with the Harley customer community. For instance, Harley's salespeople are so mentally intertwined with their customers that it can be difficult to tell them apart. Not surprisingly, Harley co-creates insights through its salespeople and managers on a daily basis. For instance, the salespeople's customer discussions are part of the strategy development and execution process. Harley is able to map and design its sales processes through the lens of experience-based interactions. Harley salespeople can literally feel the customer's pain points and aspirations. At Harley-Davidson, the customer and the company converge.

This convergence extends all the way up Harley's business network, through its tightly knit $1 billion-plus supply chain, with over 300 suppliers. Key suppliers have not only access to Harley's facilities but also to its internal management system, dubbed Ride. They have access to minutes of meetings, plans, schedules, and other internal processes, facilitating dialogue with Harley managers and employees in product design and manufacturing. In the spirit of openness and full disclosure, there is a detailed contract among key suppliers that spells out expectations and obligations on both sides of the company-supplier dialogue. For instance, when developing the electronic fuel-injected (EFI) engine for the V-Rod bike, Harley engineers and managers had to collaborate with key supplier Delphi Automotive and with European firms, including Porsche and Magneti Marelli. Later, when Delphi's initial attempts to adapt an automotive-based system to a motorcycle failed, the team had to redesign the system from the ground up—which meant trusting the development of a critical component to an outsider.

Harley attempts to balance focus and flexibility. The development of the EFI engine for the Harley V-Rod certainly called for experimentation. Engineers both within and outside the firm had real-time access to plans, files, pictures, and audio and video clips, as well as the ability to create new knowledge continuously. But the co-experimentation process and the positive experiences it generated produced a new level of trust that in turn catalyzed new efficiencies in product development. The dialogue increased dramatically as the development of the project unfolded. Moreover, Harley also has an underlying process of engaging customers in co-creating the product itself and the community at large if there are significant changes to its brand. A case in point is getting the approval of the community when Harley sought to partner with Ford on its Special Edition Harley F-150 truck. Harley owners were involved in this strategic decision, from its design to branding.

In short, Harley acts as a nodal company, partnering deliberately with both suppliers and customers in end-to-end fashion, letting insights flow from the community all the way up the supply chain and back. Harley commanded as much as a 30 percent price premium on its motorcycles between the 1980s and early 2000s, while generating a phenomenal 20-year run on consistent return on investment, with continued growth and a total shareholder return as much as 25 times the S&P 500 index.[116]

However, the median age of a Harley buyer had shot up from 45 to 49 at the turn of the millennium.[117] Harley faced the challenge of a somewhat saturated segment of baby boomers in the United States, as it also pursued rising foreign sales. Ex-CEO Ziemer saw no reason to battle the youth-conscious imports head on, saying, "The type of customer who chases the latest race-winning, forward-pitched sport bike is hardly brand-loyal." Genevieve Schmitt, founding editor of the e-zine WomenRidersNow.com, notes, "[Harley has] responded to the needs of smaller, less muscular riders by offering motorcycles with lower motors. They realize women are an up-and-coming segment and that they need to accommodate them. They don't market to a specific gender, but are gender-neutral. They market a lifestyle, with daughters and moms, dads and sons."[118]

And then the 2008–2009 financial crisis hit. The recession was not kind to Harley, which lost almost 40 percent of its profits and volumes from the peak of 2006. Harley was forced to restrategize to deal with the many new strategic risks, including customer, market, and brand risks; supply chain and operations risks; employee and other stakeholder risks; and R&D and innovation risks.[119] For instance, its brand value fell about 43 percent (according to Interbrand) to $4.3 billion and had to revitalize itself. As Matthew Levatich, global president and COO notes, "The idea of personal freedom, adventure and commitment is what all Harley riders love about the brand, irrespective of age, country, or region."[120] Harley is now attempting to engage with the younger population. Having been perceived as a brand for the 40-plus segment, Harley is "fattening the tails" as Levatich puts it. However, the core values remain the same in striking up conversations with the younger set. As Levatich notes, "We have people who have an attitude about life and they want to lead with a purpose." Harley has to manage new market risks as well; for the first time, it will have more dealers outside of the United States. That also means engaging and energizing the dealer network. In addition to a focus on global markets, its restructuring under new CEO Keith Wandell involved closing two factories, a 25 percent cut in its workforce, and the implementation of lean management at its factories.

Only time will tell if Harley can continue to grow and maintain superior returns and continue to keep its motor—and the Harley lifestyle—running. For instance, Harley and community engagement partner Jump set out to decode the different types of communities that existed under the Harley umbrella and then develop a metrics system to gauge the health of those communities. In particular, the team hoped to come away with a new strategy for brand community engagement. The team studied the dynamics of groups like the Red Hat Society, Burning Man, Weight Watchers, Fantasy Football, and Apple to learn more about the implicit rules that governed these communities. Harley and Jump uncovered three forms of community engagement, dubbed as "Pools, Webs, and Hubs," entailing different types of community-building initiatives most likely to have the greatest positive impact. The Jump team then collaborated with Harley to develop three strategic imperatives for using services to build community engagement and a set of design principles for implementing each imperative. One thing is for sure: Harley's ability to make a comeback will depend on its successful management of deep engagement with all its new stakeholders in co-creatively valuable ways.

The Harley-Davidson example shows how embracing co-creation with internal and external stakeholders is necessary for strategic risk-return management of enterprises in an increasingly complex competitive environment. Harley—like any co-creative enterprise of the future—will not only have to engage in co-creating value to drive superior returns but also manage its corporate reporting and valuation, given the new scrutiny and activism of today's investors, to communicate more effectively its navigation of the road ahead to its shareholders and other stakeholders.

MANAGEMENT CO-CREATION

As the examples in this chapter vividly illustrated, successful co-creative enterprise transformation requires building co-creative management systems to engage stakeholding individuals as co-creators everywhere in the enterprise ecosystem. Enterprises must create opportunities for managers in large organizations to understand and viscerally experience the business as their customers do. Customer-facing employees can be more actively engaged in the new product development process and in fine-tuning marketing of new products, along with customers. In fact, customer-facing environments can be a rich place for customer experimentation and generating insights through customer experiences. In instances where distributors and dealers still play a significant role in the value creation process with customers, some aspects of their roles may need to be redefined through multisided co-creative interactions. In community-based platforms, personal engagement in community co-creation can place individuals at the center of market- and brand-building processes. Senior executives can also play a critical role in stimulating and leveraging stakeholder communities. Established enterprises must also exhibit openness in co-creatively managing new product development with external talent and connect this external engagement all the way through its activity chain to sales and delivery. Collaborative innovation can occur as much in public services as in the private sector.

Co-creation can spread all across the value chain system in making partnerships much more effective than in the past by deepening engagement with stakeholders. In diversified enterprises, internal co-creation across businesses can increase the benefits of collaboration, as well as reduce its costs. Interaction of people from lower levels within enterprises can enable identification of solutions for day-to-day shared problems. Operational planning processes can be co-created in "win more–win more" ways.

Co-creating strategy requires that top management and senior managers in charge of the strategy process no longer view themselves as the sole experts in developing, evaluating, and implementing strategy. They must adopt a distributed view of strategy involving a process of engaging multiple stakeholders in the interactive resolution of complex issues. They must encourage the continuous coevolution of strategy across a wide spectrum of themes and supporting initiatives launched between themselves and the people who have the most at stake with their enterprise.[121] In the new strategy framework, the distinction between strategy formulation and implementation disappears. There is no handing-over process between thinking and acting.

Organizations have to find ways to engage employees in reconfiguring resources on demand, especially across multiple geographies and time zones. They must encourage co-creative leadership at all levels of organization. Further, enterprises must move toward designing co-creative performance management systems, where senior management only sets a few broad themes and top-level measures and then invites all managers to build their own individual strategy map and scorecard within the broad context that has been set.[122] The other role of senior management is to set up processes and tools that allow individuals to connect their scorecards with those of other people whose participation is required for them to succeed. Sustainable value creation also requires balanced risk taking by focusing on co-creation opportunities that can generate superior returns while simultaneously reducing risks for both enterprises and their stakeholders. Embracing co-creative engagement with internal and external stakeholders is necessary for strategic risk-return management of enterprises in an increasingly complex world.

In the next chapter, we discuss the crafting of the technical, social, and organizational architectures in building co-creative enterprises of the future.

6   CRAFTING CO-CREATIVE
ENTERPRISE ARCHITECTURES

Building a co-creative enterprise is a direct function of the co-creative capacities of the architecture of the enterprise that supports value creation as a co-creation. By enterprise architecture, we mean the approach to developing enterprise-wide capabilities through the structuring of relationships among its tangible and intangible resources and assets, as well as management systems, in a planned, principle-based manner. Such relationships ultimately enable co-creative engagements among customers, partners, stakeholders, and employees everywhere, every day, in the enterprise ecosystem.[123]

As information and communications technologies (IT) become embedded in business processes, the enterprise *technical* capabilities must be connected to the demands of internal employees/managers and the demands of external stakeholders as they leverage resources, access competence, and engage together in the co-creation of unique value(s). The strategic architectures of co-creative enterprise ecosystems, as a nexus of multiple co-creation platforms, entail high-level blueprints that diagram the design of new platforms of engagements, the redesign of existing ones, and the building of enterprise and network capabilities and resources to support platforms.

The primary focus of this chapter is on co-creation platform innovation—the innovation of capabilities for co-creation platforms. We start by examining IT-based capabilities. We then discuss the harnessing of network resources in building individual-to-network-to-individual interaction capabilities. Co-creative enterprise architectures must allow the building of new sources of value creation advantages across the activity chain system.

In the co-creation view, the organizations themselves are assemblages through which agency takes place. Hence, in addition to the technical architecture, this requires paying attention to the *social* architecture—the management structure, training, skills, beliefs, decision rights, performance metrics, rewards, and values of the organization—to enable the co-creative enactment of value creation. Further, building a co-creative enterprise rests on co-creative capacities of *organizational* architectures that enable extended enterprise and open/social network resources to be harnessed effectively by the organization. We elaborate upon the social and organizational architectures of co-creation in detail.

TECHNOLOGY AS ENABLING CO-CREATION PLATFORMS

Ubiquitous information and communications technologies in the hands of ordinary individuals have already transformed the societal and business landscape. Consider that in the near future, ordinary people are expected to have terabytes of storage capacity in one hand—the one holding the cell phone—and with a flick of a finger on the other hand access the Web, get informed or communicate, and bring one's "presence" in space and time to the purview of one or many, whether through text, voice, pictures, or video. The content and context of a Web-infused physical and simulated world are but the backdrop against which "creative recombination" of content and knowledge happens. Everyone can interact with this system, whether as a "giver" or "taker," to co-create their own experiences of value through engagement platforms facilitated by enterprises. These enterprises are themselves evolving IT-enabled co-creation capabilities inside their organizations and across the various interfaces of multiple other organizations in their enterprise ecosystems.

A variety of artifacts, as products, already contain embedded sensors and intelligence. With smart radio frequency identification (RFID) tags, products can report on ambient environmental conditions and also enable the tracking and maintenance of items as they move through enterprise supply chains. Moreover, smart artifacts are also increasingly internetworked, allowing them to communicate with one another and with human agents. From the perspective of human agency, wireless sensor networks are creating new spaces of experiences and transforming how we as individuals and communities interact with everyday objects.

The Internet of Things (IoT) is enabling any physical artifact in the world to potentially become a "device" that is connected to the Internet. IoT extends the Internet into everyday objects, giving them the ability to connect to a data network, interoperate with other objects, and intercommunicate with other entities, with the potential to generate new sources of agential value. IoT is a convergence of the digital world of "bits" with the physical world of "atoms," embedding the "computer" everywhere—with hardware and software becoming "everyware," as it were. This does not imply digital computer interfaces in every object but rather embedding intelligence into objects that make them "smart" and Internet addressable and interfaceable, with smartphones emerging as the ubiquitous computer at hand. Applications on smartphones are already linking smart things with resources on the Internet relevant to agents in the context of space and time. IoT augments the reality of everyday objects through "interdevice internetworking." IoT is allowing any artifact to become a device for detection and communication, as well as storage, computation, and display, and to exchange information and interact with other entities in the same representation. Light switches and thermostats that communicate with lightbulbs and heaters, pill bottles that order refills from pharmacies, early warning systems that predict forest fires and earthquakes, bottles of wine that provide information about its vintage and wine connoisseur reviews, and artwork in museums equipped with tagged text, images, and audio and video streams are all realities.

As Web users, when we click on an object on a Web page, we are clicking on a digital artifact. In the world of software development, programmers use many digital artifacts during the development process, and they are also its by-products. Open source software is software that is available in source code form and that is often developed in a publicly collaborative manner. This is the case with open source hardware, as well, which, given advances in 3D printing, is doing to the world of physical artifacts what open source software did to digital artifacts. When combined with the IoT evolution, it means expanding how we map reality as such and how artifacts in the process map us. Physical artifacts can become embodied with social data as people interact with them, augmenting their identity and heritage in the process. The artifact's data—its "memory"—can be carried and shared with other entities independently of the physical artifact itself.

Human beings, on their part, are social animals, instinctively inclined to connect with one another and belong to a social network. They want to be unique, but they also want to be connected. The underlying impulse is familiar, but the emergence of more opportunities for humans to enjoy self-created, externally influenced experiences in the social fabric is new. The burgeoning mobile Web enables new forms of sociotechnical interactions that make it possible for people to participate in thematic communities, which are distinct from spatially defined communities. For instance, PatientsLikeMe allows people to share their medical condition histories and experiences. Sharing among thematic community members promotes informed, effective collective action.

Co-creating individuals partake in events in real, temporal, animating, and sense-giving layers of manifolds of human experiences. A football game, a business seminar, a wedding, and a breakfast meeting are all examples of *events* as we use the word in daily parlance. From the perspective of enterprise agential action, events can be disaggregated into subevents. For example, a seminar meeting can be divided into two subevents: a large-group presentation in the morning followed by a small-group discussion in the afternoon. An NFL football season can be divided into 16 games, each game can be divided into quarters, and each quarter includes 20 to 40 separate plays, each a subevent of its own.

If I have a marginal interest in sports, I may track Sunday's game at a very superficial level. I might note the score and look at a filmed highlight or two. Even if I actually attend the game, I may experience it superficially if my primary interest is to enjoy some time with my friends and down a couple of cold beers. But some of my friends who are serious football fans may want to analyze all the details of every single play. Indeed, fantasy football leagues open up whole new spaces of experiences, layered on top of the actual games as it were, based on the statistics of the game and involving different compositions of teams picked by individual fans playing with one another.

Some event and subevent hierarchies are well defined by rules. Sports is an example with relatively well-delineated hierarchies of season, game, quarter, and play. In other cases, event hierarchies are not so clearly defined or well understood. Health care professionals would have difficulty breaking down the treatment of a patient (the hierarchy of events) entering the emergency room into a clear hierarchy of subevents. Moreover, hierarchies shift with changing contexts. A football fan who joins one of the popular fantasy leagues reconstructs the fan experience of the sport by drafting and trading players from various real-life teams, selecting starters and making substitutions, and tracking and comparing weekly performance statistics in competition with other fans in a thematic community. In this context, the score of a particular game is often less relevant. What matters more are the performance statistics of a player in one individual's fantasy team and contrasting and discussing the player's performance in a subcommunity of team fans. Thus, enabling interactions among individuals in assemblage systems is critical to affording the meaning that individuals attach to events.

For enterprises, closing the gap between the promise of co-creation and its reality is a direct function of the evolution of the co-creative capacity of the *enterprise IT architecture*. Three broad sets of architectural IT capabilities are required. Smart assemblage systems must have event-centric activation of interaction environments, dynamic process capabilities, and collaboration capabilities. All three must be centered on individuals and their environments and the innovation potentials with multiple other enterprises that are part of the extended value co-creation network.

Smart Assemblage Systems with Event-Centric Activation
of Interaction Environments
Following our discussion in Chapter 3 of individuated co-creation experiences (see, for instance, the OnStar example), enterprise architectures must

enable event-centric activation of interaction environments and be adaptive, flexible, and scalable with interoperability across supporting partners in the network. It is important to recognize that the same individual can activate different environments of interactions in the event-based network. The key for the firm is to understand the "envelope" of different activated environments and then build the underlying system, infrastructure, and capabilities to accommodate heterogeneous experiences.

Consider the case of Medtronic, Inc., a world leader in cardiac rhythm management that seeks to offer lifelong solutions for patients with chronic heart disease.[124] It developed a system of "virtual office visits" that enables physicians to check patients' implanted cardiac devices via the Internet. With the Medtronic CareLink Monitor, the patient can collect data by interacting with the implanted device. The captured data is transmitted to the Medtronic CareLink Network. On a dedicated secure website, physicians can review patient data and patients can check on their own conditions (but no one else's) and grant access to family members or other caregivers. Medtronic's CareLink system goes beyond the cardiac device itself and unleashes opportunities for an expanding range of value creation activities. As Dr. Kenneth Riff, vice president of strategy and business development for Medtronic's Patient Management Division, put it about a decade ago, "Once you stop thinking of a pacemaker as a therapeutic device and begin to think of it as a health care information and interaction platform, all kinds of new ideas open up." For example, each person's heart responds to stimulation slightly differently, and the response can change over time. Doctors can respond to such changes by adjusting the patient's pacemaker, and this can now be done remotely. Furthermore, Medtronic's technology platform can support a wide range of devices and remote monitoring/diagnostic systems that can be used for monitoring blood sugar readings, brain activity, blood pressure, and other important physiological measures.

From the enterprise side, Medtronic needs to understand how patients actively participate in the process of engaging with Medtronic's pacemaker constituted engagement platform, which is embedded in the patient's domain of lifestyle experiences. How do the quality of the patient's interactions with the doctor and the hospital staff affect the quality of the patient's overall experience? What roles do the combined network of related

products, services, and caregivers and the patient community play in creating value? How can any one of them create unique value with the patient
at any given point in time? What if the patient values the whole experience co-created with the network and not simply with the pacemaker?
How does the network's ability to accommodate different situations affect
the patient experience—different time, date, and location of an irregular
heartbeat? Moreover, the same individual can have a different experience
with the network under different circumstances, depending on the context
of events and the patient's personal preferences at that moment in time.
Given the same network, individuals can have different experiences, depending not only on the situational context (time and space) of events but
also on the social and cultural context of events. How much do intangible
aspects of a patient's context, the meanings they attach to outcomes, and
their involvements influence the experience?

Each individuated co-creation experience, in effect, activates multiple
stakeholder interaction environments afforded by the Medtronic engagement platform. As shown in Figure 6-1, the IT application layer provides
the link to the enterprise-stakeholder value level through the strategic architecture of enterprise engagement platforms, which ultimately enables
intended value outcomes to be realized. But the application layer also entails supporting event-centric capabilities from an enterprise perspective.[125]
To illustrate, consider the *interaction layer* of engagement platforms not
just from the patient's perspective but from the perspective of doctors and
other stakeholders as well.

Consider the scenario of a "crisis out of town." The patient may activate and engage with an emergency call center, medical support, and
hospital emergency services. The patient may need directions to the closest hospital, and the attending physician may need access to the patient's
medical history. How do the two doctors—the primary care provider back
home and the physician on call at the out-of-town hospital—coordinate
their diagnosis and treatment? How can the patient recognize and assess
risk-reward relationships and best cooperate with medical professionals?
The doctors, the facilities and services, and the pacemaker are all part of
a network-based engagement platform centered on the patient and the patient's wellbeing. The challenge is to identify a "core" set of stakeholder

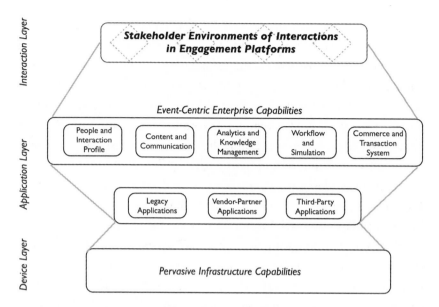

FIGURE 6-1   IT as enabling co-creation platforms

interaction environments and build event-centric information and communication infrastructures to support a portfolio of co-creative engagements and associated experience outcomes.

Note that the co-creation experience emerges from the "constellation of interactions" in the network.[126] It cannot occur without a resource network of firms collaborating to create the platforms and the interaction environments they afford that allow the patient to undergo that unique co-creation experience. In this regard, Medtronic also invites individuals as innovators the world over to submit ideas. Its Eureka platform initiative is designed to foster interactions between potential inventors or engineers and Medtronic, linking new product ideas with Medtronic's research, development, engineering, and, most important, its competence base in commercializing medical technologies. Medtronic recognizes that its enterprise ecosystem multiplies the value of the pacemaker to the patient, the patient's family, and the patient's doctors.

Simultaneously, the patient, by co-creating with network resources in its ecosystem, is an active stakeholder in defining the interaction, involvement, context of events, and meaning attached to outcomes. Value ultimately lies at the intersection of resources and opportunities, in the actualization of co-creation experience outcomes of a specific patient, at a specific point in time, in a specific location, and in the context of a specific event. The total co-creation experience with the network results in more personal and unique value for each patient; this is the case for all the stakeholding individuals besides the patient, from the doctor to the nurse to all other participating entities. The common denominator for value creation is the co-creation experiences of all individuals that enterprises must connect with, understand, and gain insights from.

Each stakeholding individual has both a demand and a supply side. Medtronic's strategic architecture of engagement platforms must enable the "demand" side of each individual to be engaged co-creatively with the "supply" side that supports that individual. Thus, rather than fixed roles of stakeholders in the system—customers, competitors, suppliers, collaborators, and investors—there are *roles of the moment* that shift and morph as circumstances change. Consider Hackensack University Medical Center in Hackensack, New Jersey, a "digital hospital" where Ken Burns, a trauma surgeon and CIO, championed the building of new IT capabilities. Doctors could access x-rays from an internal website on any computer inside or outside the hospital and could even control a life-sized robot (a "digital doc" wearing the typical white lab coat and stethoscope) from their laptops at home. Doctors could direct this digital doc into hospital rooms and use two-way video to discuss patients' conditions. Nurses could use a PC that rolled around on an IV-like stand and log into patient electronic records through a wireless connection to review vital signs—temperature, heart rate, and so on—entered into the system earlier by a nurse's aide. Nurses could pull up medication orders, check the accuracy of medications and dosage levels, and even interact with other sources of medical expertise to learn about patient therapies. The system enhanced the quality of the patient experience and allowed nurses to spend more time on caregiving. Before, nurses spent a lot of time on the phone with pharmacies, trying to get medication refills, or with doctors, trying to decipher their handwriting. The IT system ensured that the pharmacy got drugs to nurses on schedule and that nurses could access almost every piece of information they needed—from insurance plans to medical tests. For their part, patients could use TVs in their rooms to access information about their medical conditions. Pervasive, "everywhere" infrastructure that allows individuals to interact and collaborate through their device of choice, whether as customers or employees, is becoming a core capability.

While Hackensack Medical Center reported increased productivity, lower costs, and simultaneously better patient outcomes from its IT systems, a technical system that the University of Pennsylvania's hospital used to prescribe drugs created new ways to make errors, according to a study. The system scattered patient data and drug-ordering forms over so many different computer windows that it increased the likelihood of doctors ordering the wrong medications.[127] Technology can be used to enable better physician, nurse, and patient interactions, but only through better design thinking and if used wisely. The DART principles of experience configuration (see Chapter 3) and the CITI principles of engagement design (see Chapter 2) are highly relevant in designing and innovating IT systems that enable and connect with co-creation experiences.

Dynamic Process Capabilities

The Medtronic CareLink example illustrates how co-creation system processes in the underlying network must be selectively and dynamically activated to enable personalized interactions and value outcomes. This result goes beyond modular, standardized processes that are interchangeable with multiple entities in the ecosystem toward "on-demand" dynamic process capabilities.

Consider the case of Cleveland Clinic, whose CEO and cardiac surgeon, Delos "Toby" Cosgrove, was instrumental in its transformation toward a more co-creative enterprise. With more than 37,000 employees and annual revenues exceeding $4.4 billion in 2008, Cleveland Clinic sought to enhance and innovate all stakeholder experiences, especially those of patients and caregivers. For example, in January 2008, Cleveland Clinic opened its medical records—the "chart"—to any patients who wanted to see their own medical information. As Cosgrove put it, "The charts really aren't the hospital's; they belong to the patients, and we think it's their right to have that information." This transparency has an effect on care because now when nurses review charts during shift changes, they do it bedside instead of at the nursing station. The patient and nurse can carry on a conversation. Dubbed MyChart, the medical chart system is transparent to the patient, and patients are urged to ensure the accuracy of the personal information.

From the perspective of the health care provider, MyChart allows x-rays, MRIs, and CT scans to be stored and viewed online with laboratory results. This display helps them routinely check patients' health statuses as well as screen for numerous disorders. Test results are available to the patient after having been reviewed and released into the system by the doctor. If the patient chooses, the doctor can schedule an appointment to first inform the patient of the diagnosis and discuss its implications and treatment options. The online scheduling tool allows the patient and the doctor to view past appointments, request appointments, and make cancellations.

Thus, the goal at Cleveland Clinic is to let patients and their families guide these dynamic processes to help caregivers help patients better through more co-creative interactions everywhere in the system. To do so, the underlying technology platforms must be designed for effective interactions of various participants and stakeholders in the network.

In 2008, Cleveland Clinic invited up to 10,000 patients (from over 100,000 using MyChart) to participate in the design of the electronic Personal Health Record (PHR) system to make it more "portable." As Dr. Martin Harris, CIO of Cleveland Clinic, explained, the pilot was intended to extend Cleveland Clinic's online patient services to give patients the ability to interact with multiple physicians, health care services providers, and pharmacies and to open the exchange of medical information to a broader network without compromising privacy. Cleveland Clinic sought to create national access to electronic medical records at no cost to the user or provider. The goal was to empower patients to become more collaborative with their health care providers.

Collaboration Capabilities
The Internet has evolved from publishing and commerce ("Web 1.0") to engagement and collaboration of individuals ("Web 2.0"). As we saw in the previous chapter, enterprises in general are already connecting communities—not only of employees but also customers, partners, and stakeholders outside the corporate firewall to generate ideas and accelerate

innovation. Younger workers growing up with social interaction tools expect the same kinds of tools in their roles as employees as workplaces are becoming more digital as well. Whether sales applications, recruiting, training, resource planning, or supply chain management, enterprise software as services is being built on the Web, much like consumer services have always been.

As collaboration becomes more fluid and interpersonal, individuals seek opportunities to work with others through various modalities of interaction—whether wikis, blogs, shared bookmarks, group messaging, or conferencing tools such as WebEx and telepresencing. For instance, at BT Group (formerly British Telecom), which has blended inside and outside collaboration, more than 16,000 employees work together on wikis to collaborate on everything from writing telecom software to mapping cell phone base stations to launching branding campaigns. These employees work across time zones; engineers in Asia can pick up on a project hatched through a wiki when their British counterparts go to bed. Traditional hierarchies dissolve as a young engineer can amend and build upon the work of a senior engineer. And although BT has its own internal social networking platform, over 10,000 BT Group employees also use Facebook. As J. P. Rangaswami, BT Group's enterprise architect, said, "The new people come infected with the new world." This infection is becoming more widespread across the entire value chain of activities as organizations engage in building collaborative and transformative IT capabilities in their extended business networks. Nor does "collaboration" mean compromising information security. The Department of Defense, for example, uses WebEx's software as a service to enhance its collaborative communications globally.

Collaborative IT capabilities are also transforming the health care business. As we saw in the Hackensack Hospital example, real-time access through the Internet and audio- and videoconferencing can help patients and providers stay connected and avert many medical exigencies. In the Cleveland Clinic example, we saw how electronic health records across interoperable health care systems can allow patients to co-shape their health outcomes by extending the capacity for collaborative care into the business network. The same is true from the health caregiver side as well.

Project ECHO is a program spearheaded by Dr. Sanjeev Arora, a professor of medicine at the University of New Mexico Health Sciences Center. ECHO (the Extension for Community Healthcare Outcomes) is a platform for service delivery, education, and training that provides specialty care to individuals (especially those who are uninsured) living in rural or underserved areas who have chronic complex diseases. For example, the primary care doctor in that area may not know how to treat hepatitis C or may know how to treat diabetes but does not have a trained team to help her manage several patients. Using what Arora terms "learning loops" and "team multipliers," Project ECHO has transformed health care in rural areas.[128]

Learning loops at ECHO entail multimedia, case-based educational experiences that use not only best practice protocols but also case-based shared telemedicine access to the ECHO "knowledge network" of specialists collaborating with community-based primary care providers. The specialists gain deep co-created domain knowledge, while the rural providers learn rapidly about how to provide high-quality treatment. Outcomes are systematically monitored over time and co-managed longitudinally.[129]

Project ECHO's "team multipliers" are about training ancillary providers to be part of the health care team. The ECHO model empowers nurses, medical assistants, and community health workers to become part of a "disease management team." This model multiplies the capacity of a physician by training other professionals who have less knowledge than the primary doctor (and get paid significantly less) but can work as a team to provide the same protocol-driven care in the outreach area. Once the doctor has prescribed the medicine and the protocol is in effect, the trained workers can execute the protocol effectively. The teams also have access to the ECHO knowledge network. Over time, the learning loop kicks in and the support providers enhance their expertise in their areas. Project ECHO relies on team-based IT capabilities to co-create mutually valuable outcomes by connecting people at low cost to global resources, engaging in teleconferenced dialogue, sharing health care data through the Web, generating new knowledge, and learning rapidly from field experiences.

Project ECHO has been awarded nearly $8.5 million over three years from the U.S. Department of Health and Human Services (HHS) Health

Care Innovation awards. It will identify 5,000 high-cost, high-utilization, high-severity patients in New Mexico and Washington State and use a team of primary care "intensivists" trained to care for complex patients with multiple chronic diseases, working with area managed care organizations and care providers. It is estimated to save over $11 million over the three-year period. Reports on the high concentration of health spending reveal that 5 percent of the population account for nearly 50 percent of health care costs ($1.3 trillion).[130] Collaborative telemedicine, with its potential to help patients with limited access to services or who are among the minority of patients that account for the vast majority of health care expenditures, can transform health care experiences through co-creation.

Thus, co-creative enterprise architectures provide the "backbone" to:

- innovating engagement platforms and designing co-creative interaction environments;

- linking IT-based capabilities with a strategic architecture of co-creation platforms to enable co-creative engagements of value;

- accelerating innovation success through internal and external co-creation with all stakeholders; and

- building competitive advantage through multiple facets of co-creation opportunities and connecting them with value creating network resources.

INDIVIDUAL-TO-NETWORK-TO-INDIVIDUAL INTERACTION CAPABILITIES

The co-creation view requires reconfiguring and recontextualizing resources around points of interaction. If the goal is to enable heterogeneous co-creation experiences and allow individuals to co-construct their own experiences, it's obvious that the entire resource network will be affected.

Heterogeneity of Co-Creation Experiences

Enterprises have the complex task of designing engagement platforms that afford environments of interactions that accommodate heterogeneous co-creation experiences. Enablers of individual experiences must be integrated into the underlying architecture of engagement platforms. For instance, the rapid spread of embedded intelligence demands a network capable of continually feeding information from points of customer-company inter-action back to the enterprise—in a form that facilitates managerial action such that both the manager and the customer can co-create unique out-comes of value appropriately. This implies a system capable of recognizing the heterogeneity of individual experiences. Co-creative systems should be able to easily scale up and down, change configurations constantly, selec-tively activate competencies, and facilitate managerial action at low cost. They must be able to facilitate the construction of a different experience for each individual—one that's fulfilling to that individual in the context of the space and time in which it is being co-constructed.

Consider electric power. Deregulation has moved this industry toward more competitive generation, transmission, and distribution of electricity. Dynamic pricing by the hour, or even by the minute (as telecom companies do), seems attractive. While this can potentially produce cost savings for all entities participating in the network, consumers must make behavioral changes in their consumption patterns, whether it is adjusting their use of household appliances or just shifting the times of day when they use energy. Smart control systems are part of the necessary network in this arena. Some of the intelligence has to be pushed out to the point of con-sumption. At the same time, the backbone of the network infrastructure needs attention. The electric grid infrastructure must also be able to recon-figure power generation and transmission to suit consumption patterns. And there is investment required to retrofit or replace household meters with the embedded intelligence to collect more real-time-of-use data and calculate more complicated bills.

Heterogeneous pricing has a profound impact on accounting and bill-ing systems. Traditional accounting was designed to reflect stable busi-ness models and fixed assets; it fostered the assumption that improving the utilization of physical assets was the key to profitability. Though still required for historical costs and public reporting purposes, they can no longer be used to manage day-to-day operations in the co-creation view. In their place, flexible, program-oriented budgeting (rather than budget-ing driven by administrative categories), contribution thinking, and cash flow analyses become critical new tools.

Closely associated with heterogeneous pricing is micro-billing, a major infrastructure capability that firms will need to compete in the new experience space. Telephone utilities have always had by-the-minute accounting and billing systems; other firms need similar systems as well. Billing systems are also repositories of embedded customer information as well as part of the customer interface—which is to say, a social instrument. Billing can no longer be treated as an obscure, back-room operation but as a potentially valuable tool in enabling a personalized experience and generating economic value through it.

Consider, for example, the implications of personalization in a billing environment. All bills are personal by definition; the bill is, after all, based on your transactions and has your name engraved on it. But if you are like most people, you may still find telecom bills or credit card statements hard to decipher and manage. What if the experience of reading and paying bills introduced an element of co-creation? What if you could choose the tools to interact with your own data the way you would want to? Suppose one has just returned from vacation or it is tax time. Why not quickly sort the transactions on your e-bill online based on a selected time frame of your choice (not company-centric billing periods), tally up amounts, and search for amounts above a certain number? Why can't the system learn how you want to categorize transactions? Why can't it use the learning from others about how they tag items and suggest attractive groupings and layouts? Co-creation is about changing the way interactions occur in mutually valuable ways.

Embedded intelligence in assemblages are often needed to facilitate the choosing of options and co-shape environments with ease. Consider the "airplane mode" feature on the iPhone. It is very useful to be able to quickly turn off wireless services in the context of being on board an aircraft. But it also useful to be able to turn off roaming services and associated charges while on the ground. However, what if I want to turn only data services off and not voice. In many smartphones, it means constantly trying to recall where the option is buried, often a couple of menu layers deep. Doing so would engender a wide variety of novel experiences. Or take another situation. Smartphone displays typically brighten up in sunlight so they are more visible. Conversely, when there is less ambient light, the display dims. But what if you actually want the display brighter in darkness as well? It often requires fiddling with the brightness options each time. Or consider the alarm clock on the iPhone. Why can't it turn off after a set time? Why can't frequently used features and options "float to the top"? Why can't embedded intelligence in the system learn how an assemblage is engaged with contextually?

What's key, in general, is the enterprise learning through co-creative engagement, understanding how individuals as buyers, users, experiencers, and co-creators think, and what options they want in creating standardized/customized products and services. In short, experience personalization is agnostic, as such, to product and process standardization or customization. Instead, it is fundamentally about the nature, quality, and purposefulness of network interactions and recognizing individuation of co-creation experiences explicitly.

Consider, for instance, the pharmaceutical industry that has long relied on the blockbuster approach to drug development, trying to create medications that can be used identically by millions of patients, thereby generating revenues measured in the billions of dollars. It's an approach that seeks to minimize the impact of heterogeneity of experiences in favor of uniformity. But such an approach has many problems. Side effects, which occur with practically every medication, are clear evidence of heterogeneity in patients' bodily interactions. So are interactions among multiple medications taken by a single patient, which can sometimes be fatal. Yet, the clinical trials used to test new drugs have not typically encompassed heterogeneous populations around the globe, leave alone heterogeneous patient interactions.

A physician, ultimately, selects a drug based on patient history, diagnosis, and his own judgment shaped by his experiences and those of his peers. How does this process of choice deal with patient heterogeneity? The conventional approach is basically one of trial and error. The physician prescribes his preferred medication for a given condition and monitors the results. If the drug works, fine. If not, the prescription is switched to a second option. The process continues until an effective medication for the particular patient is found. It's awkward and potentially even dangerous.

Today this process is rapidly changing. Take Herceptin, a breast cancer treatment made by Genentech, which works well—but in only a small percentage of patients. Herceptin became a successful medication because those patients can be identified through a test developed and administered by small diagnostic companies. What's interesting here is the ability to identify one product from the options available that is uniquely suited to me, using a method that is more efficient and safer than the traditional trial-and-error method. With new advances in patient screening and gene-based testing techniques, physicians will increasingly be able to determine whether a given drug might be effective for me specifically—an example of adapting to individual heterogeneity.

From an enterprise perspective, the quality of an experience outcome is conditioned by the quality of the underlying processes in fulfilling that experience. From an individual's perspective, however, the particular form of content that is exhibited by the experience outcome drives experience quality. Traditional quality management is about stamping out variation in a bid to control quality of products and services. But experience quality means combining heterogeneity of contexts of individuals and events in space and time—in other words, *outcome variability*—coupled with reliable quality. Thus, there are two key aspects of affording engagements based on the quality of co-created experience outcomes. On the stakeholder side is the ability to free up outcomes that are "baked" into conventional rigid processes and then co-shape outcomes of value to individuals. On the enterprise side is the ability to (re)design processes based on desirable co-creative experience outcomes of value to individuals. Enterprises have to distinguish between the "quality of a process" and "co-created experience outcomes." The latter must guide the former. Moreover, the goal is to maximize variation in types of engagement experiences (i.e., accommodate a wide variety of co-created experience outcomes), while minimizing variation in the underlying quality of processes (i.e., classic Six Sigma).

Thus, the traditional quality management principles do not go away. Rather, enterprises must be able to design engagement platforms that selectively activate assemblage systems to facilitate a variety of contextualized interactions that generate mutually valuable outcomes, while ensuring the quality of fulfilled experiences. The same individual who demands a unique, personalized experience also demands responsiveness, speed, reliability, and cross-channel consistency in actually experiencing events underlying engagements with assemblages. To illustrate, consider the fashion company Burberry.[131] As Burberry CEO Angela Ahrendts said, "Our vision is that a customer has total access to Burberry, across any device, anywhere. They get exactly the same feeling of the brand and feeling of the culture." Based initially on a sketch that Salesforce.com CEO Marc Benioff drew on a napkin during a meeting with Ahrendts and Burberry CTO John Douglas, Burberry aims to combine Burberry's customer portal, social marketing, Burberry's supply chain world, the Burberry world of fashion, retail experiences, social product offerings, custom mobile apps, and insights and analysis in a unified social enterprise architecture. As Ahrendts notes, "You have to create a social enterprise today. You have to. If you don't do that, I don't know what your business model is in five years."

With over 10 million Facebook followers, Burberry is attempting to integrate its technical architecture of engagement platforms with its social architecture, building common ground between its customers and fashionistas and its employees, especially customer-facing sales, service, and marketing personnel. Employees not only have access to CRM-type data, but they can also connect with customers' social media activities, from Facebook comments to Tweets and blog postings. Customers can also initiate conversations on a variety of lifestyle issues, make store appointments to check out a new collection, and even attend fashion shows remotely with a "front seat" view and order items in real time directly off the runway. Customers can also suggest (re)design ideas for products. Burberry, in turn, can experiment with changes to its offerings and test its marketing communications with the Burberry community.

In its flagship retail stores, Burberry is transforming the retail experience through several enabling technologies deployed throughout the store to engage individuals. For instance, a key enabling technology is an RFID system, which provides both sales associates and customers with immediate access to a rich stream of content when an RFID-tagged item is activated. The content includes up-to-date information on every item, such as what sizes or colors are currently available, which enables the sales associate to spend more time attending personally to a customer rather than disappearing into the back room to check the stock. The content also includes the heritage of the product, sketches, color swatches, and video clips that customers can view on display units throughout the store. The net result is a retail store engagement platform architecture that lets consumers co-construct a compelling new retail experience. The challenge for Burberry is to afford interaction environments that enable a variety of novel, personalized experiences on the one hand, while ensuring a high quality of individuated co-creation experiences on the other.

Capacity to Rapidly Reconfigure Resources
Whether high fashion or commodity products, balancing the diversity and quality of experiences requires the capacity to rapidly reconfigure resources on demand. Consider the remarkable transformation of a very traditional industry—cement—by an innovative Mexican-based company, Cemex. In the cement industry, customers (chiefly builders and contractors) demand definite delivery times on which they can rely. But almost half of these customers can be expected to change their orders, usually close to the original scheduled delivery time. Under the circumstances, forecasting does not mean much, and a firm like Cemex cannot change the way its customers work and behave. The key challenge is to develop the ability to respond quickly to changes in customer demand.

To tackle this problem, Cemex had to reconceive its operations around giving customers flexibility. That meant that Cemex itself had to become flexible, while continuing to ensure dependable, on-time delivery of cement. To achieve this goal, the company invested in CemexNet, a satellite communications system that links all the cement plants, coordinating Cemex's far-flung production facilities. It then installed a logistics system called Dynamic Synchronization of Operations, which uses GPS technology and onboard computers to link the delivery trucks and coordinate them. Like FedEx, it built transparency into its operation, allowing dispatchers to see the location, speed, and direction of each truck and obtain information on weather, traffic conditions, inventory, and customers' locations. The result: trucks can be quickly rerouted to coordinate orders, production plants, and deliveries in response to last-minute changes requested by customers. Now there's an online engagement platform where Cemex's suppliers, distributors, and customers can check order status and make changes up to the moment of delivery. Customers can specify characteristics like color, strength, texture, and elasticity, which are critical to using ready-mix cement. The access of Cemex's managers and customers to real-time information centered on events is fundamental to the company's rapid response capabilities.

Of course, all this did not happen overnight. It took Cemex several years to build its current infrastructure, starting with the communications network and the IT infrastructure, and followed by the logistics infrastructure that enabled Cemex customers to be part of the value creation process. In the case of Cemex, rapid resource reconfiguration involves the ability to turn on a dime in response to changing customer requirements. It can also imply being proactive, as in the case of Zara, another fashion company like Burberry, that built its strategy on "fast fashion." Zara uses its employees to spot trends in fashion. To stay current with the latest fashion ideas, trends, and tastes, Zara encourages retail employees and its designers to socialize with consumers. They then utilize the company's internal communications network and wireless devices to send real-time information to Zara's commercial group and design center in Spain. If a shop manager sees that a particular garment is selling well or that a different color or style variation is needed, she alerts the company. Thus, new designs are created continuously, not just more of what's selling off the racks. It takes as little as two to three weeks for Zara to move from a design sketch on a notepad to store displays of new garments. As one young Zara shopper said, "Fashion is so transient that you just want to get the look of the moment at a really good price." This is what Zara provides.

To make this possible, Zara has developed the ability to reconfigure its supply chain elements very rapidly. Zara cuts the raw material themselves, and its workshops in Spain do the final sewing and assembly. Because it manufactures garments close to the market (rather than in a cheaper but more distant location, such as China), the chain can replenish store stocks twice a week, minimizing inventory and adjusting quickly and flexibly to trends. Another benefit is that transportation costs are also reduced. Thus, slightly higher manufacturing costs are more than offset by savings elsewhere in the system and especially by the increased inventory turns that are generated by offering cutting-edge fashion.

In the case of Cemex, this reconfiguration is triggered when a customer telephones the company with an order or a change in plans. Because calls come in all the time, the process of reconfiguration has to be continuous. In the case of Zara, the company drives the fashion intelligence gathered by its employees into decisions regarding style, designs, fabrics, shapes, colors, and so on. In both cases, the capabilities have to coevolve with co-creation experiences to selectively access competencies on demand in the network.

Access to Competence

A nodal enterprise is one that provides the intellectual and technical leadership needed to establish an effective resource network, as well as the incentives that hold multiple participating enterprises in the network together. Li & Fung in the textile business is a classic example. This Hong Kong–based company has become a nodal enterprise by accessing a network of 7,500 suppliers in 37 countries. It uses this network to enable clients to rotate their fashions at very short notice—often within three weeks. Li & Fung manages the information in the entire system as well as the relationships with the supplier network to deliver products faster, cheaper, and with less risk. When an order arrives, Li & Fung uses customized websites, e-mail, and other communications methods to work with the customer to fine-tune the specifications. It then creates an optimal "supply chain on demand," finding the right suppliers of raw materials and the right factories to assemble the clothes. Thus, the fabric may be woven in China, if that's where the appropriate dye is available; durable fastenings may be produced in Korea; and the garment may be sewn in Guatemala. It also balances the workload among its portfolio of suppliers in various regions of the world.

As the garment moves through production, a retail customer can make last-minute changes (just like a Cemex customer). In this case, however, the change may impact a global supply base. The customer can alter the design until the fabric is cut, change the color until the fabric is dyed, and even cancel the order altogether until the fabric is woven. Li & Fung's competence lies in its deep understanding of the competencies resident in its vast supply network, its mastery of the economics of production, and its ability to create a customized supply chain suited to a customer's specific requirements. It illustrates how access to competence can be a critical element in creating the infrastructure that enables flexible and resilient individual-to-network-to-individual capabilities.

If enterprises are to embrace the co-creation paradigm, they have to build enterprise architectures that recognize the centrality of internal *managerial* co-creation experiences as much as external stakeholder co-creation experiences.

Capacity for Managerial Action
Events such as a machine breakdown, a customer query, or a change in inventory levels are triggers for experience configuration. IT systems must be oriented around events that are not only stakeholder relevant but managerially actionable. The systems must facilitate queries and navigation based on how managers want to utilize information, not on arbitrary rules and procedures. IT systems must unfold in time and space, cutting across the divisions between applications, processes, and the data sources. Information must be indexed in a unified manner and accessible based on the events to which they refer. For example, a car accident sets in motion many processes involving data from many sources: police, insurance companies, onboard computers, hospitals, repair shops, and so on. The common thread is the event—the accident. The manager needs access to all the relevant event-centric information in a single unified view, including the ability to access data across many accidents to examine trends or patterns of interaction.

Efficiency and the Capacity to Change
The co-creation-based view of the enterprise demands a flexible infrastructure that supports both the capacity to change (via experimentation, innovation, and flexibility) and efficiency (via support for standardization, as in subprocesses). Experience-based innovation can simultaneously bring efficiencies with it, with judicious investments in experience configuration enablers. A mere pile of data does not produce insight any more than putting lettuce, tomatoes, cucumbers, and salad dressing in the same bowl

automatically produces a salad. We need contextual organization of data from multiple sources, types, and streams, all navigable via effective managerial interfaces (whether we define them as "dashboards," "cockpits," or whatever metaphor we prefer). The system should facilitate event-centric and experience-based interaction with data so as to generate insights on which managers can act.

The information infrastructures must not only support the best practices embedded in current business processes but also enable managers to experiment, discover, and evolve the next practices. This means the ability to change the business logic embedded in applications quickly without significant resource implications. The technical architecture must entail a capacity to support hypothesis generation by managers and to help them identify weak signals and exceptions in masses of data from multiple sources. These tools must help generate contextual insights for decisions rather than merely presenting trends. Enterprises need engagement platforms that let managers collaborate effectively, access competence from a wide range of sources, generate knowledge rapidly, and build consensus on action, especially internally.

The technical architecture must enable information—audio, video, images, text, statistics—from multiple, heterogeneous, and legacy databases to be readily and seamlessly available. Navigation must be easy enough so that busy line managers can explore databases themselves rather than delegate the task to analysts. The data interface must be easy and intuitive. The infrastructure must facilitate not just hypothesis testing but also hypothesis generation. Knowledge threads connecting managers with one another must be protected. It must be possible to revisit data, add new information, and continuously generate new insights in co-creative fashion.

Managerially Experiencing Stakeholder Co-Creation

The information infrastructure must allow managers to experience the business in the same way the stakeholder does, thereby achieving a new level of personal managerial effectiveness. The managerial experience domains of business—on a real-time, continuous basis—must be as close as possible to the experience domains of customers, employees, suppliers, and other stakeholders. Managers must be able to interact in real time with systems and communities of practice in order to discover, understand, and respond to critical situations as they occur. Just as it is critical for consumers to be able to interact with consumer communities, managers must be able to communicate with employee communities, and not just to share best practices within the system but to create "next practices" through real-time, problem-solving collaboration as well. As a manager, I should be immersed in the experience as it is happening. But I also want the ability to view it later for more detailed analysis. I need the ability to reconstruct the experience using an event-centric information system that can help me search for patterns, formulate hypotheses, and respond effectively to opportunities and problems.

Such capabilities must be available to every stakeholder-facing staff member. In the co-creation view, every employee who has the ability to directly influence the stakeholder experience and facilitate the co-creation of value is a line manager. In a world of discontinuous change, line managers learn in the context of events; they learn from one another, from customers, from suppliers, and from broader communities of interest and expertise. Technology can support this learning process. The generation of new knowledge in a systematic fashion around events is indeed a significant managerial challenge. It requires coming to terms with the "learning disabilities" that mark the social infrastructures of so many organizations. For communities of practice to flourish, we must understand how managers want to interact with one another and the technical infrastructure. Managers need to get as much real-time data as possible on the nature of co-creation experiences, and they must understand and intervene selectively in critical individual consumer events while they are managing the overall operation.

Capacity for Agility and Accommodating Managerial Heterogeneity
Managers must have the capacity for agility to co-create value effectively. Agility is the ability to act fast—to improve the cycle time for managerial action. It's a capability that is critical to co-creation. Agility depends above all on the readiness of line managers to respond quickly to environmental change. And line managers, like all people, are a heterogeneous lot with individuated managerial experience domains. Therefore, organizational

agility is largely a function of the capacity of the managerial engagement platforms to respond to the needs of heterogeneous line managers.

Line managers differ in how they access information, how they develop insights, and how they build consensus for action. Yet, in developing information systems for managerial use, IT groups have tended to ignore or minimize the problem of managerial heterogeneity. For example, the information needs of "sales managers" (a functionally and hierarchically defined group) are usually treated as monolithic—even though, in reality, the information needs of "sales manager Jill" may be quite different from those of "sales manager Jack." When IT groups try to accommodate variations in needs, they usually do it by building a large variety of features and functions into the system. Unfortunately, this approach often increases the complexity of the system without improving its ability to meet the heterogeneous needs of managers.

"Individuation" is different from catering to a user group or customizing an application at the level of the organization. It's about being sensitive to my "context of the moment" as a manager and to how I want to access, visualize, and use information. It's about giving me the capacity to collaborate in the enhanced network of suppliers, partners, and customers, as well as to reconfigure resources for rapid co-creation of value. To achieve true individuation, it's important to understand the basic sources of managerial heterogeneity. Because managers differ in their levels of sophistication and domain knowledge, one manager may need only one hour to learn a particular information system, whereas another manager requires two days to learn it. Furthermore, while the sophisticated manager can get at the features she wants and be pleased, a less sophisticated manager may spend endless time navigating through features, feeling increasingly frustrated and alienated. Obviously, IT systems that require the manager's active engagement will have to deal with heterogeneity in sophistication and domain knowledge if they are to be effective. For managers to co-create value, they must have the capacity for contextual dialogue, which will vary across individuals and from one project to another. Individual managers vary in their willingness to experiment, due in part to their varying responses to the efficiency versus innovation trade-off. Management processes have traditionally been focused on increasing the efficiency of transactions and business processes. But agility requires willingness to experiment as well, which generally reduces efficiency (at least in the short run). Whether and how a particular manager trades efficiency for experimentation depends on the context for managerial action. Ultimately, efficiency and innovation must both be accommodated.[132]

Consistency and Flexibility of Managerial Actions
The actions of managers at various levels in the enterprise must be consistent. As a manager, I must be able to personalize my actions, but I also want to be in sync with others. The interactivity needed to strike this balance consistently is a very critical systemic capability. Managers must also be able to have a visceral understanding of the co-creation experience—a "gut" sense of stakeholder reality. Simply reading a written report rarely conveys this sense. Information systems should also provide video and audio inputs integrated with textual data and, ideally, capable of capturing, in real time, the nature of the activities taking place in a specific location. This kind of rich, multisensory information enables managers to refine and clarify their questions about the activities they manage. However, it's also critical to provide a common event context. Remember, the same manager may be involved in different roles at different times. One day, she may be focusing on managing day-to-day operations; the next day, on resource optimization; and the day after that, on resource allocation and planning. Thus, the system must provide continuity and consistency, while also permitting the manager to shift focus at will, calling up varying sets and styles of information as her changing roles demand. One of the most important value-adding activities of any manager is the asking of new, nonroutine questions. These will often be stated in vague form, supported as much by intuition and hunches as by hard data. Unfortunately, most traditional information systems are geared toward answering known questions presented in standardized forms. Well-crafted information systems enable the manager to contextually collaborate with others who may have to act on this hypothesis or who may have a different perspective on it. Collaboration in rapidly building a consensus around a hypothesis is a critical capability in the co-creation view.

BUILDING NEW STRATEGIC CAPITAL

There are times when improvements to an existing system will not do—when you just have to discard what you know. For generations, ships were gradually improved by adding and redesigning sails, refining hull designs, modernizing navigation systems, and so on. But the development of the steamship rendered most of those incremental improvements worthless. We still have sailboats, but they are no longer economically viable for commercial transportation anywhere in the developed world. The lesson is clear. The emerging model of value co-creation is an inflection point. Thus, you as the manager must decide whether to just add more sails to your ship or build an entire steamboat instead.

We hope you decide to build a steamboat. We believe the new competitive space, as we have described it, demands it. We suggest that managers fold the future of competition in, starting with the experience co-creation space. Extrapolating existing capabilities will not get us there. In short, managers must create new strategic capital—new sources of innovation, value creation, and competitive advantage. New strategic capital is about challenging the traditional and established approach to value creation and competition. It entails new ways to think about opportunities, new ways to access competence, new ways to reconfigure and leverage resources, and new ways to engage the organization.

The current capabilities of organizations—including your organization—reflect an implicit theory of how to compete, based on the traditional paradigm of value creation. The concepts and ideas we have discussed in this book collectively embody an emerging theory of an experience-based view of joint value creation. By implication, they also direct our attention to new sources of competitive advantage. Harnessing the new sources of competitive advantage requires crafting the strategic architecture of co-creation platforms as we have illustrated through the various examples in this chapter.

From an enterprise point of view, strategic architectures of co-creation provide a potential sense of strategic direction on what new platforms will be built where in the enterprise ecosystem, how they will provide access to competence and reconfigure resources to facilitate intensive engagements, and what kind of transformation in capabilities are needed to build the co-creative capacities of the enterprise ecosystem as a nexus of interactions among multiple enterprises in the same ecosystem.

Consider the case of the trucking and logistics industry. The Class 8 highway truck segment of the transportation industry, which consists of the largest long-distance trucks, is a complex business involving multiple business-to-business customers and sophisticated information systems. Freightliner, a heavy- and medium-duty commercial vehicle manufacturer, offers software packages that allow fleets to monitor their costs, and it has become more involved in its customers' quest for maximization of efficiency as they face rising fuel costs to vehicle maintenance to uneven driving performance.[133] At the same time, Qualcomm, an industry leader in wireless, satellite-based positioning, and communications hardware for the trucking market, offers a suite of hardware, infrastructure, and software solutions (through certified partners) for truck fleet management and driver performance monitoring. Likewise, Detroit Diesel Corp. offers a system that Freightliner's customers can install at their fuel island or exit gates that automatically downloads information from the engine electronic communications module, including idle time, fuel consumption, and percentage of time in top gear. In principle, Freightliner's customers can use this information to make decisions on how they can improve performance, increase fuel efficiency, and reduce downtime. Many small to medium-sized fleets do not have the capacity to support these types of systems, however, and even if they do put these systems in place, they might not have the expertise to determine what the information means and how it can be utilized in a valuable manner.

As a "nodal" enterprise—that is, one that builds and maintains the co-creation network and provides its intellectual leadership—Freightliner can co-create mutual value with fleet customers and an extended network of engine monitoring systems, powertrain and subsystem modules, and service-repair constituencies (e.g., selected dealers, travel centers, diesel centers, garages). This can happen by being both the platform through which vehicle telematics information is sent and facilitating best-practice interactions on truck fleets.

For instance, imagine that Freightliner determines that a particular engine is exhibiting behavior that indicates a need for maintenance. Freightliner knows that customers value information on engine maintenance needs before a truck breaks down. Now imagine Freightliner being able to pinpoint a particular truck that shows excessive fuel use. Its customers value the assurance of a local dealer assessing the situation before the next scheduled maintenance period. But while large fleets have the capacity to analyze this information, they typically do not know how they compare with other fleets and how those Freightliner customers are analyzing their own information. They don't know the best practices for usage and maintenance of the Freightliner trucks, so one customer who may have "worst-in-class" uptime or fuel economy has little or no insight into what another customer may be doing to achieve "best-in-class" operational measures. Could customers compare operational measures with other fleets (anonymously) and learn what steps those fleets are taking to achieve better performance? To what extent can fuel efficiency be correlated with driving style, engine, tire, road, and load conditions? On the supply side, can Freightliner summarize problems for suppliers that relate to their supplied components? Can suppliers provide repair or diagnosis methods directly to the service centers and the Freightliner call center?

Going one step further, consider a breakdown experience. Say a truck is traveling from the U.S. East Coast to the West Coast. The truck starts exhibiting low power somewhere in the middle of Utah. Typically, the driver has two choices: continue on, hoping that the truck makes it to the final destination (which will most likely result in a breakdown situation), or call for help. If the latter, the call may be made to any or all of the following: a Freightliner dealer, an engine distributor, a fleet maintenance breakdown department, or the Freightliner Customer Assistance Call Center. In most instances, the driver will be told to go to the nearest Freightliner dealer. But there are only four in Utah, and this truck is 150 miles from the closest one. If the driver attempts to make that trip and breaks down, he incurs a towing bill that is not covered by Freightliner. The driver is left with many questions and issues: Even if the truck ends up being towed, will the dealer have the parts and the mechanics necessary to make the repair? Even if they have the parts on hand and the mechanics on-site, how long will it take to fit the truck into the service schedule? Will the load still get delivered on time, or should the trucking company send another tractor to pick up the trailer? Could Freightliner, the driver, and the fleet maintenance manager engage in a dialogue based on the fault codes generated and the nature and urgency of the load being carried to co-create an appropriate course of action? What is the nature of transparency and access to information that will be required by the different constituencies in the service-repair and call center network that will be selectively activated? (Freightliner could provide the service center with proactive repair information and truck diagnostics prior to the truck showing up at the dealer facility.)

The building of platforms by Freightliner, however, depends on the opportunity to leverage the capabilities of other enterprise platforms in the ecosystem of services (recall the GELI principles of capability leverage from Chapter 4). Consider that customers of Freightliner such as third-party logistics (3PL) and trucking companies (e.g., Ryder) in turn provide logistics services to their business customers (e.g., HP). From Ryder's perspective, companies typically outsource the logistics function to 3PL companies because they prefer not to invest in truck fleets, maintenance, and the IT infrastructure that is required to support fleet logistics operations.[134] They want to invest instead in their core products and business processes. Moreover, as contract supply and logistics chains have become increasingly sophisticated over the years, companies such as HP can get a better return on their logistics costs by outsourcing to 3PL companies such as Ryder. Most companies like HP have predetermined requirements that they want the 3PL partner to fulfill. There isn't much co-creative engagement in the classic relationship between Ryder and HP. Both companies believe they know best about how their business should be run, with typical interactions being predominantly bilateral exchanges and, at best, conventional collaboration entailing sharing resources and working together in common teams. In other words, this collaborative interaction between parties has traditionally been largely passive, with considerable potential to generate mutual value through co-creation.

Ryder is one of Freightliner's primary customers and relies on it heavily for the purchase of trucks for its fleet. Ryder's fleet size is over 150,000, and its annual consumption of diesel is over 400 million gallons. Thus, Freightliner is an important enabler for Ryder's operational success: trucks are a critical element in its supply chain, since they make the final delivery of shipments. Typically, fleet managers and owner-operators of Ryder trucks deal with the sales department or the dealers at Freightliner. These interactions are focused on ensuring that trucks are purchased at the desired prices and specs. The current state of interactions is typically geared toward making the sale efficient for both parties involved. Freightliner's design teams have little visibility into the interaction space across the downstream customer chain.

Managers of Ryder's Fleet Management Services already work closely with Freightliner's design team so the trucks can have the desired capabilities Ryder seeks. To be able to meet the complex and diverse requirements of Ryder's customers, Ryder's Fleet Management Services have to be on top of maintaining and servicing its trucks. Maintaining such a behemoth fleet economically and with limited resources requires innovation. For that reason, Ryder collaborates with Freightliner in product development. One of their collaborative initiatives was the "RydeGreen" project. These trucks were specially designed for long-haul fuel efficiency, equipped with direct drive transmission, fuel-efficient drive tiers, and a battery-powered sleeper system to eliminate unnecessary and wasteful idling, as well as meet the EPA's new fuel efficiency standards. While these are indeed useful product feature innovations, Freightliner still lacks insight into the engagement experiences of Ryder's customers, and even when information does flow upstream, it often gets lost in translation and filtered through engineering design-think.

For effective co-creation between Freightliner and Ryder, consider an exploratory strategic move by Freightliner to make its product development process more inclusive with co-creative inputs from Ryder and its downstream customer chain via a co-creation platform. This platform has to facilitate corrective feedback from the customer chain. A shared infrastructure for dialogue is critical for the potential benefits of co-creation to be realized. This dialogue can even be extended to Freightliner's supply chain, such as the engine manufacturers. One of the most important components of a truck is its engine, and Freightliner has partnerships with many suppliers like Detroit Diesel. Engine configurations vary based on the commodity to be hauled, geographic area of uses, and emission standards.

Freightliner and engine manufacturers collaborate by sharing technology, making joint investments in research, and sharing information. This association primarily focuses on developing engines that comply with the emission standards enforced by EPA, the specs desired by Freightliner, and the outcome of the engine research by the engine manufacturer. This association can be made more co-creative by elevating the interaction to the next level—that is, by facilitating the engine manufacturer's ability to understand the truck drivers' needs. Since the process is R&D-intensive, deviations can be very expensive. Yet, the engine designers have to keep in mind not only their immediate customer, such as Freightliner, but also the customers further down the value chain, such as Ryder. Features like idle time performance, fleet maintenance, carbon footprint, and so on can be incorporated effectively in the design through co-creative interactions along the entire activity system.

Nodal companies like Freightliner and Ryder must take leadership roles in co-creating the strategic architecture of engagement platforms across the activity system that is built on interaction linkages. Parties that are working together in this type of activity system have many opportunities for co-creation. To enable full co-creative engagement, there must be a willingness to forgo traditional "contractual" roles. For example, Freightliner could have a role in defining the performance goals of HP. Each player plays the role of a customer as well as a "company," depending on what or whom they interact with in the activity system. Each of these entities perceives the same interaction very differently, depending on whether it is a service *receiver* or a service *provider*. It is like looking at the same goal from different vantage points.

A strategic architecture of co-creation can thus bring all parties together on the same portfolio of platforms to facilitate mutual goal alignment, co-creative interactions, and both enterprise-specific and joint outcomes. The challenges faced by each managerial function in the respective enterprises across the activity system can be very diverse and difficult to understand at an industry or corporate level. The success of co-creation across the organizations in the value chain system relies heavily on enabling co-creative interactions between the frontline managers—the individuals representing their respective companies—in addition to co-creative management capabilities at higher levels inside each organization. Co-creation between frontline managers facilitates goal alignment between the collaborating partners at the operational level and eventually at a strategic level. It provides an opportunity to better understand the capabilities that each player brings to the table. This might not be achieved in a traditional collaborative setting where the customer makes requests for certain products or services and the provider tries to fulfill them. This sort of relationship is typically not used as a springboard to explore all the strengths and resources that all the players can bring to the table. Thus, opportunities for innovation co-creation among the companies are available both at strategic and frontline managerial levels in building co-creative management systems.

SOCIAL ARCHITECTURES AND ENTERPRISE ECOSYSTEM GOVERNANCE

The environment of the individual manager is a subset of a broader culture of co-creation that embraces an entire ecosystem, starting with the individual enterprise. The social architecture in the co-creative enterprise must recognize that heterogeneous individuals are at the heart of internal engagement processes. Thus, the starting point must be respect for individuals and their uniqueness. Meritocracy, not hierarchy, must rule. The focus must be on discovering and mobilizing expertise, regardless of descriptions or titles. Knowledge must be organized around communities of practice, not administrative or organizational silos. The social architecture must enable painless and continual hooking and unhooking of talent based on tasks and skills. Rigid structures cannot impede access to expertise from various organizational homes. Contributions must be recognized across organizational boundaries—both vertical and horizontal.

Employees at every level must be trained in the art of collaboration and in dynamic negotiation for value creation. An organizational capacity to learn, nurture, share, and deploy knowledge across traditional boundaries (personal and institutional) is an important skill, and intercultural and interpersonal competence among managers is a critical dimension of this skill. Managers must learn to manage the migration paths of both customers and technologies. Product migration must keep pace with customer migration, if not anticipate it. The managerial mindset is probably the most potent tool when it comes to making the transformation to the new co-creation-based view. The mindset required is one that embraces change and accepts that "shifting roles of the moment" are critical. Understanding the organizational demands—demands on individuals, the firm, and the extended network—is quite critical to managing the mindset. This process is not just about an intellectual understanding of the nature and dimensions of the mindset. It needs a deep understanding and commitment to recognize the emotional and behavioral traumas associated with changing a vast majority of individuals and teams who have worked with a different set of assumptions. It is changing the way people are socialized. The challenge is to get managers out of their "comfort zone" and into an "opportunity zone." The skills for managing the new co-creation space are twofold. The first is substantive knowledge—knowledge of both the stakeholder and the technologies underlying the business, which is informed as much by personal knowledge as by "proxy analysis" via staff groups. The second is the sheer ability to get things done, including interpersonal and intercultural competence, team skills, and a capacity for ongoing learning. Investment in personal excellence is critical for individuals with ambition to lead in the new competitive space of value co-creation.

As business relationships and models undergo dramatic and rapid change, individuals yearn for stability. The organizational pivots, which provide stability, are values and beliefs. While many firms have tried to articulate a system of values and beliefs, few have been successful in living by them consistently. For example, a professed belief in the value of diversity is hollow if individuals within the system frequently demonstrate bias, whether overt or subtle, against people on the basis of age, gender, race, ethnicity, or even intellectual heritage. (Intellectual heritage may surprise you. But suppose, for example, the dominant intellectual heritage of a bulk chemical firm is chemical engineering. How well does such a system tolerate geneticists?)

Needless to say, no single individual or group can accomplish all the tasks required in creating value. But team management is a complex challenge. Accountability must be clearly established even as team managers are free to change the mix of team members and tasks at short notice.

Our performance evaluation and reward systems must reflect this emerging competitive reality. Managers will be forced to gravitate to a project/management-oriented approach rather than depend on more traditional quarterly and yearly reviews for assessing performance.

Increasingly, rapid reaction time and all the component skills—such as the ability to amplify weak signals, interpret their consequences, and reconfigure resources faster than competitors—will be a critical source of advantage. It's not just running faster but thinking smarter that makes the difference. Becoming a co-creative enterprise puts a premium on the governance process for co-creation of value. A wide variety of collaborative modes are needed in the new co-creation sphere, including arm's-length contractual relationships, information-sharing arrangements with suppliers, and internal collaboration partnerships for deploying resources against new opportunities. This implies that managers operating at multiple levels in the organization must learn how and when to collaborate and how and when to compete. It's not easy to learn to balance self-interest and common interest, individual recognition and shared success, the need for a separate identity and the need for teamwork. It requires a readiness to move beyond the comforting structural clarity of an organization chart to deal with difficult and often ambiguous relationships on a constant basis. Unless the enterprise has a clear and shared agenda, continuous and opportunistic collaboration cannot work. Many enterprises are intent on standardizing their global business processes. Their leaders often say, "Once we standardize our processes, we will have visibility into what everyone inside the business is doing." That may be true. But it reflects an internally focused, efficiency-based point of view. Given the state of constant flux in the competitive environment, standardizing business processes appears counterproductive. We need the ability to continuously monitor our processes and modify them as needed. In some cases, standardization is desirable—but it's not a worthwhile goal in itself, and it's certainly not the total solution for any company. Moreover, in a co-creative enterprise, operating only through a hierarchical chain of command is no longer acceptable. Rather, it is about approaching zero latency—the ability to continuously monitor the environment and respond rapidly—which suggests a highly decentralized management approach. Line managers must have the tools to understand what is happening around them and make relevant, appropriate decisions based on what they know.

In the co-creation view, flexibility, teamwork, ongoing problem solving, constant searching for process improvements, and collaboration with suppliers are the norm. Yet, the greatest strength of the old fixed-process system—accountability for performance—is still necessary. Sacrificing accountability cannot be the price for flexibility, collaboration, and teamwork. It is easier to rely on clearly defined organizational charts, where the focus is on accountability and ease of performance measurement. But the intangible costs of overlooking the unforeseen and the unplanned can be enormous. As business processes get embedded in the information systems of the enterprise, they can be harder to change. Formal structures and business processes are necessary but are not sufficient tools for dealing with a world of change. In fact, they can become obstacles to the necessary flexibility. The co-creation view demands *protocols and disciplines* as well as structures and processes when organizing activities. It is like building a sandbox for managers. The managers are not restricted in how they can use the sandbox. They can do anything they want in it—as long as they stay in the sandbox and play nicely with the other managers. Thus, protocols and disciplines provide a framework for innovation and creativity. Without a clearly defined and consistently practiced system of values, no large system can survive. Values provide the emotional anchor that lets individuals cope with change. When these values are violated, the trust of consumers, managers, and investors can be quickly destroyed, as major crises over the years, such as Enron and the Catholic Church scandals, have reminded us. Every manager can legitimately interpret weak signals differently. A manager living in California's Silicon Valley has different views of market and customer evolution from one living in Hamburg, Germany. A technical specialist is likely to view change through a different lens than a marketing expert or a financial manager. While such differences are important and must be taken into account, a single framework for market evolution must be shared among all members of a firm. In a decentralized, global organization, priorities cannot be dictated from the top—hence the need for forums to debate, discuss, and establish priorities. Communities of practice from around the entire enterprise and other ad hoc combinations of knowledge, expertise, and perspective can ensure that priorities are set on the basis of dialogue. The criteria for inclusion in those groups are merit and accomplishment, not hierarchical position. In establishing protocols and disciplines, senior managers must, in consultation with operating managers, establish a few "nonnegotiables." That is their job—and a crucial part of the value they add. Without clearly established rules of engagement, empowerment is not possible.

Co-creative ecosystem governance thus entails a judicious mixture of formal structures, flexible business processes, and management protocols and disciplines. Rather than legal boundaries, strategic and operational boundaries define the co-creative enterprise. The nodal firm with its extended network is an operational and strategic notion, subject to constant reevaluation and redefinition. A nodal firm may reject a supplier, and a supplier may opt out of a nodal network. These relationships are flexible, and the boundaries of the network are also flexible and evolving. This may have a significant impact on the way we think about reporting results. Accounting rules, for example, are based on what the company "owns" legally. Yet, in co-creation, an enterprise ecosystem may effectively be using more resources than it owns. Rules governing an enterprise's access to network resources that a company only partly owns or does not own at all must be put in place. The economic efficiency of the entire ecosystem, rather than the efficiency of particular enterprises, must be accounted for. The critical importance of management protocols and disciplines in building co-creative ecosystems of capabilities cannot be underestimated.

ORGANIZATIONAL DESIGN

Taken from the Greek word *organon*, meaning "organ" or "instrument," organization is about individuals creating structures to support agency and a purposeful collaborative pursuit of collective goals.[135] Organizations provide purposefully designed engagement structures to human interaction. They are groups of individuals bound by some common purpose to achieve collective goals. In reality, organizational assemblages are combinations of rational, natural, and open systems.[136] As rational systems, organizations are assemblages oriented to the pursuit of relatively specific goals, exhibiting relatively highly formalized social structures.

As natural systems, organizations are assemblages whose people pursue multiple interests, both disparate and common, but who recognize its perpetual value. The relationships that develop among the participants are very influential in guiding the ongoing behaviors of the participants. As open systems, organizations are assemblages of interdependent flows, activities, and interactions linking shifting coalitions of participants embedded in wider environments of matter, energy, and information flows. Organizational *design*, then, is about engagement design of assemblages with purposive intent in consequence of the value creation opportunities—given the existing set of institutional constraints on the one hand and attempts to leverage resources as the organization accomplishes value creation goals on the other.

Efficiency and Innovation

Over the last century, cost reduction and efficiency have been central themes in strategy. From the Colt revolver to the Model T assembly line at Ford, standardization of components, vertical integration, and process efficiencies were at the heart of effective management. Later, the pressure to create differentiated products forced managers to devise new ways to manage costs: process reengineering, outsourcing, modularity, use of common platforms, and embedded software. The desire for economies of scale drove expansion into national, regional and global markets. All these strategic approaches were based on the *cost* imperative—one of the fundamental assumptions built into the traditional view of value.

Under pressure for cost reduction, most managers may focus on efficiency and regard innovation as an attractive distraction. However, firms do innovate continuously, and they disrupt markets by exploiting discontinuities. In reality, efficiency and innovation are not opposed but are interconnected. For example, consider efficiency as exemplified in today's hyperefficient global supply chain system. Implicit in building and operating a global supply chain are a host of technical and organizational innovations. The sheer logistics of component movement among multiple countries require innovations in information sharing, component tracking, transaction management, pricing transfers, quality assurance, and global workforce management. Underlying all this effort are the innovative IT networks, databases, and applications that support the system. Thus, efficiency at a twenty-first-century level is impossible without innovation.

Conversely, successful innovations must have efficiency embedded in them. Suppose Apple wants to release a new product. The innovation will not be successful unless Apple applies efficiency criteria, whether in scaling production, reducing costs, or operating multiple manufacturing facilities around the world. The success of the innovation depends on the operational efficiency with which it is executed.

Efficiency and innovation go together in the co-creation view, where we increase the capacity for experimentation and generating insights, reduce risk (in both experimentation and in exploiting a good opportunity), reduce investment (by leveraging resources of the entire enterprise and its enhanced competence base), and reduce time (whether it is for experimentation or for scaling up). Organizations as assemblage systems must therefore be designed for *both* efficiency and innovation.[137]

Institutional Frames and Organizational Forms
As organizational assemblages coevolve with their offerings (which are themselves components of assemblage systems) and with other organizations, they alter institutions over time. Institutions are "humanly devised constraints that shape human interaction" and emergent economic, social, and political orders.[138] They entail formal constraints such as "rules of the game" that human beings devise and informal constraints such as unwritten codes of conduct, conventions, customs, traditions, and behavioral norms. Institutions are a creation of human beings. They evolve and are altered by human beings, and they begin with the individual. Simultaneously, existing and evolving institutional frames impose binding constraints on individual agency.

Moreover, it is the interaction among institutional frames and enterprise strategy that shapes the direction of change in the reality of joint value creation. New organizational forms emerge from multiplicities of potential forms in the virtual, from millions of potential assemblages, which through a process of intensification by enterprising individuals are embodied as social structures to support purposeful collaborative pursuits (e.g., the evolution of the Apple enterprise from its garage days). The intensive process of *organizing* is the entrepreneurial process that continues as the actualized organization evolves as it mobilizes and harnesses resources, from materials and energy to information and personnel. The coevolution of organizations with their environments "revirtualize" new potentialities and "reactualize" new forms in a cyclical process of "creative destruction" over a period of time.[139]

The process of creative destruction is not only about new forms of competition evolving among organizations and the emergence of new business models of value creation. It also includes the evolution of different types of organizational forms (e.g., the rise of flatter, networked organizations and new blends of markets, networks, and hierarchies) that are made possible by new engagement platforms of global resource leverage and their connection with value creation opportunities.

Organizational Environments

Organizations are "sense-making" assemblage systems that entail engagement in continuous cycles of agential enactment and strategy formation.[140] What we call "organizations" are the consequences of human actions. And if the organization is an emergent phenomenon, so is the environment that is created within it, since it is a result of the actions of organizational agents.[141] Organizational performance reflects the interaction of organizational outcomes and an environmental response that is much less under the actors' control.[142] Further, as "autopoietic" systems, organizational systems are closed with respect to their own organization and structure but nevertheless maintain intense interactions with their environments.[143] People's relationships form routines, involving roles, procedures, and the use of resources that constitute stable forms of integratable interactions. The emergent routines and mechanisms of these interactions constitute the organization's structure. Just like any autopoietic entity, organizations as social phenomena are characterized by both identity (an organization) and structure. The various institutional systems that make up a social system become closed domains of communication, autonomous and independent, while maintaining forms of interdependence (structural and loose couplings) with organizational environments. Such organizational "operational closure" also provides the conceptual and practical foundation for studying systemic "feedback loops."[144]

Embodiment of Value in Human Experiences
What distinguishes a co-creative organization from order is that the former involves an active intensification from the virtual in the process of its actualization. Hence, feedback loops are not only about learning and knowledge but are more fundamentally about desire-power relationships. Organization entails the embodiment of multiple of parts of assemblages into a larger, more coherent desire-power complex.[145] Embodiment happens objectively to bodies when they come under a constitutive relationship, but it is also the subjective experience of *becoming* organized or embodied. Corporeal and corporate bodies are similar in that they have extension (body) and thought (mind), and they can affect and be affected by other bodies.[146] Institutions translate thought to action and desire to gratification. Co-creative organization is an immanent, productive process that can turn passive reaction into creative reaction, whereby encounters between bodies are transformed into a co-creative process of value creation. Co-creation implies an efficient force that constitutes the organization itself as a corporate body with capabilities of intensifying powers of action, passion, and intellect, or an autopoietic system continuously reinventing the terms of its own actualization.

Organization, in the co-creation view, entails a complex process of embodiment involving (joyful or sad) passions. These passions are feelings-effects that are experienced throughout the corporate body and mind (culture). The power of an organization is characterized by its capacity to affect and to be affected, to act and to be acted upon—in short, its power of existence—as is also true for all other agents. This power is a virtual that gets intensified and charges the actual, fulfilled by active and passive affects. The net balance of these affects determines whether an organization is active or passive. An organization enhances its power to exist from within by engaging other bodies and organizations that result in joyful passive effects and by forming shared ideas that transform those passions into positive action.[147] Co-creative organization entails the purposive design of joyful engagements between bodies and the transmutation of that joy from passive to active affects through the formation of relations, decisions, ideas, and offerings.

Positivity

Positive Organizational Scholarship (POS) "seeks to understand positive states—such as resilience or meaningfulness—as well as the dynamics and outcomes associated with those states—such as gratitude and positive connections." POS focuses on positive dynamics that entail "excellence, thriving, flourishing, abundance, resilience, or virtuousness," representing an "expanded perspective that includes instrumental concerns but puts an increased emphasis on ideas of 'goodness' and positive human potential."[148] Human beings pursue positively deviant virtues despite institutional pressures and constraints that might mitigate such behavior. Positive organizational behavior is, hence, sometimes evidenced by a relative absence of mistakes and crises rather than by extraordinary or positively deviant behavior. However, emergence of more enduring positive organizational states of expanded value creation entails the transformational becoming and embodiment of positive affections.

The co-creation view provides a theoretical framework for how positive value outcomes emerge from virtual co-creative capacities, are enacted through co-creating actions, and are actualized in positive value outcomes. Co-creative engagement design, co-creation experience configuration, and co-creative building of capabilities provide the structural means by which latent capacity can be unleashed, human possibilities enabled, and positive value outcomes achieved through the portfolio of co-creation platforms in the ecosystem in which enterprises operate and are enveloped.

In the next chapter, we discuss how leaders in any enterprise, whether in the private, public, or social sector, can go about engaging stakeholders to achieve the transformational change to build a more co-creative enterprise.

7

CO-CREATING
TRANSFORMATIONAL CHANGE

Any enterprise seeking to migrate to co-creation with its customers, partners, and other external stakeholders should begin by examining the nature of the relationship between management and all the co-creators during the transformational change. Establishing co-creation as a way of organizational life requires challenging and mutating the organization's DNA toward co-creation thinking, by innovating and designing engagement platforms that allow everyone to create the change together. Following the principles of co-creative engagement design, the co-creativity of enterprises is a function of purposefully designed engagements from within an organization that harness the personal and collective intelligence of individuals. After decades of experience with organizational change and jump-starting innovation, it has become abundantly clear to change agents that successful transformational change is best achieved through engagement with those it affects.[149] The best way to build co-creative enterprises is to co-create the transformational change.

Co-creating transformational change entails a fundamental change in mindset toward co-creation thinking that begins at a personal level.[150] A good starting point is to think about all the enterprises you have interacted with where your personal experiences were frustrating, but the enterprise insisted it was creating value for you. Think about the following:

1. How could more valuable experiences have been created for you? Are there things about the offerings and their delivery that could have been changed? Would the respective organizations have been better off if they had connected with you about your experiences and made appropriate changes to their activities and processes to generate outcomes of greater value to you? How?

2. What if you were offered an engagement platform where you could connect with the enterprise through better dialogue—before, during, and after your engagements—in order to take more control of your experiences and outcomes? What if the products-services themselves became a purposefully designed platform of engagements that enabled you to do this?

3. What if you could offer your own ideas for changes? What if the actions taken to implement them were more transparent to you? What if you could have more of a say in the actions and decisions taken that you care about, and perhaps even participate in the enterprise's redesign of activities, processes, and offerings?

Engaging individuals by tapping their personal experiences is one of the best ways for an organization to start a conversation about the design of experience-based engagement platforms, which are central to co-creation thinking. Ideas about how to connect value creation opportunities with resources must be harnessed in organizations through involvement of the many.

In this chapter, we first discuss organizations that have successfully begun the journey to implementing co-creation thinking. We first look at Mahindra, whose leaders facilitated co-creation thinking from the inside out, while also bringing in ideas from the surrounding ecosystem. Next, we discuss Predica, which is owned by Crédit Agricole; its story serves as an example of how co-creation is an organizational "silo breaker" in achieving alignment across management functions. We then discuss the role of senior management in leading enterprise-wide transformation to co-creation by first examining the Hospital Moinhos de Vento (HMV) enterprise ecosystem, an instance of strategic innovation transformation from the inside out. Then we look at Hindustan Computers Limited

(HCL), which achieved organizational transformation by engaging its employees and increasing their willingness to participate in creating change. Subsequently, our discussion of Intuit demonstrates how co-creation with stakeholders can be proactively stimulated from inside the organization and tried out experimentally at first and then introduced more widely over time. The HMV, HCL, and Intuit examples also suggest a process of enterprise transformation in evolving the technical architectures of co-creation.

Our next two examples come from the public sector, one at a local city level (Seoul, South Korea) and one at a more national level (Brazil), which together suggest how co-creation thinking can contribute to more democratic changes in governments. Finally, we conclude our discussion with the example of Infosys, which demonstrates how IT enterprises are increasingly taking architectural innovation one step further in a process of "innovation co-creation" that facilitates the rapid evolution of co-creative enterprise architectures with minimal investments, including collaborative innovations in private, public, and social sector partnerships.

BUILDING A CULTURE OF CO-CREATION THINKING

Let us start our discussion with Mahindra & Mahindra Ltd, one of India's largest vehicle manufacturers and a subsidiary of the Mahindra Group, an industrial conglomerate that has its headquarters in Mumbai and operations throughout both the Indian subcontinent and the rest of the world. Until one afternoon in August 2010, Naveen Chopra, then senior general manager and head of Plant Quality for the Automotive Division, had never heard of co-creation. Little did he know that the concept was about to transform his outlook and career—and the culture of his organization—over the ensuing two years. That afternoon, Chopra attended a seminar that was just one module in a successful ongoing Global Program for Management Development (GPMD) involving Mahindra's senior executives. The topic was the co-creation paradigm.

Chopra was instantly taken with the idea. "It's such a simple, commonsense concept once grasped, but it provides a structure and principles that we don't always use in life," he said. "I realized that it could change the way we think and deal with each other, leading to improved performance." Initially, Chopra saw some strong parallels with the work he was already doing in the company's quality function. Co-creation emphasized the need for enhanced communication, coordination, and collaboration among stakeholders, and he was constantly striving to improve precisely these practices across the five operating sites of Mahindra's Automotive Division. At the time, he thought, "I can use co-creation in the quality function. Let's apply the principles and see what happens."

Chopra set to work immediately. In September 2010, he drafted a short presentation about what he had learned, sharing it initially with his immediate colleagues and then spreading the word to his wider quality team across the five plants. Chopra's initiative was fully supported by Allen Sequeira, then executive vice president of Group HR & Leadership Development, laying the groundwork for further progress. Very often, existing institutional structures impede the execution of co-creation initiatives. General managers have to rise to the challenge because so many things need to change. Chopra was lucky to have support, but he was also captivated and persistent.

As head of Plant Quality, he was already collaborating with multiple functions of the business, such as manufacturing, marketing, and customer service, in a quest to enhance and enrich the company's quality culture. With the co-creation mantra of "win more–win more" at the forefront of his mind, Chopra started to tackle the practicalities of implementing co-creation among the stakeholders, together with a core team representing the different functions.[151] The first step was to consider who the stakeholders actually were, from suppliers and dealers, to of course, employees inside Mahindra. The second was to select one group of stakeholders to get started. He decided to begin with employees. The third was to consider what needed to change to help them become more effective. "We looked specifically at building employees' capability by building up their knowledge and skills," said Chopra. "Of course, the staff already had access to some training through our HR department, but there was room for us to do more to enhance their potential." Using co-creative principles and methods, he decided to enable a small group of engineers, each with up to 25 years of specialist automotive experience, to pass on their knowledge and expertise to dozens of younger colleagues. Again, Chopra cycled back to the second step: identifying specific stakeholding individuals from the pool of engineers who could benefit from this type of knowledge sharing. With this accomplished, he was ready to establish an engagement platform—in this case, monthly workshops—where the whole group could meet to share their knowledge and experiences. These were led by a voluntary cadre of experienced engineers who took on the role of trainers. The meetings were more than just about talking shop. To be effective, they required an honest approach from all participants, based on mutual respect, openness, and willingness to experiment.

Typically, a workshop would focus on a specific theme, with one or two seasoned engineers in, say, fuel supply systems passing on their expertise to their junior colleagues. Between them, the groups proceeded to document their learning and create an internal training module on the subject, which could be run at any time and updated as necessary. The co-creation process is essentially that simple to get started, although it requires constantly engaging stakeholders in ways that enrich their co-creation experiences. In just two to three months, this process had enabled specialized knowledge sharing and training to be rolled out at high speed and at no cost to the company.

This early success soon caught the attention of senior management levels in Mahindra, particularly Pawan Goenka, president of the company's Auto & Farm Sector and a member of its senior leadership team. As Chopra notes, "His support boosted morale and encouraged us to work with more zeal." In the 18 months since, Mahindra has created around 50 similar modules, with 400 to 500 employees benefiting. Says Chopra, "Using traditional classroom training methods, this would have taken us ten years."

Nachiket Kodkani, head of Manufacturing and a participant in the GPMD 2011 executive education program, joined the co-creation journey. Co-creation initiatives have less chance of scaling up and succeeding without other co-creation champions. Together with Naveen, Nachiket engaged his management team and achieved great success in manufacturing operations. He began with noncore areas such as engagement of contract labor (as a way to experiment) and then tackled core areas in the production process, including redesigning the manufacturing shop floors through the lens of engagement platforms and harnessing the creative capacity of individuals as never before. As Kodkani notes:

I realized co-creation has a different kind of power that is latent in it. It actually gets into a "win-win" situation and achieves right customer-centricity at the end of it. We have now been able to move toward a better, focused approach. In the past, we made assumptions in our thinking about what creates value. If you consider co-creation, it is really a joint approach. It is about being there, right on spot, together with stakeholders. In this age of resource shortages, the right way to tackle problems, issues, and challenges is through co-creation. The results have been exceptionally good. We have solved problems faster, generated new ways of doing things which have also been adopted faster, and overall, become not only much more efficient and effective at the same time, but have a new team spirit in the organization.

Chopra then looked to replicate the process with other stakeholder groups in Mahindra's quality function—namely, suppliers and dealers. In the case of suppliers, Chopra and his team considered how supplier meetings could be leveraged to improve mutual understanding, cooperation, and collaboration. If supplier capability could be improved, it was reasonable to conclude that quality would improve, too, with both parties "winning more." Instead of taking the traditional approach of finding fault with the suppliers and urging them to take corrective action, such as training, efforts were made to consider how they experienced interaction with Mahindra. Suppliers were encouraged to share their experiences. There was initially some suspicion, which was natural because Mahindra was their customer, but by the end of 2010, some 80 suppliers were on board, with this effort producing the desired results.

In the case of dealers, as with the suppliers, traditional meetings were reformed into a more effective engagement platform, with emphasis placed on seeing issues from the dealers' perspective and supporting them. Again, both Mahindra and the dealers reaped the benefits, from addressing vehicle defects to shaping new product features, including more productive relationships and faster cycle times. Some dealers duly initiated co-creation in their own businesses. Stakeholder experiences like this can be very powerful. Suddenly, people were all seeing cultural change taking place right in front of their eyes—quite a magical change with inclusive relationships and real human involvement. People felt like they were part of something and became much more motivated.

By early 2011, word of Chopra's success with co-creation was spreading within Mahindra, with other executives—including many who had taken part in GPMD—beginning to see its potential to transform their own functions. Momentum continued to build during the year. In April, the company held a co-creation workshop for 350 executives. In August, after the next annual GPMD, six more executives acted on the idea. Finally, in November, there was a huge workshop involving over 1,000 Mahindra employees, dealers, suppliers, and other stakeholders, such as banks. As a step toward sustainability, Mahindra's co-creation journey was shared with wider business and social stakeholders, including banks and educational institutions, "which in turn got a lot of benefits by implementing co-creation principles at their end," says Chopra. For example, the Nashik branch of India's leading nationalized bank, State Bank of India, implemented the concept and "reaped huge benefits in increasing home loan distribution." Even local colleges became involved, benefiting from collaboration with Mahindra, with the company "winning more" by fulfilling some of its wider social responsibilities and goals. This viral spiral of expansive value creation in the enterprise ecosystem is a unique characteristic of co-creation as people grasp its inherent potential.

The next big question for Mahindra was whether the approach would continue to evolve to become embedded throughout the enterprise. It has been a remarkable "bottom-up" approach, starting with the crucial building of a quality culture at plant and process level, which has been spreading into the company's ecosystem. Now there is the potential to rejuvenate many key areas, such as strategy, performance management, and customer-facing functions. But top-down commitment is needed, too, because co-creation brings many changes and further implications. The signs so far are encouraging. Says Anand Mahindra, chairman and managing director of Mahindra & Mahindra, "The co-creation mantra is now embodied in the three basic tenets of the Mahindra Group—accepting no limits, thinking alternatively, and driving positive change in everything we do." Mahindra's vice president of Operations, Aher, notes, "Co-creation has become a unique practice in Mahindra. We are now able to solve any issue with a great spirit. We are making efforts to take it through all the sectors, and even to all our stakeholders, where we can co-create even their organization. It is a great concept where we can work together and create something new where both parties are immensely benefited."

The next steps at Mahindra are to harness the power of technology and social media to move the crucial engagement platforms beyond face-to-face workshops, with wider geographical and enterprise ecosystem impact, given a widely diversified conglomerate that is Mahindra & Mahindra. This will enable the enterprise ecosystem to scale co-creation and share its best practices and make its principles, methods, and tools more easily accessible throughout its many functions and divisions, and harness "internal synergies across businesses" (the "conglomerate premium"). The challenge is to achieve a balance between scaling co-creation and enhancing the management systems of the conglomerate enterprise. As with any real transformation, it takes time. The hope is to create new champions. In the meantime, Mahindra's first co-creation champion, Naveen Chopra, is already expanding his part. Having taken on a new role in 2012 as senior general manager, head of Vehicle Engineering, he is enthusiastically encouraging his new colleagues in Mahindra's Automotive Division to adopt the principles of co-creation in their specialization of vehicle design. Chopra says, "This is a culture I want to spread. I recognize it is a huge challenge. But we have a lot of ground to cover over the next few years. What I would really like to see is Mahindra become known as a co-creative enterprise."

BREAKING ORGANIZATIONAL "SILOS" THROUGH
CO-OWNERSHIP AND ORGANIC ALIGNMENT
One of the biggest hurdles in established organizations is enabling all internal stakeholders and immediate external stakeholders to participate more easily and more substantially by allowing a two-way flow of engagement, rather than streamlining sequential processes and straitjacketing outcomes. The traditional representation of processes only tells half the story, and it is told from the vantage point of the enterprise's process. From Kaizen to Lean and Six Sigma quality methods, all prescribe how process owners should design their processes based on specifications set by their internal or external stakeholders. Once these specifications are gathered, the process owner designs and executes the process against them. This presupposes that the enterprise's process creates something of value that the stakeholder pas-

sively "receives" in the form of predictable and repeated delivery of a result that is assumed to be satisfactory. This is also one of the major reasons why "silos" exist in enterprises. Co-creation thinking opens the door to a new approach to operations where the role of enterprises is no longer to design processes in the traditional sense but to set up engagement platforms where the enterprise and the stakeholder converge to co-create humanized value.

Consider the case of Crédit Agricole, Europe's second-largest banking network, with over 7,000 branches.[152] Organized as a federation of 39 regional banks in France, Crédit Agricole is at its core a retail bank that also sells asset management, investment banking, and insurance products. Predica, one of its divisions, designs life insurance products and manages sales through the Crédit Agricole retail banking network. In 2007, Isabelle Steinmann, head of Product Development at Predica in charge of a team of about seven product managers, was tasked by then-president Jean-Yves Hocher with developing and launching a new product, Cap Découverte. It was to be a unit-linked life insurance product, which is a life insurance policy whose yield is indexed on a series of mutual funds rather than in euro-denominated bonds. The product was for younger customers and was meant to act as the first step in teaching them how to save money for the future. Steinmann wasn't sure how to overcome the challenge of getting consumers to understand its relatively complex functioning. Predica did not sell its products directly but supplied them to the regional banks, which in turn trained their branch advisors to sell them to customers. Although Predica "trained the trainers," the regional banks ultimately decided on the product launch strategy. And branch advisors were swamped with products promoted by the various divisions, from simple checking or savings accounts to credit cards, loans, or other investment products.

Having been exposed to co-creation thinking, Steinmann began to see the value of using it to align stakeholders all along the new product development and launch process. Crédit Agricole employs about 40,000 bank advisors in the branches, and about 60 percent of them were the junior advisors Steinmann wanted to focus on, as they tended to be the face of the bank for young people starting their financial life. Each of the 39 regional banks also had an insurance specialist. Since each bank is itself a large organization, the insurance specialists acted as product managers within the regional banks, orchestrating all insurance training and support for the retail branch advisors and playing a particularly important role at launch time. Branch managers also had a critical role because they set the performance goals for the branch advisors. If managers were not on board with a new product like Cap Découverte, they could set goals that would lower the product in the advisors' list of priorities, and its golden goose would be cooked. An even more important protagonist was the regional bank top management, who had the power to accept or turn down the new product. Each bank was an independent entity, and collectively the 39 regional banks owned the product divisions, including Predica, so the bargaining power was in their hands.

There were five other "co-creators" within Predica, counting Isabelle herself. Predica salespeople handled the day-to-day contacts between the regional banks and Crédit Agricole, calling on the retail branch advisors to foster interest in their products. They could convey different levels of enthusiasm for a new product, greatly influencing its success. They also developed all the sales support material used by retail branch advisors. The Predica Communications Department controlled the resources dedicated to customer-facing communications and advertising, so they could boost or slow down new products that competed for their promotion dollars. Two other stakeholders were even farther removed than Steinmann from the end-customer. The Actuarial, Financial, and Compliance Department was where the financial and legal integrity of new products got tested, ensuring that Predica would make money with the proposed design and guaranteeing that all regulatory requirements were met. Finally, Predica's top management, Jean-Yves Hocher and his team, played a key role in vetting new product design, introducing new offerings to the regional bank top managers and valuing them in the context of the firm's overall strategy. As one would expect, they had life-or-death power over the design of a product like Cap Découverte.

What was missing was a joint engagement platform, where all parties could see the design of the whole new-product complex and participate in building it together. Steinmann pointed out that her interactions with market experts and external sources often suggested product features—for example, little or no loading fees—that differed greatly from the demands from actuarial people, for whom generating fees was an integral part of the financial model. While there was an inherent conflict between customer desires for affordable products and company requirements for profits, Steinmann imagined that if both parties could look at a live model of the product, it could result in a better-integrated, co-created design. This later became the simple product design and product launch platform now used by Predica, a representation of the latest design and launch process for the product at a given time, offered in one place and visible by all. Along the way, they also attacked narrower but still irksome issues buried in product management interactions. For example, the team examined more closely how the print materials used to explain the product to the customer were being developed, as well as the support material provided to the sales staff. The participants agreed that their current back-and-forth process of developing both the customer-facing communications package and the advisor-facing support material was suboptimal because it did not create mutual transparency for the product manager and the external agencies developing the communications and sales support packages. As a result, the product manager was frustrated because she could not influence the design of either package. Similarly, the two external agencies were often rebuffed in their desire to interact with the product designer and hear her intentions. The product team also concluded that the two external agencies should have a way to make their designs transparent to each other, since they wanted the advisor tools and the end-customer communications package to have a common look and feel. There again, the solution proved fairly obvious once the culprit interactions were identified: build a simple advertising and communication co-creation platform that creates transparency and reusability for graphics across the various promotion packages being developed, and that allows the product manager to guide them toward a more common look and feel.

Continuing to examine its interactions with other stakeholders, the product development team recognized a major shortcoming: Steinmann worked very little with both the retail branch advisors and the customers during product design, except for an occasional focus group. She lamented that her interactions stopped at the point of delivery of the sales tool to the retail bank's insurance specialist. The team then decided to turn the tables and see what the world looked like from the vantage point of the retail branch advisor. They realized that advisors are split between two fronts: they spend part of their time working with customers and another part dealing with other bank employees. The employee-facing interactions frustrated them much like those of the product manager in that the advisors never had access to the actual developers of the training and sales tools but typically got a filtered version from the insurance specialists instead. What lay beyond the insurance specialist was as opaque to the retail branch advisor, as their world was to Steinmann.

From the retail branch advisor's perspective, it also struck the product development team that advisors were quite isolated. All of their customer interactions were one-on-one discussions. The team reflected it must not be terribly comfortable for a young advisor, two or three years into their professional career, to go head-to-head with customers on products as complex as life insurance without any support from their colleagues at the bank or Predica experts. Yet, the advisors were held accountable for strict sales goals, which occasionally incented them to venture into uncomfortable sales pitches. In contemplating the quality of interactions, another key point struck the team: once customers had purchased a product, there were no further interactions. Customers could thereafter seek out their advisors with questions about products, but for the most part, the bank's contact consisted of sending them statements and managing routine issues such as a change of address or beneficiaries. Steinmann realized the company could provide more value to the customer both before and after the purchase of a product. The Predica team quickly identified two other areas for improvement: the retail branch advisor's participation in the design of her own training and sales tool development and the delivery of the salespeople's communication and support packages. "The product manager suffers from the lack of access to the retail branch advisor, and the retail branch advisor deplores the lack of contact with Predica people," the product development team reflected. "Somewhere in there must be a way to build an engagement platform that links these two populations and unleashes powerful co-creation forces." As the former general manager of a Crédit Agricole Regional Bank turned head of Predica, Hocher was excited about the prospect of involving both retail branch advisors and their customers in the new co-creation approach, and he supported the team in moving to the next step: launching co-creation workshops in the field, with the ultimate intent of conceiving new engagement platforms linking players together better.

Steinmann looked for a retail bank among the 39 in the Crédit Agricole network that was willing to experiment with co-creation and launch the workshop process. The Centre-Loire Regional Bank volunteered to be the pilot case and offered the Predica product management team a workshop with about 20 advisors in Bourges, a small town known for its medieval history and spring festival. The advisors group consisted of mostly junior employees, supplemented with two midmarket advisors, one private client advisor for high–net worth individuals, and one branch manager. The day played out as a systematic and lively exploration of what a retail branch advisor does, fleshing out the nature of their customer interactions as well as their interactions involving other bank employees. They videotaped the proceedings of a co-creation workshop and later played back the results, especially observing emotional responses that could become part of the rallying cry for the co-creation effort. At one point, the group began to discuss career development for young advisors, and one young lady complained, "There aren't a lot of opportunities to advance our careers as a starting-level advisor. We're not permitted to touch 'risky' products like mutual funds because we're not trained in handling those. But nobody ever takes the trouble to teach us. So, yes, we stay ignorant, our career hardly progresses, and many of us leave the bank to go somewhere else." Crédit Agricole, like many large retail banks, suffered from high turnover, a fact well known to Steinmann and the team. Two colleagues of the advisor followed her in the breach, saying, "The new Cap Découverte product that Predica is designing could be the opportunity for us to cut our teeth and learn about this securities stuff. Maybe it could be like training wheels on a bike. We could advance our career with Crédit Agricole and grow with the bank." The branch manager somewhat defensively explained the legal and fiduciary limitations in letting young, inexperienced advisors work with risky financial products. He was instantaneously counteracted by a group of young female advisors who told him in no uncertain terms that one had to start somewhere, that the new product was an opportunity to learn, and that they wanted to be involved with it. "We'll learn together," one of the young advisors said. "We'll figure it out together within each branch. We'll support each other."

Thus a spontaneous community of passionate young advisors was born. The older private client advisor, who worked in the same branch as a couple of the junior advisors, offered herself as a coach in teaching how securities work. The community was getting stronger already. The film of this moment became widely circulated within Predica and popularized under the name *Les Demoiselles de Bourges* (*The Damsels of Bourges*), which was a takeoff on a well-known French movie called *Les Demoiselles de Rochefort*. The film captures the moment where the Predica product manager grasps that if an engaged community of entry-level retail branch advisors could be built around the new Predica product, they would do a much better job of selling.

If Predica could capitalize on the greater aspirations of the young advisors to grow professionally, a whole world would open in front of them. But how could they devise an engagement platform that does that? Steinmann reflected that a Web-based platform would provide an efficient means to scale up the workshop process and allow for larger-scale co-creation among the multiple constituencies involved. Determined to fan this spark of co-creation into a flame, the Predica team started conceptualizing how it could build a platform that would help the community of young advisors capitalize on Cap Découverte and make it into a passport to a new career. The team subsequently developed a Web-based platform prototype where bank advisors could learn about finance, securities, and life insurance; share their "lived" experiences of selling the Cap Découverte product; and provide feedback to Predica on customers' reactions to it. The site has suffered through the ebbs and flows of Crédit Agricole's and Predica's IT funding cycle, but it is now gaining stature in the firm. A throwaway remark by one of the "Demoiselles de Bourges," captured on camera at one of the workshops, caught Steinmann's attention. "By the way, our customers will learn with us," the junior advisor had said. "After all, the customers we want to attract with this product are very much like us—young, trying to learn how to save. We'll do it together."

Steinmann then began to explore how Predica could build yet another engagement platform with and for end-customers, together with advisors. Another risk for the retail branch advisors was failure to meet quotas. The new Web platform addressed that issue as well, allowing advisors to share their recipes for sales success on it. The new platform also enabled some co-creation of training, producing a cost reduction for Predica and a higher-quality experience for the advisor. Traditionally, Crédit Agricole and Predica would publish written manuals, send trainers into the field, and run sessions with advisors all over the country at a high total cost. But some young advisors have taken over some of that role. They are now writing their own life insurance manuals by accumulating best practice experiences, sometimes referred to as a wiki-like accumulation of practical knowledge for Predica products. The risk of nonacceptance of training materials is also very low, since the advisors are developing this material in the first place.

The development team also attended to "inside-out" co-creation. The best instantiation of this was when the Predica product management team made the entire product design process transparent to the retail branch advisors. After the Bourges co-creation workshop, it was clear to the product management team that the young advisors preferred being more involved in the design of products and that they were eager for Predica to open up the design of the Cap Découverte product to them. These advisors had many ideas and a good deal of passion about how to develop the offerings. One of the most telling moments was when advisors recommended against lowering the product loading fee to match the competitor ING's offering. "The customers I'm dealing with won't be looking at us versus ING," a young advisor explained. "You guys in Paris don't understand. Most of the time, I will be educating my customers on life insurance. They won't come into the branch and demand a particular loading fee versus ING or whoever. They'll be learning to save with me. They will not care one bit about loads." For these customers, the quality of the interaction would outweigh any concern about fees. The development team was astounded by this perspective, since they had always believed that advisors always wanted as cheap and competitive a product as possible.

Co-creation has been on a steady roll at Predica. As Steinmann put it, "What a difference co-creation makes to the experience of all players along the activity chain, starting with our own product managers! Not to mention the money we save by avoiding the constant reworking of designs we used to have." For the junior advisors, these combined co-creation projects have increased their access to customers and reduced the costs involved in getting and qualifying leads, since they could build on the market buzz around the Cap Découverte to find more of them. And because customers are partly educating themselves through the community Web platform, the new prospects are better qualified than cold leads. The risk of having an inconclusive discovery interview has been reduced, as has the risk of customers letting their policy lapse over time. In addition, Predica measures the number of advisors who have participated in either live co-creation workshops or Web platform interactions, and through a variety of formal and informal measures, tracks retail branch advisors' excitement about Cap Découverte (and more broadly Predica). While much remains to be done to formalize this feedback process, Predica clearly has moved from the back of the pack among Crédit Agricole product divisions to one of the leaders in terms of appeal to advisors. The Cap Découverte product, in particular, rose to the top of the list for entry-level advisors, who gave it high marks on multiple dimensions, including personal interest about the product and the product's strategic role in advancing their knowledge. In other words, the strategy of making Cap Découverte the platform on which young advisors could advance their careers worked.

The ultimate yardstick of success, however, is sales in the market. By that measure, Cap Découverte is considered a tremendous success. About 80 percent of the banks decided to sell the product in the first year, with all banks adopting it in the following year. This rate of adoption is much higher than for similar products. It has generated a lot of sales enthusiasm at the retail level. Predica sold 330,000 contracts in 2008, against a high-end estimate of 300,000 for the first year. This result is particularly remarkable given the extremely negative financial situation in 2008. By the end of 2009, more than 500,000 products had been sold. The greatest value of the co-creation effort is in the continuous buildup of new strategic capital created through the increased engagement of all stakeholders.

A key source of revenue growth is faster learning, and Predica has put in place a learning engine where new insights are continuously generated so that good new product ideas can be crafted. The new sales tools and communications packages can be updated and renewed continuously, and the Cap Découverte product (and future products) can be quickly redesigned as new ideas are generated. Customers continuously add to the collective body of knowledge of the firm, and retail branch advisors' rate of learning has dramatically increased through the co-creation platform that links them together with Predica. Co-creation is a "silo breaker" across different organizational functions through mutual stakeholder engagement and organizational connectedness, helping achieve "buy-in" through co-ownership and organic alignment. As Steinmann notes, "Co-creation ultimately results in cultural transformation."

THE PROACTIVE ROLE OF SENIOR MANAGEMENT IN ENGAGING STAKEHOLDERS

Senior leadership is crucial in facilitating and guiding large-scale, co-creative organizational change, as the previous two examples also suggest. Consider the example of Hospital Moinhos de Vento (HMV) that illustrates the proactive role of senior management in engaging stakeholders from the inside out in a process of strategic innovation.[153] Founded by German immigrants over a hundred years ago, HMV is one of the most important hospitals in Rio Grande do Sul, a southern Brazilian state, and among the five hospitals chosen by the Health Ministry as a reference institution. It has around 400 hospital beds, 2,400 employees, 4,400 doctors, and 9,200 patients per month; about 16,000 surgical procedures are conducted there each year. Its main focus has been highly complex procedures, for which the organization has won several awards. Despite this, when Dr. João Polanczyk became CEO in 2006, HMV's annual turnover was about $176 million, and its bank loans exceeded $60 million. It had a negative cash flow, operational difficulties, a high percentage of unmotivated employees and dissatisfied doctors, and a hospital occupancy rate of around 60 percent.

Dr. Polanczyk's first tasks were to fix internal process management and operational issues, align strategy execution with formulation, and make the performance management system more effective, using "balanced scorecard" principles. HMV came out of the red in 2007, boosting employee confidence and morale. In 2008, however, Dr. Polanczyk realized that there was little low-hanging fruit left and that the initial turnaround actions that focused largely on operations were reaching their contributory limit in the sense of achieving a more complete turnaround. Dr. Polanczyk began a search for innovation models, something that had never been applied on a large scale to hospitals before and that could give him value creation and a real competitive advantage moving forward. That is when he began to explore co-creation concepts as a means toward developing sustainable strategies. At that time, the health care sector did not appear to be the most attractive arena for co-creation, with conflicts of interest and misunderstandings between hospitals and health insurance plans (most of them had been opening their own hospital units) or even patients and health insurance plans (an average of 50 percent of health insurance plans actually do not cover general patient health expenses).

But Dr. Polanczyk felt that the hospital had been too "inward focused" in its initial turnaround. He very much wanted HMV to innovate and differentiate its offerings and for it to expand its value proposition, so it was not limited to just having patients as stakeholders. Seeing the power of co-creation, he strongly believed that a multistakeholder engagement process was the key to transformation. Many different types of external and internal stakeholders were identified, including patients' families, corporate clients, health insurance companies, doctors, and commercial and marketing people who were in touch with doctors and other internal stakeholders. The first step to engaging these different stakeholders was to have a dialogue with them about their experiences with existing interactions, in a bid to also increase their own motivation and commitment and imagine new ones that would create mutual value. Co-creation workshops were initiated separately for each stakeholder type, which allowed everyone to become more aware of the others' experiences. Then all internal stakeholders participated in a dialogue with patients, where openness and active listening were encouraged. Finally, in an attempt to internalize the patient experience, separate sessions were conducted where internal stakeholders, through role-playing, simulated situations that allowed them to gain a better understanding of what patients typically experienced.

Subsequently, a live engagement platform was designed to generate new ideas with internal stakeholders about different environments of interactions. Separate customer workshops were run for patients and corporate clients. In each workshop, participants included employees with a direct contact with customers, as well as leaders and internal coordinators, executive directors, and even the advisory board, making the engagements more inclusive. Participants were encouraged to not just think out of the box but to "change the box" completely and come up with new business models. Following this, the various ideas were refined and discussed in the context of HMV's strategy map and its themes. The participants then discussed and held votes on the ideas, for which they also began developing execution solutions. A Co-Creation Fair was held where the emergent ideas and solutions were communicated through posters, playful presentations, movies, and prototypes, with an open dialogue reflecting on the changes promoted by the ideas and solutions and identifying key challenges for their strategies.

Following the Co-Creation Fair, the new innovations were summarized and integrated into the strategy map, which underwent further refinement through an internal co-creative process. For instance, a preventive health care program environment was designed to turn the not-so-pleasant experience of annual checkups ("finding problems") into a positive health improvement program ("becoming an active person"). New maternity and surgery environments were established, whose development from concept to execution entailed further co-creation with their respective stakeholders. In some cases, an extended resource network of partners had to be engaged: the Patient & Family Care platform, for example, aimed to enhance the experience of patients and families before their arrival and throughout their stay at the hospital by providing information and logistical support, doing prebookings with hotel partners, and clarifying information about treatments. A new business model gave corporate clients HMV kiosks on their own premises to engage with clients' employees as customers. Together with an HMV health consultant, client companies could customize specific packages for their executives' needs, using a network of clinics in the HMV network. HMV would expand its brand and services through certification of partners, offering a "complete solution" to its corporate clients and increasing executives' use of the health package to more than 50 percent, while lowering health care costs for its clients. These were just some of the innovations that were successfully implemented.

As Dr. João Polanczyk notes, "About half of the strategic initiatives for 2010 came from co-creation with our key stakeholders. Co-creation thinking is being utilized to generate new ideas with them, to evaluate the value of older ideas and their implementation, and to make future interactions more continuous and dynamic. It has increased the engagement and commitment of the people involved." The co-created strategy map from 2010 encompassed four different value propositions, each representing the "voice" of the stakeholders involved in the co-creation process:

- Patients and families: "I want to be engaged by a unique experience of attention and health care."

- Client companies: "I want to access a complete portfolio of health solutions, with Moinhos de Vento as my partner, in managing my employees' health."

- Doctors: "I want to be recognized as part of this institution, in an environment that promotes innovation and excellence in the practice of medicine."

- Health insurance companies: "I want to give my clients options of medical services with high standards of effectiveness and competitive prices."

In 2010, the annual turnover of HMV was $259 million, with a positive cash flow and a surplus. Its occupancy had increased to 95 percent, and its employee motivation and satisfaction had steadily increased as well. As Dr. Polanczyk commented, "Co-creation doesn't end. It is a journey we have begun. We have more work and innovation ahead of us, in different areas of the value chain." The HMV example illustrates the significance of enterprise-wide CEO leadership in engaging internal and external stakeholders, especially in a time of tumultuous change in business environments.

We now come to the example of HCL Technologies and its organizational transformation under the leadership of Vineet Nayar, who was CEO from 2007 until early 2013.[154] This example illustrates how organizational transformation can be achieved through co-creating the involvement of employees and increasing their willingness to participate in creating change together. Viewing the organization of the HCL enterprise as "pivoting" around the interactions that employees have with customers—the "zone of value," as Nayar has called it—he understood that in order for the organization to co-create a unique customer experience, it must first co-create one for employees inside the organization. While leaders talk about employee engagement inside the organization, it has come to be defined in terms of fulfilling what Nayar refers to as "the existential needs of an employee," such as compensation and employee benefits, rather than "the aspirational needs of an employee." The latter, he says, is about every employee as a professionally self-seeking individual looking for a larger cause. Employee engagement with the organization, its customers, and its stakeholders carries the secret of a more sustainable and lasting enterprise. In an industry where people and their tacit knowledge are your most important assets, co-creating unique employee experiences is essential to sustaining the continuous human capital intensity of the organization. And that means putting "employees first." "Customers first" can remain a mere slogan if the organization is not able to deliver on that promise with its employees, from customer-facing employees whose sales and service delivery interactions directly impact customers to other employees inside the organization that support the customer-facing employees.

Nayar's first initiative was dubbed "Mirror, Mirror." It invited employees to look into a mirror and candidly discuss their daily experiences in the organization. It was aimed at learning from employees and communicating with them. Nayar also set up a communications and marketing team of about 30 young people called "Young Sparks," which reinforced their inherent desire to succeed. He sought a brand mantra that captured his desire to change the employee experience, and thus the Employees First, Customers Second (EFCS) tagline was born to capture this inside-out transformational process. Using an intranet-based technology platform, Nayar then launched a program called U&I (for "You the Employee and

I the CEO") to create an open dialogue with his employees and begin engendering "trust, transparency, and management accountability." Any employee could log into the intranet site and pose a question to Nayar that could be read by everyone in the company.

This engagement platform opened the floodgates. Over 400 questions per month poured in. Nayar personally responded to many of them, e-mailing his thoughts and inviting responses to be publicly posted. In addition, weekly polls gave a sense of how employees felt about various issues. Nayar also created a blog where he shared his strategic thoughts with the entire organization. He engaged in frequent dialogues with employees through videoconferences, and he launched "Directions": live, town hall–style meetings where employees could speak candidly. The presence of these multiple engagement platforms created what Nayar refers to as a "common language and shared vision and actions across the company." Soon he was beginning to change how employees experienced the company and how they got work done.

The Smart Services Desk initiative is one outcome. This ticket-based system allows employees to flag anything they think requires action in the company, from "my chair is not working" to "my salary is off kilter" to "my boss is driving me crazy." The issues these tickets raise can only be closed by the employees themselves, who can watch what actions are being taken for their resolution. Employees feel empowered to initiate, accept, or reject problem resolution, thus contributing to transparency and empowerment.

As part of his drive for management accountability to employees, Nayar told HCL's Executive Management Council that he would post his own 360-degree feedback process online so it could be viewed by the entire organization. His system allows all employees to rate the performance of their boss, their boss's boss, and any three other peer managers they choose, on the basis of about 18 questions using a five-point scale. Initially, employees learned that Nayar was seen as being good at motivating employees and committed to team building but a little shaky in execution and getting things done on time. Eventually many managers followed his example of public ratings. Today, employees at HCL are not only able to see the ratings of their bosses but also those of their peers.

Nayar views management as being beholden to the employee, not the other way around. In fact, Nayar believes in what he calls "inverting the management pyramid," starting from the value zone and back into the organization. The point is to get away from rigid command and control structures to a form of management that enables employee experiences across all interactions, whether with customers, partners, stakeholders, or fellow employees. It means recognizing the centrality of the individual employee inside the organization and co-creating their experiences, one at a time. It also means "inverse accountability of CEO to employee" and nurturing a culture of transparency.

Nayar notes that the need for restructuring the office of the CEO is even more critical today. In 2009, following the global slowdown in the economy, he said, "It is now time for the organizational structure to become flat. Rather than directing from the top, or leading from the front, CEOs need to assume the role of a coworker and adopt more effective collaborative techniques. In short, responsibility and accountability will need to flow both top to bottom as well as the other way."[155] Such management transformations are, of course, a long-term coevolutionary process, and HCL's commitment to co-creative engagement is ongoing, as it expands the sphere of co-creation to co-innovation of IT service offerings together with its enterprise customers and their stakeholders.

Senior executives can also play a critical role in stimulating and leveraging customer communities. Consider Intuit, a maker of popular business software. Scott Cook, who cofounded Intuit, recognized the impact of co-creation with customers when the Intuit customer service team began experimenting with online support forums moderated by employee enthusiasts. As chairman of the Executive Committee, he thought there was great potential in these "user contribution experiments," as he called them, and in 2005, at the company's annual outing, he put the following question to the company's top 300 executives: "How might we leverage user contribution at Intuit, both to enhance existing businesses and create new ones?"[156]

Right away two executives came up with an idea for enhancing the company's tax preparation software for tax professionals. Intuit has long included tax help tutorials and tips in its products. But could the company build a new community around in-depth advice on obscure tax issues, getting professional tax preparers to interact with one another and collectively answer one another's questions? A team cobbled together a wiki-forum site for this purpose and launched it just five weeks later. Cook was skeptical of even a minority of tax professionals spending time on the site in the midst of the busy tax season, but to his surprise, the wiki quickly attracted a following. It evolved into TaxAlmanac, an online platform that has been used by over 400,000 visitors (about equal to the number of tax preparers in the United States), containing over 170,000 pages and drawing on the collective expertise of thousands of tax professionals.

The site has proved to be of direct value to Intuit in several ways. The company has been able to learn continuously about the kinds of tax prep questions that its professional customers have, and these customers often go on to buy tax prep software. Intuit has embedded a Q&A community into TurboTax, which is for nonprofessional tax filers; every page of TurboTax now has a user forum with questions and answers relevant to the topic of the particular page. Originally, Intuit moved cautiously, including the user forum only with the least popular product variants of TurboTax Online in 2007. Within just five weeks, however, a third of the questions posed already had answers. The team moderating the forum was surprised to see the quality of the answers, particularly as users built on other answers in an organic process of continuous improvement. The TurboTax Live Community has spread to other Intuit products, inspiring others within the company to experiment. The Intuit example shows how co-creation can be proactively stimulated by good leadership and tried only experimentally at first and then introduced more widely over time.

DEMOCRATIZING DEMOCRACY
Co-creation is not just about bringing "democratic" principles to the private/social sector. The public sector and citizens at large can also benefit from a co-creative change. Consider two examples from the public sector, one at a city level and one at a national level. In October 2006, Seoul's mayor, Oh Se-hoon, launched an online open-ideas platform called OASIS to "enhance creativity and imagination in administration," and bring in citizens as active participants in government policy and decision making. Its

genesis was an internal intranet initiative dubbed Creative Seoul Project Headquarters, where the mayor encouraged civil servants to suggest ideas on three topics: improvement of work practices, encouragement of citizen participation, and transparent city administration. Over 3,000 ideas per month were received in the first year and evaluated by the Seoul Development Institute. The Institute forwarded the best ideas to the relevant civil servants. The performance evaluation system for city employees, which previously had been based on seniority, was revamped to include a merit rating system that reflected how ideas from the intranet had been adopted. This paved the way for engaging external citizens in generating ideas for better governance.

The new platform, named Ten Million Imaginations OASIS, invited creative policy-making ideas from Seoul's 10.3 million citizens. Between October 2006 and May 2009, over 4.25 million citizens visited OASIS, submitting 33,737 ideas (about 1,050 ideas per month on average). OASIS (oasis.seoul.go.kr) is a dynamic engagement system involving three key stakeholders: citizens, civic bodies, and public enterprise employees. A select group of prequalified participants, including policy experts, civil servants, and a volunteer Citizen Committee, assessed and developed ideas. Of the 1,050 ideas proposed per month in OASIS on average, about 120 ideas made it to the discussion phase. At this point, OASIS consolidated similar ideas, followed by an Offline Preliminary Examination, where selected ideas are evaluated based on feasibility and viability. About 40 ideas per month reached this phase. Then the top levels of city government took part in a brainstorming process to develop the ideas into policies. The director general, directors, and external experts participate, with the deputy director in charge of implementing the idea and policy joining at the appropriate time. After the discussion, the city government holds a working-level meeting to decide which ideas to take to the final policy adoption meeting.

About seven ideas on average made it to the fourth and final phase of the engagement process: the Seoul Policy Adoption meeting, a live public meeting of some 200 people, which included the idea's provider, Citizen Committee members, NGOs, external experts, citizens, and the city's top officials. The meeting is chaired by the mayor and broadcast in real time over the Internet. A voting process follows. Close to a hundred ideas have been adopted through OASIS, such as providing free baby carriages and wheelchairs in parks, narrowing the slits in drain covers, and installing a footbridge across the Han River. The adopted ideas are posted on the OASIS website with a due date and progression bar showing the percentage of completion. Ideas not adopted are also posted on the website, with an explanation and details on any alternate policies in process. The website allows further discussion on alternative solutions or related problems. While other institutional systems around the world tended to focus on citizens' complaints, usually on a one-off basis, OASIS allowed for continuous reform of responsive government, while enhancing the image of civil servants and improving citizens' trust in the institutions of government at large. Seoul's new mayor, Park Won-soon, a former human rights lawyer who believes in investing in welfare as an investment in the future, in people, and in creating new jobs, pledged to allocate as much as 30 percent of Seoul's budget to welfare projects. Despite political differences in balancing welfare and growth, the common multiple is a more citizen-inclusive participatory democracy.

The Ministerio de Agricultura e Pecuaria (MAPA) in Brazil is another interesting example.[157] Over the last 50 years, Brazilian agriculture has become a global benchmark in terms of productivity and innovation, thanks to the triple helix,[158] in which research institutes (like EMBRAPA) offer new seeds and crop technologies. The ethanol technology, a clean source of energy, is made of sugarcane (one of Brazil's core crops). It began its development in the late seventies, with the federal government playing an active role in defending Brazilian commodities (like sugar and orange juice) at the World Trade Organization commercial disputes and the willingness of entrepreneurs to build strong export-oriented businesses. Consequently, in Brazil, agriculture shifted to agribusiness. The Lula government's first term in Brazil (2002–2006) somehow brought this triple helix thinking by inviting Roberto Rodrigues, himself an agribusiness engineer and management professor, to be the minister of MAPA. One of the first moves by Rodrigues was to facilitate the co-creation of a strategic agenda for MAPA by inviting the agribusiness representatives of the triple helix. The MAPA strategic agenda soon became a reference among the other 35 Brazilian federal ministries. To implement the objectives, targets, and initiatives of the strategic agenda, the MAPA organization decided to advance even further by installing sectorial and thematic chambers.[159] The vision behind the chambers was a systemic view of connecting different actors (private, public, and social) related to the agribusiness value chain. Since then, 24 sectorial strategic agendas have been co-created with the participation of their stakeholders.

The rubber sectorial chamber is one of the most active, having evolved into a series of interactions with the government, entrepreneurs, service providers, and education institutes. In 2012, a live co-creation platform enabled the emergence of two strategic initiatives with the joint collaboration of public, private, and social organizations. One of them is related to agribusiness statistics in the country and to make available scarce data on rubber production areas, using data collectors all over the country coupled with GPS and sensor-based technologies. Another initiative is beginning to transform the career of rubber technical professionals by giving more options for technical training, looking for professorial expertise, and partnering with career centers to expand career possibilities. The sectorial and thematic chambers of MAPA have become more than just extensions of the Brazilian government but instead have become their own governance system. The MAPA has broadened its strategy execution capacity beyond its resource limitations by enabling live engagement platforms and the development of co-created strategic agendas to articulate the implementation of strategic initiatives. It has also accelerated the pace of strategy execution by assuming that the government alone will not be able deal with the complex agribusiness challenges of the next 20 years.

The OASIS and MAPA examples suggest that societal democracies can engage citizens, who are otherwise not engaged, in the design of management and governance processes that shape citizen environments, and can do so in a process of more co-creative democratization through a focus on human experiences.

CO-CREATING THE CO-CREATIVE ENTERPRISE OF TOMORROW

IT companies are increasingly taking business innovation one step further in a process of "innovation co-creation" that facilitates the rapid evolution of co-creative enterprise architectures across the private, public, and social sectors with minimal investments. Consider the case of Infosys, known for its expertise in IT services, with about $7 billion in revenues in 2012, most of it from large companies outside India. Infosys maintains an internal R&D arm, Infosys Labs (previous known as Software Engineering Technology Labs or SETLabs), whose goal is to anticipate technology evolution and its impact on business. In 2006, the president of SETLabs, Subu Goparaju, began recognizing a need for innovation co-creation (of enterprise co-creation platforms). Several clients had approached Infosys seeking help in identifying and pursuing new innovation opportunities and in augmenting the capabilities of their organizations to keep up with the breakneck pace of IT change. Kris Gopalakrishnan, who was then COO, encouraged SETLabs to engage the sales and delivery constituencies within Infosys on the topic of co-creation. Goparaju set up an Innovation Lab within SETLabs to focus specifically on co-creation.[160]

The Innovation Lab team immersed itself deeply in co-creation research, practices, and strategies, and created a model for innovation co-creation that shifts the core tasks of brainstorming and problem solving outward—beyond individual proposals to co-creative interactions, beyond features and processes to engagement experiences, and beyond the networks of a particular enterprise to a wider community of co-creation. Infosys believes that organizations adopting this model of innovation co-creation can generate faster, smarter, cheaper, and more effective innovations.

At Infosys Labs, co-creation with partners, academics, and customers sits at the core of innovations in emerging technologies to build tomorrow's enterprises. With a defined ideation framework and a robust platform through which members of the co-creation ecosystem can connect, collaborate, and share ideas, Infosys harnesses strengths in research and development to accelerate innovation, optimize operations, and transform business outcomes. The focus is on implementation of co-creation models with a clear vision of joint investments, opportunities, and outcomes.

The Infosys innovation co-creation model contains five key pillars. The first pillar entails access to contextual knowledge and information. Because next-generation innovations now occur predominantly at the intersection of different cultures, domains, and technologies, Infosys has found it important for innovators to have access to a diverse set of technologies and disciplines that create insights into industry trends and emerging business models, rather than relying on expertise in a single domain. When innovators lack access to contextual knowledge and information, Infosys has noticed that their innovation process tends to be slow, expensive, and "trailing edge."

More often than not, such diverse competencies do not reside within a single department, or even within a single organization, so these competencies need to be brought together from different parts of the organization, and from beyond organizational boundaries (i.e., external experts and partners). This is the second pillar of innovation co-creation: a collaborative network of experts and partners. In reality, timely access and sharing of knowledge are seldom achieved in organizations. Expert knowledge and information are typically in silos within organizations. Co-creative innovation, in contrast, is about including more stakeholders, especially those who can bring and debate new points of view, share technological breakthroughs, and identify "next" practices. Bringing together capabilities of different stakeholders from around the world and beyond the boundaries of an organization, with different interests and diverse motivations, to co-create on a single integrated platform dramatically changes the paradigm of how innovations are generated and, with it, the technology-enabling environments required.

The third pillar of innovation co-creation is integrated methodologies and tools. This involves collaborative and communicative tools for idea generation, simulation, and evaluation of innovations. But this pillar is not so much about the variety of tools as it is about the challenge of focusing on the engagement experience of innovators—that is, enabling easy access to these tools and helping them apply the most appropriate methods in a given context.

The fourth pillar is inspiring events. This involves various mind-stretching exercises for divergent thinking, experimentation, learning and enhancing creativity, and making the innovation experience exciting and fun. By engaging internal and external stakeholders to drive ideation, prioritization, and solution conceptualization, and then realizing innovations through rapid prototyping and obtaining feedback and buy-in during rollout, co-creation takes place throughout the innovation cycle.

The combination of these four pillars enables individuals both within and outside organizations to achieve innovation. The four pillars revolve around the central fifth pillar: an integrated and co-creative technology platform that provides various collaborative, visual, communication, and information tools for enabling Infosys and its clients to co-create valuable experiences with their customers and stakeholders. Infosys's innovation co-creation platform, Infosys Labstorm, entails a rich media destination for Infosys clients and other stakeholders to experience tangible innovations and research concepts from Infosys and its partners. It enables collaboration and facilitates co-creation of ideas and innovative solutions among its community of users. With access to Infosys Labstorm, a client CXO is transported to the world of innovations—real, tangible, and inspired. As the CXO checks a video or a demonstration related to the immediate discussion, Labstorm recommends related innovations, and the CXO discovers adjacencies. The CXO can visualize innovations as well as experience them "live" through their interactive demos. Such an engaging experience encourages the CXO to join the Infosys journey of innovation co-creation. Infosys Labs has set up a Centre of Innovation for Tomorrow's Enterprise that manages research on seven core themes for Building Tomorrow's Enterprise: digital consumers, emerging economies, health care economy, sustainable tomorrow, new commerce, smarter organizations, and pervasive computing. One case involved a large banking organization in North America that wanted to enhance its innovation capabilities during the 2008 recession. Infosys set up what it calls "co-creation workouts," first between the client and its customers and then between Infosys consultants and the client's internal stakeholders (from both the IT and business sides). These workouts entailed live engagement platforms that were central to the client's co-creation experience with Infosys. Infosys and its client first came together to share new ideas, knowledge, insights, and perspectives that were relevant to the client's business domain. Then, once the objectives of innovation were agreed upon, the five pillars model provided a platform through which the client, Infosys, and other invited participants could co-create. Infosys and its client agreed on the governance process and rules of engagement for different participants with different rights and roles. Various tools (e.g., social networking and collaborative workflows) were provided to facilitate productive and creative interactions among the platform participants. As innovative ideas were generated, Infosys helped all parties to visualize the experience of new, cutting-edge technologies and services (e.g., mobile banking services).

Over a hundred new ideas were generated in this fashion, including opening an account, transactions, fund transfers, and small business services, in some cases enabling new types of co-creative experiences for bank customers. One idea, for instance, was an easy-to-understand yet comprehensive representation of an individual's financial health through an indicator that constantly monitors banking transactions and contains alerts about certain events (such as hitting a specific balance). Customers can set the alerts, and they can edit and personalize their individual health indicators with fine-grained transaction details. Another idea was an on-line bank social network, where customers could invite family members or anyone with whom they were willing to share personal information to discuss financial matters. A related idea was linkages between joint accounts and community members—for example, allowing parents to approve children's transactions on a "watch list" created through a parent's cell phone. Another idea was for the bank to offer more services to its existing B2B customers—for example, helping business consultants create profit-and-loss statements and invoices with data that a client provided them.

While these ideas by themselves may be interesting, what is more important is that they are the outcome of what Goparaju refers to as an "innovation co-creation capability." He notes that the goal of Infosys is to co-create a unique engagement platform with each client enterprise, partners, and participating innovators, and then jointly build the technology that will make it possible. As another example, consider InfosysEdge, a suite of about 20 cloud-based business platforms that are built around specific themes in building tomorrow's enterprise, like the rise of digital consumers, the drive for smarter organization, and the growing potential of emerging economies. Infosys BrandEdge, in partnership with Fabric, for example, is part of WPP, the world's largest communications services company, and coevolved with client organizations. The BrandEdge platform is a comprehensive cloud-based offering that simplifies digital marketing by bringing together integrated marketing and technology expertise on a single unified platform, transforming the full spectrum of digital marketing activities, including creation and management of digital properties, data management, coordination with multiple partners, and campaign execution. As Samson David, vice president and global head of Business Platforms, noted, "There is a fundamental and tectonic shift in the world of the CMO, and it is primarily led by digital consumers." Martin Sorrell, CEO of WPP, explained, "The traditional approaches of technology and marketing rarely speak the same language. Infosys BrandEdge provides a comprehensive solution to bridge this divide and help our clients create unique personal experiences for consumers."[161] In June 2012, S. D. Shibulal, chief executive officer and managing director of Infosys, said:

Over the past two years, we have partnered with our clients in over 100 co-creation workshops to co-create products, platforms, solutions, and services to help them differentiate themselves in the marketplace, spark growth, and remain competitive. . . . Our research and experience clearly indicate that the success of tomorrow's enterprises will be strongly linked to the inclusiveness of their strategic ecosystem—an ecosystem which drives innovation through active co-creation with key stakeholders. . . . Co-creation is the future of innovation.[162]

Infosys believes that innovation co-creation is now the most preferred method of performing innovation all over the world. Its innovation co-creation ecosystem not only includes clients, technology partners, top academic institutions, and industrial bodies across the world, but it also enables joint innovation co-creation across the public and social sectors in the economy and society. For instance, consider the Sankalp initiative, which was formed in 2012 in support of the United Nations secretary-general's "Every Woman Every Child" movement, committed to preventing 200,000 child diarrheal deaths in India by 2015. Sankalp has 50 members from state and central governments, nongovernment organizations, academic and research institutions, corporations, and communities of faith, who are committed to drastically reducing such deaths in India and other developing countries through the intervention of oral rehydration solutions. The Sankalp platform, built on Infosys's innovation co-creation engine, brings together stakeholders from the United Nations Foundation; the MDG Health Alliance, which works in partnership with UN agencies; the private sector; nonprofit organizations; academic institutions; and other entities. All of these stakeholders work together and with the Infosys enterprise ecosystem to meet health-related Millennium Development Goals. Infosys offers tools and platforms built on cutting-edge technologies to design innovative frameworks and processes that help organize, manage, and assist interactions. The members can use this platform to share videos of best practices, test new ideas, challenge existing ideas, codesign solutions, and build new connections.

The Sankalp example illustrates how convergent "private, public, and social sector multienterprise/multistakeholder" capability ecosystems can build co-creative capacities that can turbocharge an even better world of more valuable co-created experience outcomes both with and for individuals.

LEADING CO-CREATIVE ENTERPRISE TRANSFORMATION

As we have seen through the various examples in this chapter, leading co-creative enterprise transformation means involving employees at all levels, as well as engaging partners and other external stakeholders. The key to successfully making the transformation to a truly co-creative enterprise culture is to begin the transformation inside. This is because, for one thing, in many organizations, especially established ones, the conventional institution-centric logic of value creation is dominant and pervades the design of the organization and how it functions and, ultimately, how individuals in the enterprise engage with one another and with external stakeholders. Co-creation has the power to transform relationships and our social realities, changing the identity of the system we live in and the quality of our human experiences.[163] In a truly co-creative enterprise, leaders *at all levels* must go beyond the conventional institution-centered "cascade and align" view of management to an individual-centered "engage and co-create" view. To do this, as we have seen through the different examples in this chapter, organizations must design and support engagement platforms for employees that give them the opportunity to debate, discuss, and establish priorities and participate in more co-creative fashion, even as the enterprise engages co-creatively with external stakeholders.

As we have also discussed, stakeholders internal to the organization won't wholeheartedly participate in co-creation with external stakeholders unless they are allowed to generate value for themselves as well. That requires giving them the opportunities to design and manage their own organizational experiences and to identify and solve problems. The reality is that most stakeholders, especially internal, feel they often get short shrift and have no significant say in the design process. But people are inherently creative and want to engage with organizations, and thanks to interactive technologies, they now expect to be able to communicate directly with one another and share and shape their own experiences. A key premise of co-creation is that by sharing experiences, all the parties involved will acquire a deeper understanding of what is happening on the other side of an interaction, enabling them to devise a new and better experience for both sides. While most organizations focus on creating economic value, successful co-creators let stakeholding individuals play a central role in designing how they work with one another.[164]

The payoffs of building co-creative enterprises include greater creativity and productivity, lower costs, lower employee turnover, new business models, and new sources of stakeholder and enterprise value. In engaging the organization to reap these potential payoffs, leaders need to ask the following questions:

- Who are the key stakeholding individuals that need to be engaged? How can their willingness to do so be enhanced?

- What engagement platforms are needed for individuals to connect value creation opportunities with resources? What new interaction environments will stakeholders want to participate in? How can existing ones be redesigned to enhance the quality of experiences?

- What potential outcomes of value would be generated for those involved, including the managers providing platform access?

Leaders of the future must be orchestrators of co-creative engagement everywhere in the enterprise's ecosystem. They must leverage network and stakeholder resources to support a strategic architecture of platforms. Senior executive leadership must also pay attention to the technical, social, and organizational architecture of these platforms. Most important, leaders must put human experiences at the center of these platforms, such that enterprises and stakeholders can jointly engage in more effective value creation, where individuals can shape their own co-creation experiences.

In the next two chapters, we discuss how private, public, and social sector enterprises can jointly build co-creative capacities of the social, business, civic, and natural communities in which they operate to enhance ecosystem states of governance, infrastructure, development, and sustainability, and thereby unleash human potential to co-create valuable outcomes of wealth-welfare-wellbeing in economy and society as a whole.

8   EVOLVING ECONOMIES AND SOCIETIES THROUGH CO-CREATION

The ubiquitous connectivity that many experience today, and that is within reach for millions of others, has fostered new social interactions, unleashing democratic and decentralized forces that take us beyond institutional boundaries. These forces continue to spawn new ways of engaging and collectively creating value. As we come to understand this new reality, the single most important shift we must make is to recognize the centrality of individuated co-creation experiences and expansion of wealth-welfare-wellbeing as the basis of value creation. It's a shift with profound implications for economies and societies, with a future that nobody can fully anticipate. Yet, if we put on the co-creation lenses that we have honed in this book, we can see the contours of "a future" as summarized in Figure 8-1.

At the heart of the co-creation-based view of economies and societies is the impulse for "becoming." Whether as customers, employees, managers, financiers, partners, or citizens in communities, every stakeholder brings "capital" to the value creation process through their "value creative capacities" and, in doing so, becomes a co-creator. As individuals' and enterprises' joint interests expand, they create value together through a multitude of channels and interactions. Co-creative enterprises intensify co-creators' acts of value creation in terms of wealth-welfare-wellbeing. As all enterprising entities and people attempt to change the way reality unfolds,

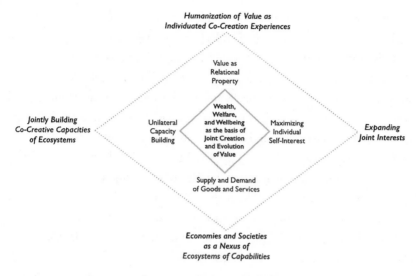

FIGURE 8-1   Contours of a co-creative economy and society

interactions coevolve through collective actions. Individuals' experience-based valuation of co-created outcomes, however, gauges their impact.

In contrast, we have traditionally had only limited conceptions of value creation—animated by the concepts of value as a relational property, supply-demand market mechanisms, individual self-interest, and unilateral building of capacities. In this chapter, we explore how a shift in thinking to co-creation along each of these four dimensions (see Figure 8-1) expands our perspective on the economies and societies in which individuals and enterprises are embedded. We first discuss the humanization of value that goes beyond seeing value just as a relational property. We then discuss how economies and societies can be seen as a nexus of capability ecosystems. Next, we elaborate on how the joint interests of individuals can be a productive basis for reframing economic growth and social enrichment in the future. Finally, we discuss how private, public, and social sector partnerships can jointly build the co-creative capabilities of enterprise ecosystems with, and for, all participating entities in expansive ways.

HUMANIZATION OF VALUE

At the dawn of a new co-creative age, it is useful to look back at how value has been constructed and how we reached this pivotal tipping point.

A traditional conception of an economic system encompasses organizations and institutions that specify "property relations" regulating production and distribution within a given society.[165] Implicit in this view is the notion that value is a relational property. Most traditional enterprises operating in market economies see value creation in business as infusing goods and services with "worth" in relation to prevailing market prices and the costs of production. Determining how worth is actualized in a given object or service is the singular challenge of any business. Furthermore, until and unless customers buy the product, by way of exchanging money, business value is not actualized. The exact same logic applies from the standpoint of any employee vis-à-vis labor. In both of these cases, value is created only when an object is judged to have the property of value in relation to the outcomes afforded and the cost of the object itself, compared to all other available objects. Hence, a tendency to valorize everything in terms of exchange value (market price or cost-benefit comparison) is the most typical manifestation of value as a relational property.

Meanwhile, the separation of work, consumption, and exchange into different spheres has resulted in a consumer society in most parts of the world. Most of us typically produce what we don't consume, consume what we don't produce, and exchange what we produce for what we consume using money and markets as media. When "exchange value" trumps "use value" and distorts "value of labor," most people are alienated from work and consume commodities for questionable uses. This much is the standard critique of capitalism.[166]

What may not be sufficiently recognized is that through markets and capitalism, people can also develop a more nuanced understanding of value as enterprises offer and communicate commodities for all kinds of purposes. Notions of value beyond rational choice for utility maximization have multiplied with new logics of consumption.[167] Individuals make value judgments in various acts of sign-object manipulations, identity practices, and social pragmatics. For instance, identity practices come to sharp relief in the world of fashion or as we adopt or construct lifestyles to enact individualism within a broader market ethic. Many of us also put "products to service" to manage relationships of prestige, power, and obligation through rituals of gifts, sacrifice, and even destruction. Alternatively, consumption is used as a special code and language to identify, differentiate, express, and affirm social alignment with a subculture. For some, it even serves as the central site of politics of difference, representation, normality, and effects. In effect, value judgment (and its discourse) can be the embodiment or expression of attitudes, emotions, desires, or an instrument for evoking similar reactions in others.[168] In this sense, value is an affect as well as a property.

Thinkers have debated the intrinsic genesis of value in many Eastern traditions and since the time of the ancient Greeks. However, the rise of relational logic of value coincides with the rationalizing tendencies of the enlightenment and the industrial revolution. Its subsequent predominance arose with the development of modern neoclassical synthesis in economics, based on marginal utility and equilibrium theories of market exchange. The arrival of a postindustrial society from 1960s onward, however, moved economies beyond production of goods toward provision of services.[169] Services can be distinguished from goods by their intangibility, heterogeneity, inseparability, perishability, and nontradability.[170] Moreover, labor involved in the production of services—that is, "nonmaterial" labor—is characterized by higher rates of information, abstraction, and affect.[171] Hence, ascribing an intrinsic logic to value is making a comeback, resonating with people's everyday human experiences.

Consider the case of Caja Navarra (CAN), a savings bank based in Pamplona, in the Navarre region of northern Spain.[172] Like other Spanish savings banks, or *cajas* (pronounced "ca-has"), CAN is a regional, not-for-profit bank designed to support its local communities through social contributions, based on a dual financial and social mission, with part of its profits allocated for local development and wellbeing. Incorporated under the legal form of "private foundations with a social purpose," cajas are actually full-credit institutions with freedom to act and compete operationally on par with the rest of the financial institutions in the well-developed Spanish banking system, which serves over 45 million people. In this era when Western democracies are grappling with deep, persistent anger over the misguided operations and aftermath of megaglobal banks, CAN's profitability and customer satisfaction are worthy of in-depth study.

In 2002, CEO Enrique Goñi arrived at Caja Navarra and immediately sought to differentiate the bank in a crowded market of over 60 savings banks, all of which made social investments (ranging from about 17 percent to 30 percent of profits for the major banks). CAN's social investment at that time was in the model of all cajas: the bank's board decided where the money went. Goñi approached the board with a proposal to put CAN's social investments in the hands of customers, in effect saying, "Those who decided had to stop deciding." In January 2004, the new initiative, dubbed "You Choose: You Decide," allowed customers to specify their preferences among the seven initiatives of social action traditionally supported by CAN. CAN personalized customers' credit cards to show their choices, reinforcing their identification with the initiative and generating a strong emotional connection.

The results of this initiative were startling. Whereas the bank had chosen to invest in welfare, sports, and leisure; culture; disability and care; research; and heritage conservation, in that order, customers allocated funds to disability and care; cooperation; welfare, sports, and leisure; research, and environment, respectively. This was a startling contrast between conventional "institutional-think" and "customer-think." Like all people, managers at CAN had been shaped by their socialization—by the dominant logic of banking and managerial attitudes, behaviors, and assumptions they learned from their business environments. Managerial thinking, naturally, is conditioned by the routines, systems, processes, and incentives that institutions pursue within the traditional framework of value creation. However, engaging customers and other stakeholders in a process of co-creation enabled CAN to overcome these limitations—to determine how to give back with their customers. Following in these footsteps requires that enterprises give customers and stakeholders the tools to "help them help enterprises to better understand them."

Through "You Choose: You Decide," bank customers revealed that their most popular project in 2006 was emergency aid in natural disasters and crises, with 12,099 supporting this. In 2006, CAN invested €42 million (about $60 million), or 30 percent of its after-tax profits, in these social programs (the other 70 percent was reinvested in the business). By 2007, over 530,000 customers (almost 88 percent of the customer base) had chosen which social initiatives to fund (with a total of €50.25 million, or about $71 million). More than 460,000 customers had selected specific projects from a portfolio of 2,707 projects proposed by 2,133 organizations. CAN's goal in 2010 was to have over 700,000 customers deciding from over 4,000 projects.

The "You Choose: You Decide" initiative was the original driving force behind the concept of CAN's civic banking—empowering people with new rights, as Goñi puts it. As CAN's pioneering initiative evolved, the bank positioned it as a customer right for "Responsible Banking": giving customers a degree of insight into and control over CAN's social investment. Since then, CAN has launched five more customer rights, continuing its relentless pursuit of consumer engagement and co-creation opportunities that extend beyond those it serves directly to the ecosystem at large in which it operates.

It was the second customer right, "Civic Accountability," that truly propelled CAN's journey toward becoming a co-creative enterprise. The first customer right, remarkable as it was, did not provide full transparency to customers on the amount they individually contributed, which resulted in them not being fully aware of the consequences of their decisions. So in 2007, over 650,000 customers received letters explaining how much profit CAN had made from their money and how much each customer had contributed to the projects they had chosen—in cash figures.

As Pablo Armendariz, CAN's head of Innovation, who works closely with Goñi in shaping the initiative, put it, "Everything is in on view, just like it is at CAN's branches. We undertake to work . . . without hiding anything, protecting our customers' interests at all times." Information on profitability—whether by region, product, segment, or individual customer—is usually one of the best-kept secrets at any bank. But CAN made its banking practices transparent, consistent with its strategic intent of social responsibility and its new perspective on the rights of customers. It provided prospective customers with an online tool to estimate how much money it would make with them, and therefore how much money the customer could direct to social projects. Besides creating a strong emotional connection with the bank (yes, a bank), CAN provided its customers with a platform to get more engaged in their society. The platform enables responsible, transparent, and innovative banking for multiple co-creators, ranging from the bank's consumers and business customers to volunteers (including company employees) and nonprofit organizations that contribute to the pool of social projects. CAN's business customers can and do use the philanthropic platform to conduct their own corporate social responsibility (CSR) activities. In effect, CAN is co-creating CSR activities with its consumers, business customers, and social project partners.

At the same time, CAN's employees have become more engaged in their daily work. James Gardner, head of Innovation and Research at Lloyds TSB in London, put it this way: "This is a testament to the power of the new world of work and inclusionism. An example of what can happen when everyone is engaged in a worthwhile journey, rather than being limited to their traditional role-defined corporate box. It is also an example of the way that customers working as partners can drive a change in the nature of the relationship."[173] Both CAN's customer satisfaction and employee satisfaction measures have continuously increased, to the benefit of CAN's reputation with customers and employees. In 2007, CAN enjoyed 8.5 percent customer growth, with over 75 percent of employees satisfied with their professional, personal, and social situation. Generating employee happiness by making banking more human is a laudable accomplishment indeed.

About 40 percent of CAN's business comes from organizations, making the bank as much B2B as B2C. Through its "Viálogos" platform, CAN engages in active dialogue with businesses—an open, live engagement platform where issues that affect business professionals can be dealt with, reflecting their needs, wishes, criticisms, and suggestions. Each Viálogos forum is focused around an important business sector. About five or six forums are held each year, with attendance averaging 200 to 250 people. CAN interacts with participating professionals in advance and then chooses a handful of issues to focus on. The key is that CAN makes public its commitments to the responses at the forum, the implementation of which it is publicly accountable for. It also encourages business professionals to share ideas with one another between forums, thereby seeding the formation of a community.

Saying that transparency is not enough, CAN introduced its third right, "Project Accountability," in 2007. The bank requires organizations running the social projects it supports to be accountable to its customers. It asks organizations to explain how they have invested their money, report who has benefited from it, and present the results "in person." CAN enables the engagement platform for these partners through its branches, where it organizes the live meetings, besides other meeting points where the project organizations can inform the public about their work. In 2007, more than 200 social organizations went to CAN branches to inform customers what they had done with the money they had been given.

CAN also transformed about half of its existing 351 branches into "canchas"—branches for social commitment (*dar cancha* is Spanish for giving an opportunity and giving exposure to someone), thereby reinforcing yet another expression of CAN's civic banking philosophy. CAN views its 175 canchas (with about 40 to 50 more opening each year) as a place where people share, with the branch belonging as much to the customers as to the bank. Besides making financial transactions at canchas, customers and noncustomers alike can have a cup of coffee, read books or newspapers, connect to the Internet with free Wi-Fi, and enjoy shows, talks, and concerts. There are magic shows, clowns, and puppets for children, and book groups are encouraged. For example, over 65,000 people have visited CAN's Pamplona cancha, surfed the Internet for over 18,000 hours, enjoyed some 12,000 hours of reading, played 47,000 hours of children's games, and engaged in over 1,500 activities. Over 20,000 people have chosen their charitable and benevolent projects in this cancha alone.

CAN also leverages its cancha-based platforms online to loop in recipients of social projects who can then share their actual experiences as recipients of funding from project partners. This transparency, access, and dialogue foster collective accountability in the entire system, and the risks of misappropriation and inefficiencies in the system are minimized. Moreover, given full transparency, individuals can make their own judgments about the relationship between the risks they might undertake in supporting certain projects and its rewards. The operating costs for each cancha are about 12.5 percent higher than for a traditional branch; however, the costs are more than balanced by efficiency gains and effectiveness in CAN's engagement with project partners. What's more, CAN sees increased sales through word-of-mouth referrals by the partners themselves and through their viral impact in the local communities. It is an investment with nonlinear market and partner impact. CAN's strategic capital is enhanced as well through its employees' experiences and insights gained from their social interactions with customers and noncustomers.

Thus, CAN's customer engagement platforms epitomize how customers can choose, decide, know, become involved, and take an active part in core company operations. Customers can even visit the project and help out as volunteers via the VolCan engagement platform, through which CAN puts individuals in touch with nonprofits. VolCan is a manifestation of the bank's fourth customer right, "Involved Banking." In 2007, 7,000 volunteer positions were offered through VolCan, with 2,750 people working as volunteers for 22,000 hours. Another 405 people were trained in five voluntary work courses organized through VolCan. Armendariz says, "We are heading toward a new society, and at CAN we are building the future together."

Under the banner of "involved banking," Caja Navarra also created EureCan, a community engagement platform of mentors, networks, and training for business entrepreneurs. EureCan Copiloto is a community of prominent businesspeople on this platform who offer advice to entrepreneurs and give them the benefit of their collective experiences with failures and successes. EureCan facilitates social networking for entrepreneurs, making it easy for them to find appropriate partners, suppliers, and support. It also holds training days exclusively for entrepreneurs, known as Eurecanforma, and facilitates an annual get-together.

Caja Navarra continues to innovate relentlessly. Its fifth customer right was "Know and Decide." Going beyond involving its customers in allocation of profits set aside for social purposes, CAN lets customers participate in how the bank itself invests customer deposits. Customers are given eight categories for investment, some of which are clean energy, youth, training and employment, family help, and entrepreneurs and innovation. Customers who invest larger sums with CAN are allowed to choose from more than 1,000 special projects both inside and outside Spain. The head of a youth activist organization described CAN as "making it quicker, easier, and more effective for activists to influence CFOs and persuading them to work with CAN (and choosing their own projects) than to fill out forms asking for government financing."

In 2009, Caja Navarra rolled out its sixth right, "Connecting Customers With Each Other"—connecting those who want to help with those who need it. CAN now puts people who want a loan in contact with people who can finance them, in peer-to-peer fashion. People can post their loan request on CAN's Web platform. Anyone who wants to finance the loan can link her deposits to the loan. CAN handles the risk through an "advanced election loan" product it has designed for this purpose, with the loan rates depending on many variables such as CD rates, loan guarantees, and payment track records. CAN's customers, the customer's borrower, and CAN are once again involved in creating mutual value. In January 2010, nearly 5,000 people received loans totaling €344 million. CAN lists each loan on its website because its civic banking is transparent.

The financial results for Caja Navarra were nothing short of remarkable. Over the six years from 2001 to 2007, profits grew 2.8 times (from €64 million to €182 million), credit investment grew 2.8 times (from €4.5 billion to €12.5 billion), resources managed grew 1.8 times (from €6.5 billion to €11.86 billion), and ROE (return on equity) grew from 8 percent to 17 percent. (Credit investment refers to the total amount of loans invested by CAN, while the resources managed are the bank's total deposits, excluding funds from the central bank.) CAN's efforts have led to an increase of 6 percent per year of the bank's customer base. By 2006, CAN had exceeded its objectives set in the 2003–2007 strategic plan. In 2007, CAN moved from 16th to 5th place in margin per employee and from 41st to 4th place in ROE among all savings banks in Spain.

The financial crisis and economic downturn of 2008–2009, which was particularly pronounced among Spanish banks, showed that this success was no mirage. Caja Navarra's financial results and bond rating remained relatively strong, in part because of its unusually tight connection with customers, who continued to flock to the bank. Funds under investment in CAN's Basque home region grew 30 percent in the first half of 2009, and the volume of funds invested in the bank's mutual funds grew 8 percent. CAN invested €120 million (about $171 million) in 2008 to support its growth. It has kept the flow of money running with over €3.3 billion in loans in 2008, up 18.6 percent in the business sector alone. Miguel Sesma, president of CAN, noted, "We might say that 2008 was the year of change; the financial sector is never going to be the same again. At CAN, in this key year, we have attained a historic record by topping the €200 million mark (about $285 million) in net profit. This has allowed us to make voluntary provisions totaling €40 million for an increasingly uncertain future." CAN closed out the 2010 FY with €11.97 billion in retail managed resources, of which €8.43 billion was within the balance sheet, rising 7 percent versus Spain's average of 0.5 percent in the financial sector.[174]

As Goñi commented:

In the future, financial institutions will have to be civic. . . . Society no longer wants outdated economic models. We have learnt that, all of a sudden, we can no longer just look to shareholders. From now on, companies will look after the profits generated by all of the role players with whom they deal, because this is the only way of guaranteeing their sustainability. . . . In Civic Banking everyone provides and everyone wins, and that is why it works. This business model attains economic and social results, which is what drives us.[175]

Caja Navarra has since been incorporated as part of a civic banking ecosystem model, entailing several other community banks, following a restructuring from a broader economic and societal perspective.

As we have seen throughout this book, the co-creative turn has manifested itself in a new generation of enterprises seeing value creation as orchestrating platform engagements for intrinsic affects in and of themselves, beyond relational properties as such. These co-creative enterprises, whose management systems and architectures continue to evolve, are enabling "markets as a nexus of differences," in which the single common element is expression, enaction, and embodiment of value as intrinsic affects through never-ending interactions and co-creation experiences.

ECONOMIES AND SOCIETIES AS A NEXUS
OF ECOSYSTEMS OF CAPABILITIES

The market as a nexus of differences presents itself as a nexus of ecosystems of capabilities centered on productive and meaningful human experiences through platforms of engagements of all stakeholding individuals in the economy and society as a whole. Consider the case of Rio Grande do Sul, one of Brazil's richest states, which nearly went bankrupt in 2005, as public investment reached its lowest level in 35 years. Since 1970, one government after another had failed to implement the necessary state reforms to reduce public debt. By 2004, 32 percent of tax revenues were tied to the pension burden and 13 percent to the increasing public debt. In the early 1990s, Brazilian commodity export–oriented states like Rio Grande do Sul suffered not only from the negative impact of the overvalued national currency but also from a severe decline in agricultural production due to recurring droughts. It became increasingly clear that no single entity could solve the state's major structural problems.

In late 2005, the Brazilian National Confederation of Industry (NCI), a powerful pan-business group, proposed a draft agenda to begin dialogue on setting goals for Brazil's sustainable development. The focus was on a joint interest engagement model that would result in a co-created strategic agenda. Several state governments and administrative departments warmed up to the concept, especially the state of Rio Grande do Sul. In 2006, leading entrepreneurs then rallied civic leaders to propose a comprehensive program for the economic and social recovery of the state. The industrial state federation, Fiergs; three trade associations, FDCL, Fecomercio, and Federasul; and FARSUL, the entrepreneurs' association, got together to begin deliberations on organizing civil society and reversing the state's economic situation. Far from playing a passive role in building public policies, these economic agents decided to propose a deep process for social and economic recovery. Political articulation began in various social and economic spheres. In order to drive legitimate change, the initiative was dubbed "Strategic Agenda 2020," so as to engage not only members of the "sponsoring" entrepreneurial organizations but rather the whole system, including representatives from trade unions, NGOs, government, political leaders, and educators. (For example, fully 30 to 40 percent of the identified programs in the NCI agenda draft were being undertaken by private entities and NGOs.).

For starters, a live engagement platform was conceived for engaging different stakeholders, building political consensus, and co-coordinating lobbying activities. The goal of this platform was to co-create a democratic means of developing another common engagement platform that could be incorporated into the government programs of elected officials. Naturally, this called for a process of consensus building and democratic goal setting by a coalition of diverse stakeholders collectively representing the interests of the public. It was coordinated and facilitated by volunteers, economists, politicians, and external experts led by Symnetics, a consulting organization, over multiple phases. In the first phase, about 950 people came together, representing all social segments—from community, union, and association representatives to business and academic leaders, NGO personnel, and government officials. Dubbed "The Future Vision of Ro Grande do Sul 2020 (the Rio Grande that we want)," it was a landmark achievement in terms of social mobilization and engagement through live meetings and workshops enabled by a "Future Search" process.

The next phase was to co-design a strategic agenda entailing long-range goals, objectives, targets, and actions (initiatives) for current and future generations and to keep government focused on strategic priorities. It was important to bring a long-term perspective on economic and social programs, while reducing the likelihood of discontinuity from one administration to the next. For instance, considering that a return on education and infrastructure programs can take 10 years or more, the strategic governance agenda—by enduring successive administrations—can help maintain the commitment to initiatives and ensure that a 15-year plan of action is actually accomplished. The agenda had to identify a societal vision and a corresponding set of long-term objectives, targets, and actions in a framework that could either be created within government or outside of it by a coalition of stakeholders. In fact, in October 2006, the strategic agenda was presented to the two state government candidates, who promised in front of over 1,000 people and the media to implement its targets.

This brings us to the third phase of systemwide implementation and performance management. While on one level, there have been roadshows and communication efforts and campaigns all over the state, on another level, there have been public discussions with newly elected government officials and reviews of initiatives and their collective progress across the board. A website was created with an online public forum and open access to every presentation or discussion topic from the agenda to democratize the governance process moving forward.[176] In effect, it was hoped that the agenda would become a "public observatory" for governance and performance management, where every public and economic entity would align its agenda with broader, strategic ones. This would also foster collective public debate and dialogue, with periodic "feedback on the feedback" via updated newsletters and blogs as part of an ongoing conversation and continuous recalibration of the national agenda.

The Strategic Agenda focuses on 12 topics: Education, Health, Security, Citizenship, Agribusiness, Regional Development, Public Management, Logistic Infrastructure, Innovation and Technology, Environment, Energy Infrastructure, and Sanitation through 31 main projects and many others spread throughout the state. This large agenda and its proposals have produced smaller, more focused movements and entities that tackled state challenges with a local approach. These independent projects show how the Agenda2020's principles have gone beyond the original initiative itself, engendering a co-creative atmosphere and spirit around Rio Grande do Sul.

We now turn to the philosophical bases of economy and society and the implications of the co-creative turn for how individuals' joint interests can be a productive basis for reframing economic growth and social enrichment in the future.

EXPANDING JOINT INTERESTS

From the time of Plato, philosophers have observed the plight of the human condition in "reconciling self-interest with the moral urge of doing well for others." In the Co-Creation Paradigm, we co-create with others not only because we want them to do well, so we, relationally speaking, will do well, too, but also because our notion of self goes beyond our own finite, embodied existence to encompass linguistic, intellectual, and communal capacities that are shared by the multitude and without which we would not even be able to function in society. We co-create in order to continuously multiply the ecosystem of capabilities that reside in the social, business, civic, and natural communities of which we are already members. We believe that people may not necessarily go beyond their self-interest if left to their own devices, unless joint interest is itself recognized to be in the self-interest of the individual. Co-creation does just that: it mandates that *we do even better for ourselves by doing well for others, too*. In other words, a co-creation-based view of economy and society is about expanding collective self-interests for you and me, and me and you, in "win more–win more" fashion.

How can we see more of our joint interests to foster this approach? The notion of enterprises in the private sector leading initiatives for the greater good has become familiar thanks to the spread of corporate responsibility practices. In previous chapters, we saw how private sector enterprises create value together with the public and social sectors (recall Nike working with Ashoka, ITC working with NGOs and the Indian government, and Starbucks working with Conservation International and the Rwandan government).[177] Likewise, social (and ecologically oriented) enterprises can benefit from working with the private sector. Regardless of who originates or orchestrates the underlying platforms of engagement, everyone benefits. Let's look at a case of a social sector enterprise providing such leadership.

Consider the example of the Ashoka enterprise. Ashoka is a not-for-profit organization focused on fostering the growth of the social sector by supporting the work of social entrepreneurs—individuals with innovative solutions to society's most pressing social problems. Social entrepreneurs are ambitious and persistent, tackling major issues and offering new ideas for large-scale change in society. Ashoka supports individual social entrepreneurs both financially and professionally. According to Bill Drayton, founder and CEO of Ashoka, "The citizen sector is halving the gap between its productivity level and that of business every 10 to 12 years."[178] With this growth has come a new set of industry drivers that are rapidly redefining the way nonprofits operate. Ashoka facilitates the creation of communities of social entrepreneurs in order to leverage their impact, scale their ideas, and capture and disseminate best practices. Ashoka has been working to build the infrastructure needed to support the growth of the citizen sector and social entrepreneurship globally, with social entrepreneurs themselves bringing in over half of the organization's funding.

The client or "Fellow" in Ashoka's case is engaged in a partnership with Ashoka. This relationship, in and of itself, is visibly different from many nonprofits that have clients that are simply "passive recipients." Unlike many nonprofits, the creation of this partnership extends to a continued interaction including follow-up analysis of key metrics of success for the donation, network building, and pro bono consulting services. First, Ashoka has created and refined a process to gauge the fit of potential Fellows on five selection criteria: the new idea itself, creativity, entrepreneurial quality, ethical fiber, and social impact of the idea. The Fellows are forced to take an introspective look at both their personal and professional strengths. Through its rigorous governance process, Ashoka seeks a plan for execution and forecasted results according to a bottom line that looks at socially sustainable process change (not necessarily profit). This process helps the Fellows to uncover risks before the project is started, thereby allowing them to mitigate these challenges accordingly. This is valuable for the potential Fellows because, regardless of whether they are selected, they would have created a solid business plan with reduced risk.

Ashoka derives increased value from the security of knowing that the donation will create positive returns not just financially but, more important, in a socially sustainable way. The governance process also provides an opportunity for the organization to view many different project ideas from potential Fellows. Being exposed to a variety of ideas is a valuable process for the Ashoka team because it helps it to learn about new trends and share best practices. Ashoka's exposure to a myriad of projects helps the team to reach a verdict on whether a project is a "knockout idea" of truly innovative quality.

Ashoka's current governance mechanisms highlight an understanding of the need to build a sound capability ecosystem in the social, business, civic, and natural communities in which its Fellows participate. The constant and rigorous sharing of not just projects but of moral and ethical fiber allows both parties to ensure they are striving toward a common goal. Following the co-creation principles we discussed in Chapters 2, 3, and 4, internal "communities" of Fellows can be developed as an engagement platform that is facilitated by Ashoka. The Fellows in these communities can work together as they move through the selection process and leverage one another's ideas and capabilities to improve upon and develop their presentations and plans for the selection committee. Each Fellow candidate has the opportunity to assume a current Ashoka Fellow as a mentor.

This mentorship can be a "win-win" for both mentor and mentee, as they can share best practices and coevolve from their ongoing interactions and actual human experiences. This would also be beneficial to Ashoka in strengthening its overall network in the field of social entrepreneurship.

Recognizing that borders are slowly eroding in the global economy, Ashoka has gone one step further and created the Global Fellows network. Global Fellows are worldwide variants of the Fellows program in the United States, with social entrepreneurial ideas that are transnational and globally scalable. Ashoka's expectation is that these Global Fellows will evolve and work together to seek international solutions. The network is designed to provide services and opportunities for Fellows to interact at all stages of the project life cycle. This program not only provides tools and resources but, more important, the ideal of creating a community of shared learning to increase the overall impact of all Fellows' work. Global Fellows benefit from this networking program because they are able to connect with others that have possibly dealt with similar issues or roadblocks through their projects. They gain the value of being part of a larger group with a shared mission and vision. The value each Fellow generates through these networking engagement streams is completely dependent on the individuals' initiative to utilize its capability ecosystem and the subsequent desire of members to engage with those reaching out.

There are also opportunities for Ashoka to work with enterprises in the private and public sector. In Chapter 1, we discussed how Nike is using Ashoka's Changemakers platform to exercise sports as an instrument for social change. Ashoka is a community of people who are intrinsically interested in social innovation. Changemakers is a platform that enables challenges to be posed to the community to surface the best social solutions. People can join the Changemakers platform in several ways. First, they can participate in one of the many "collaborative competitions" that are sponsored by Ashoka and various nonprofit and for-profit organizations, such as Nike. Each competition focuses on a different social issue and lasts about a quarter. At the end of each competition, a panel of judges chooses the finalists, and the online community gets to vote for the winner. All entries are posted online for the community to view and critique. For example, take the Global Water Challenge, an online competition to discover and support entrepreneurs with groundbreaking approaches to the world's water and sanitation challenges. Anyone could review entries and get involved through open online discussions. More than 100 innovations poured in from 35 countries, including an innovator in Sudan who launched a bartering system to exchange a local natural resource for water treatment equipment that radically reduces waterborne diseases and a Nigerian entrepreneur who created cheap, clean, and sustainable energy from human waste. Thus, Ashoka is not only fostering and channeling human ingenuity by organizing human agency as a nexus of its own socially driven engagement platforms, but it is also acting as a nodal enterprise embedded in the context of economies and societies as a nexus of private, public, and social sector ecosystems. Nike turbocharges Ashoka's efforts, as does Ashoka Nike's efforts, and jointly they not only boost overall productivity in the system, but they can have much more impact on economy and society as a whole. In the process, both the Ashoka and Nike enterprises benefit in their own self-interests with minimal fixed investments on each other's part by accessing each other's competencies. Nike, by finding "bottom-up" solutions for using soccer for social change, is able to expand the value creating potential of its enterprise ecosystem, and Ashoka is able to expand both its entrepreneurial pool of potential Fellows and the social impact of its current Fellows by using sports to drive social change. In other words, sports become a common ground for "win more–win more" outcomes of mutual value to both enterprises, while simultaneously accelerating economic and social development. As the late South African activist and Nobel Peace Prize laureate Nelson Mandela said, following his fight against apartheid where his involvement through sports played an important role in healing racial tensions, "Sport has the power to change the world. It has the power to inspire. It has the power to unite people in a way that little else does. It speaks to youth in a language they understand. Sport can create hope where once there was only despair. It is more powerful than government in breaking down racial barriers."[179]

The public sector can also have far more economic and social impact through partnerships with the social and private sectors. Although there are many public-private partnerships, this does not necessarily mean they are all designed through co-creation thinking or that they are necessarily inclusive with respect to engaging the social sector. Let us now consider the public sector example of UIDAI (Unique Identification Authority of India), which, though still finding its way, highlights both the opportunities for generating "win more–win more" outcomes and the potential pitfalls of less considered inclusivity. Established in January 2009, in liaison with the Planning Commission and backed by the prime minister's office of the Government of India, UIDAI was conceived as a public-private organization with a chairman from India's IT private sector, a director general from the government, and almost 400 officers and subordinates staff.[180] As noted by UIDAI, "A crucial factor that determines an individual's wellbeing in a country is whether their identity is recognized in the eyes of the government. Weak identity limits the power of the country's residents when it comes to claiming basic political and economic rights."[181] While the Indian government has made efforts in the past to provide clear personal identification documents to its residents, it has not managed to resolve issues related to the "uniqueness" of identification within its national systems. Several different identification systems had been created for different purposes, with cards including voter identification cards, ration cards, driver's licenses, and income tax cards.

Absent a nationally accepted, verified identity number that both residents and agencies could use with ease and confidence, individuals underwent a full cycle of identity verification every time they tried to access a new public or private sector benefit or service—increasing overall economic costs of identification and causing extreme inconvenience to individuals.

The plethora of different identities for different institutions and different states in India has been a significant hurdle for the more than 30 million poor migrant workers who are denied services and benefits when they move. With high levels of corruption, ghost and duplicate identities in various systems have been common, with more than a half of all Indians paying bribes or engaging in influence peddling to facilitate the completion of tasks requested of public offices. Due to identity issues, the government loses about $24 billion per year due to welfare schemes alone. The ability for an individual to easily obtain and maintain fraudulent identities also contributes significantly to the existence and growth of untaxed money in India, estimated at $1 trillion (equivalent to 60 percent of India's GDP in 2010). Moreover, according to UNICEF, only about 40 percent of children younger than five are registered at birth. This lack of identification becomes a significant barrier for underprivileged residents who cannot access benefits and subsidies from government welfare programs. Thus, immense benefits could be derived from a mechanism that uniquely identified a person and did so instantly, securely, and accurately.

The UIDAI's purview was limited to the issuance of a 12-digit Unique IDentification number (UID) branded as *Aadhaar* (meaning "foundation" in Hindi), which is linked to a person's demographic and biometric information. The UID infrastructure collects only basic Know your Resident (KYR) information (name, date of birth, gender, and address) for each individual and a photograph together with their biometrics (fingerprinting of all fingers and scans of both irises) during registration. The Aadhaar number itself is randomly generated and does not reveal any personal information about the individual. Moreover, the UID guarantees only a person's identity, not rights, benefits, or entitlements. While enrolling for Aadhaar is optional as such, the central government of India budgeted approximately $380 million to fund UIDAI, and enrollment commenced August 2010, with a goal of enrolling 600 million people by 2014. As of this writing, over 200 million Indian residents have registered with registrars in the 35 states and union territories that enroll residents, and over 180 million Aadhaar numbers have been issued, making it already the largest and most advanced biometric database in the world.

At a fundamental infrastructure level, UIDAI Aadhaar illustrates how the public sector can potentially enable and foster the building of capability ecosystems for all enterprises in the economic and social system, whether private, social, or public. This foundation is both technological and social. On the technical side, it provides a universal identity infrastructure over which private, social, and other public sector enterprises can build services and applications that benefit residents across India. Enterprises that become part of the UID applications ecosystem get an authentication service via UIDAI confirming almost immediately the identity of any individual through an advanced technology infrastructure that checks incoming UIDs and biometric information against its database. On the social side, it represents a new dawn of equal opportunity for each individual.

(Aadhaar's logo is a sun in red and yellow with a fingerprint traced across its center that communicates just this.)

The UIDAI Aadhaar initiative is not without resistance from within the government and external critics and opponents. Aadhaar's potential to eliminate duplicate or "ghost" beneficiaries threatens rent seekers across the existing system who will no longer be able to exploit the system to their advantage. Although Aadhaar will act only as an enabler of services and systems, it does eliminate redundant systems and processes that duplicate work across government states and departments, sparking resistance from those who feel it will take over the function of existing personnel. Further, some existing government systems are not up to date and will need to be overhauled to enable the effective application of Aadhaar. For example, in some states, existing databases of the Public Distribution System, the Indian food security system, exist only in the form of offline document files. These files must be converted into an online database before they can be linked to Aadhaar. There is resistance to this change from some quarters.

The concept of Aadhaar as an electronic cardless identity has also spawned concerns about data privacy, viability, intent, and risks of the initiative. Some have argued that most of the poor get deprived of what they need because of corruption and not lack of identity. Leakages, it is argued, stem more from officials taking bribes and charging more for the transport of goods (e.g., grains). Others have called into question the huge amount of money being spent in the name of the poor and without any legal and constitutional sanction for it as yet. Although UIDAI has repeatedly emphasized its avowedly pro-poor mission, there has been backlash from civil society activists and leaders who work with the poor.

The scale of the Aadhaar initiative demands a deeper level of engagement with its myriad stakeholders for it to be successful in the longer term. Although it was set up with a pubic-private organizational structure, the lack of inclusivity of social sector stakeholders from the start appears to have contributed to social discontents. Public initiatives are as much a social as a technical challenge. While policy makers need to focus on technical implementation, costs, and delivery issues, concerted efforts are necessary to include social sector stakeholders in order to nurture public trust. Traditional communications efforts to educate the public of the benefits of the initiative are not sufficient anymore in an age where the influences of conventional and social media can take on a life of their own. Citizens need to be actively engaged in a dialogue about the initiative to ensure that concerns about functionality, security, storage, and privacy are addressed. This requires a focus on transparency from the citizen's perspective. It is crucial to connect with human experiences of openness and accountability and to establish dialogic engagement platforms to nurture public trust. This is not easy by any means, but without due diligence and purposeful design around co-creation principles (creative, intentional, integrative, and transformative engagement design), public trust can dissipate easily.

On the one hand, as the Ashoka-Nike example suggests, public sector enterprises could benefit from public-social partnerships as much as public-private partnerships.[182] Simultaneously, such partnerships can benefit from more co-creative engagement to generate more mutually valuable outcomes. For instance, one of the strengths of the UID system is that it is based on both an open technology architecture and an open applications programming interface that allow any service provider to participate in the Aadhaar ecosystem by developing an application that utilizes Aadhaar as an authentication method. UIDAI could build an applications design engagement platform that fosters co-creation of key applications. Doing so, however, requires codesigning the engagement design of this platform together with stakeholders both in the communities in which applications are designed and in the communities in which the applications will be used. In addition to the applications developers, service providers, and served customers, there are other key stakeholders such as public/private sector banks, nonbanking finance corporations, microfinance institutions, National Payments Corporation of India (enables interoperability between banks), Reserve Bank of India (the banking regulator creating the regulatory environment promoting financial inclusion), and state governments and departments that enact policies and create systems and processes to deepen financial inclusion. UIDAI, as a nodal entity, faces the challenge of leveraging the capabilities of these stakeholders to support the strategic architecture of multiple engagement platforms in the financial inclusion application ecosystem. These engagement platforms will have to bring together the various stakeholders to engage in multifaceted dialogue aimed at generating new ideas in the ecosystem; discussing benefits, costs, and risks; and fostering active discussions and experience sharing and consensus building among stakeholders, all to enable significant co-creation of expanded value in the ecosystem. Further, continuous stakeholder engagement with the various users of applications service platforms would allow the ecosystem to evolve based on feedback from DART-configured stakeholder experience domains, to minimize conflicts, and to lead the design of platforms toward more transformative engagement and actualization of unique value all around.

JOINTLY BUILDING CO-CREATIVE
CAPACITIES OF ECOSYSTEMS

Jointly building co-creative capacities of ecosystems necessarily entails a convergent engagement of private, public, and social sector enterprises. Consider the real-life applications UIDAI is piloting as part of Aadhaar's application ecosystem. Consider, specifically, the goal of financial inclusion, which seeks to give people the ability to control their money, enabling them to gain access to basic financial savings, affordable credit, remittance services, and insurance and investment products. (Only about half of Indian households have a bank account.) The economically disadvantaged pay a poverty premium, as it were, because they have no means to store the cash they earn and because they are unable to apply for bank accounts due to a lack of identification. Furthermore, in rural areas, people often have to spend hours, and sometimes an entire day, traveling to the nearest banking facility and end up spending a significant portion of the money they had hoped to save for the journey.

Now consider an Aadhaar-enabled Payments System as a means for achieving the goal of financial inclusion. This is a prepaid system that includes a Business Correspondent (BC) operating a micro-ATM device and a process that enables cash transactions for the customer. The micro-ATM device is essentially a fingerprint authentication device that communicates with the UIDAI and the banks through a payment switch to access the bank accounts of the resident and the BC. The BC starts by depositing a predetermined amount, currently around $200, in the bank that owns the micro-ATM device. This amount or "prepaid" balance changes with every transaction that the correspondent conducts for a resident. When a resident makes a withdrawal from his account, the correspondent pays the resident cash. This amount is credited to the correspondent's account and withdrawn from the resident's account. The opposite happens in the case of a deposit where the resident gives a cash deposit to the correspondent. The first step of the process is authentication of the resident done through the UIDAI's authentication application. Once the resident is authenticated, the Aadhaar-linked bank account is accessed, and the account balance is announced in the local language through a speaker interface in the ATM device. Similarly, the withdrawal or deposit amounts, both pre- and post-withdrawal/deposit balances, are announced through the speaker, ensuring complete transparency and helping to mitigate any attempt by the correspondent to skim income from the resident's withdrawal. Although this is only in the early stages, the platform capabilities have to evolve as a function of experience-based engagement to connect with the social milieu in which the platform is embedded. For instance, the current design makes the details of the transaction clear to mitigate leakage, but it also raises the security risk of large withdrawals, notwithstanding privacy concerns. This is an instance where open ideation of the design challenge can generate new potential solutions.

Further, UIDAI's financial inclusion capability ecosystem and the private sector can also intersect in mutually opportunistic ways. Consider ITC's agribusiness capability ecosystem discussed earlier (see Chapter 4). With the government's push for financial inclusion and the banks' struggle to develop viable BC models, ITC has recognized the business potential for providing financial services through its eChoupal network and is piloting a BC model with its Sanchalaks and learning how best to design a BC-based engagement platform that may well evolve with non-Sanchalak BCs. On the farmer side, a BC-based model provides easier access to government schemes and the opportunity to build credit faster, not to mention lower transaction costs that allow the farmer and the community to increase savings and investments in income-generating activities, ultimately improving their quality of life. Further, collective financing models with a community-based approach can offer access to equipment services that would otherwise entail significant capital expenditures.

Thus, through the example of UIDAI, we can see how private, public, and social sector enterprises can converge on building joint co-creative capacities of enterprise ecosystems. In projects with a similar scale, there is growing awareness that no enterprise can act alone or achieve success alone. Rather, all enterprises are inextricably linked in an interdependent, globally networked geometry that represents both the opportunity and the challenge of jointly building co-creative capacities.

Going back to Figure 8-1, the examples discussed in this chapter point to a co-creation-based view that can expand value creation in economy and society by seeing it as a nexus of private, public, and social sector ecosystems with heterogeneous modes of human experience-based value creation that go beyond mere modes of "production" of goods and services and "relations of production." Further, expanding joint interests, especially by jointly building co-creative ecosystem capacities, provides for a far more productive basis for reframing human agency and markets, and economic growth and social enrichment in the future, by considering wealth-welfare-wellbeing as the very basis of joint value creation and evolution (as shown in the center of Figure 8-1). The late Nobel laureate Ronald Coase, who at age 101 (in 2012) witnessed more structural changes in economy than most of us, called for reconnecting "Man and Economy."[183] As he wrote in the *Harvard Business Review*:

When modern economics was born, Adam Smith envisioned it as a study of the "nature and causes of the wealth of nations." His seminal work *The Wealth of Nations* was read by businessmen, even though Smith disparaged them quite bluntly for their greed, shortsightedness, and other defects. The book also stirred up and guided debates among politicians on trade and other economic policies. Even at the turn of the 20th century, Alfred Marshall managed to keep economics as "both a study of wealth and a branch of the study of man." It's time to reestablish the connection between economics and the ordinary business of life. . . . Knowledge will come only if economics can be reoriented to the study of man as he is and the economic system as it actually exists.

Although we prefer the term "Human Experience" to just "Man," Coase's point is more than well taken.

The co-creation paradigm bridges "human experience and economy" as it were, providing a way to put back human experiences into the economy in central fashion, and beyond to "individuated co-creation experiences in society at large" by expanding wealth-welfare-wellbeing in society as a whole. The convergence of private, public, and social sector co-creation on wealth-welfare-wellbeing is the subject of the next chapter.

9   WEALTH-WELFARE-WELLBEING AND PRIVATE-PUBLIC-SOCIAL SECTOR CO-CREATION

Central to the co-creation view of the enterprise as a nexus of engagement platforms is the "quality of life of human beings," regardless of the nature of the economic system in which enterprises operate. Enterprise, as organizing human agency, can exist and flourish under many different economic systems. Capitalism, for instance, is a whole economic system that has a particular perspective on value and its creation/appropriation. Further, within capitalism, there are different variants with different connotations of "capital"—for example, financial—with different emphases on stakeholders—for example, shareholder capitalism that emphasizes financiers, managerial capitalism that emphasizes managers, employee capitalism that emphasizes employees wherein labor and financial capital are not separated (as in some cooperatives)—and so on.[184] More generally, stakeholder capitalism encompasses recognition of different types of stakeholders who contribute "value creative capital" (including their creativity) and not just financial capital and who, in the co-creation view, must all be engaged jointly as human beings.

The key point is that all stakeholding individuals as co-creators who contribute to experience-based value creation, as we have discussed in this book, *exist equally, although they do not equally exist*; in other words, the primacy of different stakeholders may vary depending on the particular framing of an economic system. Most important, stakeholders must be recognized as human beings in all their complexity, whose ideas about value can go beyond just narrow conceptions of "left-brained self-interests," as it were.

As noted by Nobel laureate Amartya Sen, "Human beings are not merely means of production, but also the end of the exercise."[185] If the actual behavior of human beings is affected by ethical considerations, then welfare-economic considerations must be allowed to have some impact on actual behavior. And further, if wellbeing is considered to be the capability to achieve valuable human "functionings," then arguably wealth-welfare-wellbeing should be a basis of joint creation and evolution of value.

In this chapter, we discuss how joint capacity building in the virtual can be intensified through co-creating actions of stakeholders through private, public, and social sector platforms of engagements, to expand wealth-welfare-wellbeing in economy and society as a whole. This has the potential to balance the invisible hand of free markets with the visible hand of governments and civil society, together with stakeholder expectations of more responsible, responsive, and effective enterprises and coevolving better states of governance, infrastructure, development, and sustainability.

STAKEHOLDER CAPITALISM

The notion that individuals as stakeholders matter and must be conceptualized as being an integral part of the value creation process has gained hold in recent years. Stakeholders are increasingly seen as contributing intrinsically to value creation rather than as entities to be merely managed by the enterprise. Stakeholder theory has evolved from seeing the firm as a nexus of complete (and incomplete) contracts to firm-specific investments by stakeholders other than shareholders with a mediating hierarchy such as boards of directors; the firm, consequently, monitors aspects that are organized via the market, such as control rights, decision rights, and responsibilities.[186] Although advances have been made in going beyond the one-dimensional view of shareholder value (profit) maximization and seeing management as beholden to shareholders, a *"Homo economicus"* view of stakeholders still lingers.[187] Stakeholder theory has evolved further to a more human-oriented "*Homo sapiens*" view. The firm is now seen as not just an economic but also a moral and human institution, where businesses are populated by and have consequences for human beings in all their complexity; this opens up the firm's purpose to a plurality of values and a social view of value as much as an economic one: 'businesses should be the best we can create together, rather than avoiding the worst.'[188] This view opens up the possibility of additional value creation rather than a zero-sum game and of competition being emergent and value expanding rather than being determined by industry structures and mere appropriation of value. But institutional-centricity persists as opposed to seeing stakeholding individuals as their own active centers.

Evolving further still, stakeholders can themselves be seen as resource owners with different kinds of contributions in a network of value creation—that is, not just the firm.[189] Extended property rights are now based on different types of contributions (benefits and risks) to value creation by participants in a network. Knowledge assumes special importance as a value creation contribution. In other words, the role of the stakeholding individual in value creation also changes from passive to active, affecting enterprises and being affected by them, opening up various kinds of causalities in the value creation process.

The co-creation view evolves stakeholder capitalism even further with its individuated agency and experience-centric view of joint value creation, wherein agency presupposes and entails value(s), is co-creative, and is coevolutionary. Agency is distributed in (organizations as) assemblage systems whose "persons" include all human beings employed by a focal enterprise and its stakeholding individuals. All co-creators are in "entrepreneurial" assemblages of persons, artifacts, interfaces, and processes, whose strategic architecture creates outcomes of value together. Value creation is predicated on access to competence in the joint resource network (with stakeholders and enterprises still "owning" particular key resources). So when an engagement platform–based offering entails multiple enterprises as part of the resource network supporting the offering, "mutuality" considerations often apply, particularly in value creation instances where there is no common "shared" value ground among resource-providing value-generating parties. The co-creation view accommodates shared, mutual, and even "symbiotic" value creation (i.e., without "reciprocity" necessarily).

In the co-creation-based view, it is not necessary to make a distinction between value "creation" and "appropriation" as such, in that the latter typically refers to co-created "economic" outcomes of value desired by managers, shareholders, and other investors who contribute to the joint process of (multistakeholder ecosystem) value creation. Stakeholders, by contributing to value creation (through appropriate engagement platforms dealing with "economic" aspects of value outcomes), are already included in economic value appropriation—that is, those outcomes that pertain to economic value(s).

Co-creation is agnostic to the locus of ownership and whether capital is separated from labor in that it can be practiced in non-labor-owned and entity-distributed ownership models as much as labor-owned models. In all cases, co-creation hinges on *how* individuals go about jointly creating outcomes of value. A more fundamental question is that of the notion of "investment" beyond the "financier." For instance, are consumer communities that facilitate the spread of a brand "investing" in the enterprise and its success? What about suppliers who share their accumulated knowledge with the enterprise? The world needs an expanded definition of *owner*, which is traditionally taken to be the basis of residual claimant status. Defining an owner solely as someone who provides (and risks) financial capital underestimates the complex mosaic of roles in co-creation. All co-creators will increasingly demand to know more about the inner workings of enterprises because of the Web and associated structural shifts in society. Today, few industries and companies volunteer to disclose risks and debate them with co-creators. Yet, stakeholding individuals as co-creators are increasingly assigning a greater responsibility to managers to recognize and discuss with them elements of risk, including personal risk and societal risk. Co-creators must trust the enterprises with which they engage in co-creation.

EXPANDING WEALTH-WELFARE-WELLBEING
IN ECONOMIES AND SOCIETIES

Although co-creation is agnostic to the locus of ownership, it is instructive to examine the case of Mondragon in the Basque region of Spain, designed as a large-scale "cooperative employee ownership network model," which has successfully managed to avoid the pitfalls of "socializing losses while privatizing profits" in the traditional capitalistic separation of labor and financial capital. Mondragon offers valuable insights from the perspective of designing multistakeholder engagement models with less volatility in the regime of wealth-welfare-wellbeing. It has done so with a "solidarity values–based governance structure" that is inherently more conducive to embracing co-creation principles, balancing stakeholder risk-reward relationships and enterprise innovation potentials on the one hand, and growth and extreme income inequalities on the other.

Mondragon is a $15 billion+ ecosystem of over 100 cooperatives, which own among them 125 subsidiaries and integrate 24 other support entities, all of which are linked as members of a structured yet flexible entity, the Mondragon Corporation, whose governance structures are accountable to members.[190] Most Mondragon cooperatives are in the "Industry Area," which consists of 12 different divisions, including automotive chassis and power trains, industrial automation, components, construction, vertical transport equipment, household engineering and services, machine tools, industrial systems, and tooling and systems. There is a "Retail Area" that consists of a network of supermarkets, cash and carries, and other consumer goods chains with more than 2,600 outlets. The critical "Finance Area" entails three specific sets of activities: banking, social security, and insurance. A series of cooperative supporting institutions are part of the "Knowledge Area," entailing R&D, education and training (Mondragon University has over 3,600 students), and consulting. The "General Council" is an "operating" executive body that provides strategic coordination to members. Unlike senior management structures in traditional multinationals, General Council members cannot "impose" a decision on a division or member company, although they do have substantial influence. Member cooperatives are legally autonomous. The General Council engages in strategic planning, new technology and business development, economies of scale and other synergies, legal affairs, internationalization, and public and media relations, while coordinating the policies of the different divisions and cooperatives through an "Industrial Council." Two governance bodies oversee all activities of the Mondragon Corporation. One is the Cooperative Congress, consisting of 650 members, that meets annually to establish priority action strategies and that defines common network principles, and protocols and disciplines. The other is a 21-member Standing Committee with a president who presides over congressional meetings, which acts like a "board of directors" overseeing implementation of congressional policies and monitoring the performance of the Mondragon Corporation as a whole.

The autonomy of individual cooperatives and their employee-owned members "inverts" the traditional conglomerate. The highest governance authority in an individual cooperative is the General Assembly based on the principle of one member–one vote. The General Assembly meets at least once a year, votes on major issues, and elects an internal board of directors called the Governing Council. The Council, in turn, elects a president and appoints, and may remove, the CEO and must approve the CEO's choices for senior managers or unit directors, as well as the Management Council responsible for daily management. This governance structure is cascaded "bottom up" with the cooperatives electing Governing Councils of the Groups and Divisions, as well as the members of the Standing Committee. Thus, the latter is *not* elected directly from the Congress. (Divisional bodies have a governance structure similar to an individual cooperative.) The general membership also independently elects an Audit Committee to monitor the firm's finances and a Social Council that deals with a wide range of personnel affairs and participates in decisions on safety, pay scale, and social welfare. Thus, the organization is rooted in principles of economic democracy, where every single member can participate in informed decision making.

At Mondragon, there is solidarity through compressed differentials: the top salary is about 6 times that of the lowest-ranking employee; in some cases, it is 7 to 9 times. In the Industrial Area, about 3 percent of the workers earn between 3.5 and 6 times as much as the lowest employee, 30 percent earn 3.5 times, and 67 percent earn anywhere from the least to 2 times as much. Hence, extreme inequality is held in check. In general, executives earn less than those in comparable positions in traditional capitalist companies, reflecting non-material incentives at work. Historical context is important here. In 1943, following the Spanish Civil War with massive unemployment and a social crisis, a young priest in the Catholic Social Doctrine, Father Jose Maria Arizmendiarrieta, set up a vocational training school in the village of Mondragon with an emphasis on cooperation, the primacy of labor among the factors of production, and an emphasis on employability as much as employment. Father Arizmendiarrieta understood that knowledge "must be elaborated with [the worker]" and was opposed to the "top-down" philosophy of social relations. He saw the "cooperative" as being built on a foundation of education for economic progress toward a better social order. He called for human action: "Those who opt to make history and change the course of events themselves have an advantage over those who decide to wait passively for the results of the change." He believed in experiential learning: "Life is a fabric of relations between the past and the present, and the future is not built in a vacuum: experience, that of others as well as our own, is enriching, a positive resource." He urged his followers to channel their actions within the range of possibilities without losing sight of their social solidarity ideals. After trying with no success to apply the priest's teachings at places where they had found employment, 5 of his 11 students started a new company in 1956, Ulgor (now Fagor Appliances), which manufactured simple paraffin cookers and heaters. Funds to start the company were donated by the local townspeople, and the business began with 24 worker-members. Ulgor initiated an evolutionary process of economic and social transformation that continues to this day. In doing so, the worker-members refrained from admonishing those who failed to support the cooperative movement. In fact, Father Arizmendiarrieta simultaneously encouraged and sought to secure collaboration with private business and government, which has persisted ever since. His vision was to develop an economy that served the people, not the other way around.

Since it was founded, Mondragon has emphasized entrepreneurship and constantly seeks innovation and growth, which is typically not the case in many worker-managed, self-governed entities (especially when political maneuverings supplant economic and social considerations). Some key aspects must be considered here. First, there is profit pooling among cooperatives at the divisional level, ranging from 15 to 40 percent of pretax profits, determined by the division's Governing Council, depending on how "integrated" the division is both in terms of shared product/markets and collaborative relationships over the years. In the meetings that determine profit pooling, managers whose co-ops are doing poorly are under intense pressure to improve performance, and a cooperative must defend and document the measure it is taking to address problems, with the divisional Governing Council providing regular scrutinizing oversight. As noted by José Luis Lafuente and Fred Freundlich, a key principle is "With autonomy, comes responsibility," and mitigation of "free riding" as such. Cooperatives understand the "mutuality of help," as almost every cooperative has had more or less serious problems at one point or another and has been assisted, and even saved, by fellow cooperatives.[191]

By law, 10 percent of the profits is allocated for education and a pro-cooperative fund, and 20 percent is placed in a reserve fund. The General Assembly decides how to distribute the remaining 70 percent of the profits after taxes, with a common practice being to allocate 50 percent to workers as capital. One of the central funds is a venture capital fund, which has been key to making investments in manufacturing expansion overseas, for instance, and investments needed for growth and competitiveness. Another central fund supports a dozen technology R&D centers that employ over 700 researchers, the development of Mondragon University, and comprehensive education and training that consists of technical, social, and business courses.

The workers cannot take out their individual profits, which are based on pay scale (there are no tradeable shares), until they retire or leave the company. Rather, the funds remain in an interest-bearing account and are managed as part of Mondragon's own banking system (Caja Laboral), which in turn provides access to capital, especially to small and medium-sized enterprises in the region and does not necessarily favor Mondragon cooperatives. Caja Laboral also attracts the savings of residents in the region. Besides financing the cooperatives, it promotes entrepreneurship through the central funds it manages. The Employment Assistance Fund finances unemployment benefits for members who lose their jobs. In the middle of the economic crisis that occurred between 2008 and 2009, the number of jobs fell by 8.3 percent, though most of these jobs were held by nonmembers (there is an upper limit of 20 percent of jobs that can belong to nonmembers). During the same period, the number of members of cooperatives rose by 6.1 percent, suggesting increased job security.

One of the remarkable features of the engagement design at Mondragon is that decisions on restructuring and the search for solutions are always made in assemblies and in participatory, deliberative, and collaborative democracy fashion. For instance, in the mid-1990s, 31 percent of workers were nonmembers, so the company decided to enact the 20 percent limit. As Mondragon has engaged in "multilocalization" globally, it is experimenting with ways of integrating overseas nonmembers in better fashion and providing pathways to membership through short-term contracts as it has done in Spain. Mondragon workers also engage in open intellectual debate on competencies and values. This organizational culture is strongly connected to its educational base and continues in other social cultural spaces outside work, reinforcing its foundation to continue to evolve and transform its economy, society, and culture, in deference to its founder, Father Arizmendiarrieta. The priest's ethical and social principles were very influential in a thorough restructuring in grassroots democratic fashion after his death, and the coevolution of its enterprise, economic, and social organization continues in co-creative engagement fashion.

Consider a typical situation when one of the cooperatives fell on hard times in a downturn. After a joint review of options and three days of meetings, the worker-owners agreed that 20 percent of the workforce would leave their jobs for a year, during which they would continue to receive 80 percent of their pay and, if they so desired, free training to learn other types of work. This group would be chosen by lottery, and if the cooperative was still in trouble a year later, the first group would return to work and another group would take a year off. Or consider a self-managed project team in Soraluce, a world leader in milling machine tool manufacturing. When an order arrives, a cross-sectional project team is formed from manufacturing and assembly workers, engineers, and sales staff. This team has full P&L responsibility from the creation of the team to onsite installation at the client site through a complex 6- to 18-month process, with the team meeting frequently to make decisions on improving any aspect of the product or process. In Fagor Home Appliances, for instance, production is organized as "minicompanies," each fully autonomous in a particular plant area associated with a specific production process. Its responsibilities include housekeeping, equipment maintenance, product quality, on-time delivery, and productivity (volume and cost). Each group of 15 to 20 employee-owners has daily and weekly meetings to follow its progress in terms of performance indicators it sets for itself and to solve problems as they arise. The traditional "supervisor" role disappears; rather, each "self-managed" team selects one person to serve as lead for a certain period of time, so everyone in the group gets that position eventually. The lead and the team work together to establish their own training needs to ensure that, over time, all team members are qualified to work in any function in the minicompany.

Enterprise innovation potentials are harnessed that include operational innovation, product-service innovation, strategic innovation, and management innovation. For instance, 16 Mondragon cooperatives co-created a new shared organization, Ategi, to achieve volume purchasing advantages, which puts together the purchasing needs for utilities and other products/services (computers, phone/Internet, etc.), selects and negotiates with suppliers, and delivers the finished purchasing agreement to the co-op member. Mondragon also fosters cross-unit collaboration to take advantage of new strategic opportunities. For instance, consider a "Sustainable Mobility" project that initially involved 35 engineers, drawn from several automotive cooperatives, who worked 18 months to produce an electric car prototype and contributed to several other "green" transportation initiatives. Currently, 130 researchers and engineers from various cooperatives are working on the development of products linked to the electric car, and plans call for a $15 million+ investment to develop these programs further in the short term. Further, conventional firms can become joint venture partners. For instance, Mondragon recently founded a new company, Smart Health Services (SHS), for managing integrated purchasing and supply logistics for health centers. This is a new type of business and is a joint venture promoted by the Mondragon Health cooperative platform, which holds 51 percent of its shares, and another Mondragon co-operative, LKS Consultancy, whose capital stake is 9 percent. Kudea, an independent external firm, which has expertise in the management of purchasing and general contracting processes in the private health care sector, is also a stakeholder, capitalizing 40 percent of SHS.

In summary, Mondragon balances local autonomy with joint capacity building in the common interest through decentralized decision making and distributed leadership. This is combined with collaborative innovation and coordinated intercooperation of inputs and profits, reaping the benefits of scale, accessing resources, and connecting with opportunities globally. At the same time, an owner-membership core that focuses on regional employment and employability is preserved, and productivity and efficiency are enhanced through worker engagement, with an eye on education and skills development for the future workforce.

Thus, the Mondragon ecosystem boosts economic and social growth, while enhancing wealth-welfare-wellbeing in equitable win more–win more fashion. While we do not imply that all the principles of co-creation as expounded in this book are practiced fully in Mondragon or that further value expansion is not possible, the Mondragon example is exemplary in illustrating a deeper, wider model of stakeholder capitalism and the need to explore the space of convergence of private, public, and social sector enterprises centered on the wealth-welfare-wellbeing of individuals and their personal and social experiences and the actualization of human potential.

PRIVATE-PUBLIC-SOCIAL SECTOR CO-CREATION

There is growing awareness that no enterprise can act alone or achieve success alone. Rather, all enterprises are inextricably linked together in an interdependent, globally networked world of open and social resources of stakeholders on the one hand and enterprises' own extended networks on the other. By harnessing collaborative innovation potentials across the private, public, and social sectors, in mutually interdependent ecosystems, enterprises can jointly build co-creative capacities in terms of *governance, infrastructure, development,* and *sustainability,* as discussed next.

Governance

Economic governance consists of the processes that support economic activity by protecting property rights, enforcing contracts, and taking collective action to provide an appropriate physical and organizational infrastructure.[192] Private institutions can outperform the state's legal system in obtaining and interpreting relevant information and imposing social sanctions on the violators of norms. But private institutions are often limited in size; as economic activity expands, a transition toward more formal institutions is usually observed. The purpose of institutions can be protection of property rights against theft and usurpation, enforcement of voluntary contracts, provision of physical and regulatory infrastructure to facilitate economic activity, or avoidance of serious cleavages or alienation that threaten the cohesion of the society itself. The nature of institutions could be formal in enacting and enforcing state laws, institutions of private ordering that function under the umbrella of state law, private for-profit institutions that provide information and enforcement, and self-enforcement within social or ethnic groups and networks.

Governance issues include how major policy decisions are made, how various stakeholders can influence the process, who is held accountable for performance, and what performance standards are applied.[193] It is about management of relationships among participating stakeholders and cultivating relationships of a wider web of constituencies about purpose and accountability.

Consider India's banking and financial systems, which benefited from a strong regulatory framework, that took shape in the early 1990s through the Securities and Exchange Board of India (SEBI)—the equivalent of the U.S. Securities and Exchange Commission. Former SEBI director Pratip Kar described how SEBI developed its framework for governance and regulation. Its work offers an important lesson in public-private engagement and how to govern stakeholders in coshaping and coevolving regulatory capacities.[194] As Kar noted, when SEBI engaged its stakeholders, it was not only prior to the advent of Web-based technologies, but the protagonists did not even realize that they were actually working on governance in a co-creative manner. It just seemed natural and the only logical way forward. Stretch goals, constraints, pressure for accountability, and urgency formed a potent mix for jointly creating regulatory governance capacities.

SEBI sought to install a new governance framework that would anticipate and be responsive to the needs of the Indian economy, which at that time experienced a sweeping and historic reformation. In some places, regulations existed but needed redesigning; in other places, a new regulatory design had to be crafted. Change threatens the status quo, of course, and the Indian stock market in 1992 was no exception. SEBI's first step was to identify the stakeholders of the regulatory architecture, who included:

- investors, because they invest their savings in stocks to make money;

- firms, because they need capital for growth;

- intermediaries, because as agents or service providers they arrange or facilitate securities transactions between buyers and sellers;

- institutions like the stock exchanges to provide the marketplace;

- regulators of all parts of the financial market (because money is fungible and flows seamlessly between markets in a liberalized economy, meaning that policies in one sector have an impact on other financial markets); and

- governmental entities, because they have to manage the economy, and the stock market is central to it.

Next, SEBI identified potential supporters among the stakeholders and recognized possible pockets of resistance. It quickly recognized the investor community as its primary constituency; investors are the bedrock of financial markets, and investor protection was the raison d'être of SEBI's existence. The regulatory architecture had to protect investors' rights, understand their problems, address their grievances, and sustain their confidence in the market. SEBI knew that its regulatory changes would not automatically enlist the support of the other stakeholders; for example, an elaborate disclosure requirement would be resisted by firms, and a strict compliance and risk-management regimen would be opposed by intermediaries, but both of these would serve the interest of investors.

SEBI's third step was to make the principal stakeholders a part of the change process and co-create the new regulatory architecture with them.

Excessive regulation would lead to regulatory anarchy, as the market would look for opportunities for regulatory arbitrage. But if the regulator and the regulated were a part of the same reference framework, it would be possible to create a mutually satisfying regulatory architecture that would maximize economic value.

SEBI then established engagement platforms on which the regulator and the stakeholders could exchange ideas. The Indian securities market had very few trappings of a modern securities market, such as electronic markets, trading systems, settlement cycles, risk management systems, regulations for takeovers, or insider trading regulations. The stakes were high for SEBI. It had to get things right the first time; failures would be expensive and could turn away domestic and international investors, disillusion firms that issue securities, and dishearten intermediaries.

Even before SEBI gained statutory powers in 1992, it used the media to reach out to investors and learn about their grievances against security market transactions involving listed companies, brokers, or other intermediaries. They heard only a few complaints in the first few weeks of the media campaign, but the number of investors writing to SEBI picked up in later months. SEBI began to publish the names of companies and intermediaries against which complaints had been files and highlighted the top ten offenders. This initiative helped SEBI understand the nature of investor problems and what needed to be mended, which helped SEBI prioritize its agenda and allowed investors to express their concerns and problems.

Before SEBI was formed, a few investor NGOs had looked after investor grievances, sometimes using moral persuasion and sometimes legal action on behalf of investors. Once SEBI became a statutory body, it began to formally recognize these investor associations across the country (using strict eligibility criteria). SEBI held periodic meetings with these groups, sometimes at their request and sometimes at the request of SEBI. These live meetings provided another platform for interaction with investors.

The stock exchanges were themselves a live platform. SEBI used the exchanges to organize meetings not only with brokers but also with issuers, investors, and other intermediaries. India's Chambers of Commerce and Industries were another platform, which helped SEBI and industry to understand each other's viewpoints.

Finally, advisory committees set up by SEBI for consultation on regulatory policy interventions became the most interactive and powerful engagement platforms. These committees consisted of representatives of all stakeholders in the regulatory process, including the stock exchanges, investor associations, intermediaries, mutual funds, listed firms, academics and other experts, professional bodies, fellow regulators, and government representatives. The advisory committees discussed problems in the market, new areas of development, market needs, and areas in which regulatory policy intervention was required or an existing policy needed to be changed. SEBI officials attended the advisory committee meetings only to give clarifications if requested by committee members, or to help prepare minutes and reports of the committee, but not to give SEBI's views on issues. Any committee member was free to place any agenda item for discussion, as is SEBI.

Today, SEBI places advisory committee reports on its public website and circulates them to all the stakeholders across the country, requesting feedback within shorter timeframes. SEBI sometimes meets with the stakeholder groups to discuss draft reports. Often some of the stakeholder groups will hold their own meetings and invite SEBI. On occasion, SEBI facilitates meetings between the stakeholder groups and the advisory committee concerned. SEBI collates the views from these meetings and sends notes back to the advisory committee to prepare a final report. This process enables the SEBI board to make decisions based on inputs from all stakeholders, which ensures that the final policy announced by SEBI minimizes surprises to the market. Many of SEBI's major public policy decisions have been adopted through this engagement process, including policies on takeover regulations, framing the integrated risk management system for the securities market, corporate governance norms, a change in governance structure of the stock exchanges, a policy of dematerialization of securities and electronic share transfer, a change in settlement cycles from account period to rolling settlement, and the introduction of derivatives trading.

Thus, SEBI used multiple platforms to frame the governance for securities market development. However, it is important to keep in mind that SEBI has had its ups and downs. Further, we do not imply that all the platforms we discussed were proactively designed using co-creation engagement principles as we have discussed in this book. Having said that, the intent at that time was certainly one of implicit, if not explicit, co-creation. As we discussed in Chapter 3, one has to pay constant attention to the DART principles of co-creation experience configuration and constantly make adjustments to continuously create experience-based outcomes of value together. The strength of co-creation governance stems from ideas and initiatives that emanate from the intersection of all stakeholder interests, recognizing different perspectives, mixing diverse interests, and blending and synthesizing them to gain broad consensus, while paying attention to stakeholders' co-creation experiences. Indeed, corporate scandals, like India's Satyam accounting debacle in 2008–2009, have only reinforced the need for more intense and broader co-creation, together with the private and social sectors, and beyond the regulatory architecture itself. It was shareholder activism coupled with media and public scrutiny that brought this debacle into the open.

The dilemma of governance in networks and communities, as enterprises deal with a large number of stakeholders from suppliers and partners to customers and citizens, involves the growing complexity of managing a network of relationships with multiple modes of collaboration and coping with rapid changes in environments. And the needs, interests, and goals all of these stakeholder groups are continually evolving. Governance based on protocols and disciplines is therefore needed in addition to structures and processes. This involves enabling a shared governance agenda that provides a framework for intentional and creative engagements; rules for interdependencies and collaborative engagements among agents; protection of intellectual property along with a clear basis for agents to act independently; a set of shared values and beliefs that are clearly defined and consistently practiced; a shared view of ecosystem evolution; forums for debating, discussing, and establishing bottom-up priorities; a shared vocabulary; and even a few "nonnegotiables," without which empowerment is not possible. While effective governance entails a judicious mixture of formal structures, processes, and disciplines and protocols, jointly framing governance must itself involve a co-creative process.

Infrastructure

Information infrastructure can turbocharge the co-creative capacities of the technological, social, and organizational architectures of enterprises. At the most general level, however, infrastructure describes the underlying foundation of the physical and social facilities of the ecosystem—both the physical systems and the technologies.[195] Infrastructure consists of the structural assets of the built environment and its physical support networks, and it includes a great deal of artifacts. In the broadest sense, then, infrastructure is everything in the built environment that is distinct from natural environments. The foundational primacy of physical infrastructure affords it a rather unique status. For instance, a city's bridges, roads, and water system are not described simply as important physical artifacts but as investments in the city building process. The history of successful infrastructure investment is less about the direct impact of technology and more about the interaction between technology and society. The returns on investments are measured in terms of a society's economy, health, and social wellbeing. Infrastructure is thus a critical determinant of co-creative capacities of an ecosystem of capabilities.

For instance, following its campaign for a Smarter Planet, IBM convened a series of conversations on how to build "smarter cities," exploring how progressive cities are modernizing and spurring economic development. The discussions sparked new ideas and meaningful actions across the entire ecosystem stakeholders of a city—from mayors, to CEOs of private companies, to citizens. Conversations initiated at the Smarter Cities events have led to partnerships like the one formed with Dubuque, Iowa, in 2009, to make it the first "smarter" sustainable American city and an international model of sustainability for communities of fewer than 200,000 residents. Similar IBM initiatives include smart energy systems, more efficient transportation and decongestion systems, and analytics for public safety and data visualization. As noted by ex-IBM CEO Samuel J. Palmisano, "Smarter infrastructure has measurably greater economic and societal leverage than traditional infrastructure."

With over 50 percent of the world's population now living in cities and this figure projected to grow to more than 70 percent by 2050, the need for adaptive and responsive infrastructure is paramount to the capacity, prosperity, livability, and sustainability of our future connected cities. The building of smart infrastructures allows cities to intelligently utilize technology to adapt to their environment, and it plays a central role in the competitiveness of cities and their capacity to grow and support sustainable living. As part of the Dublin collaboration on Sustainable Connected Cities, Intel Labs Europe, Dublin City Council and Trinity College Dublin have collaborated on a variety of programs, including City Watch and City Sensing. As Martin Curley, vice president of Intel Labs Europe, notes:

The innovations delivered through the quadruple helix of interaction between knowledge institutions, industry, government, and civil society will help set Dublin apart and propel it on its path to become a truly sustainable city. Central to our collaboration will be the engagement of citizens and comprehension of the challenges they face living within a modern city. As innovative solutions are developed and validated, they will be used to form design patterns, which can be exported and replicated to solve similar issues facing cities and communities throughout the world.[196]

The City Sensing and City Watch programs combine the use of fixed and mobile sensors to create a real-time picture of what happens within the modern urban city environment—for example, providing information on flooding that disrupted its citizens' lives. The mobile sensing component is enabled by a participatory sensing application for use on smartphones and mobile devices, allowing citizens to participate in developing technological innovations that will improve their environment, systems, and local services. The smart infrastructure allows the city manager to see when a citizen reports a flooded drain and matches this with a drain sensor and weather data to create alerts. This allows the council to remotely take action such as closing roads and dispatching cleanup teams. The experimental nature of this new value creation relies on the citizen as a co-creator in the innovation process, and information on what is successful and what isn't can be gathered quickly, which makes finding solutions through the innovation ecosystem faster and more successful.[197]

Airports, like cities, also require a common open operating system that allows for the sharing of data between artifacts and presenting that data as information in the right way and on the right devices to benefit and engage citizens.[198] For instance, the PlanIT UrbanOS is an open standards software platform that provides a connectivity infrastructure that facilitates the interactions among people, places, and things and accelerates the development and deployment of smart urban technology–enabled engagement platforms. The London City Airport, in collaboration with Living PlanIT, TSB (the United Kingdom's innovation agency), Milligan (real estate developer), Cisco, Hitachi, IBM, Philips, SITA, SITC, and Springboard, envision these new platforms as essential in measuring and improving flights and engaging frequent flyers in particular. This active, integrated, and intelligent relationship management system enables and connects more closely with passenger co-creation experiences, while combining airport operations, baggage handling, retail, food and beverages, foreign exchange, and security through a single infrastructure.

The European Union Open Innovation Strategy and Policy Group unites industrial groups, academia, and private users to support policies for Open Innovation at the European Commission. The Group is developing co-creative innovation ecosystem models based on collaborative engagement among all participating enterprises and actors in economy and society, spanning organizational boundaries and going beyond normal licensing and collaboration approaches to create a circle of sustainable growth that will lead to new services, improved quality of life, and more jobs.

Infrastructure networks, in addition to blending the social and technical, also operate to continually transform the natural into the cultural.[199] Urban infrastructures cannot be reduced to a set of technical objects, but instead need to be seen as complex assemblages that link human, nonhuman, and natural agencies across territories and communities. Paradoxically, making space for the mobility and flow of some stakeholders might also mean erecting obstructions and barriers for some others. In fact, mobility and circulation of energy, transport, communications, or water across territories imply construction, operation, and maintenance of material assemblages immobilized across space. When the former serve the interests of certain powerful stakeholders, whereas the latter impose externalities on the less powerful, infrastructure networks become politically charged. We get a better view of this when we recognize infrastructures as complex assemblages instead of merely technical constructs for engineers. However, in the past, we have rarely defined sites in a way that would permit joint exploration of organizational or network architecture.[200] The emerging alternative position operates from the premise that the real power lies within the relationships among multiple distributed sites that are both collectively and individually adjustable. Further, the dynamic achievement of a functioning energy, communications, water, or transport network requires constant effort to maintain the functioning system. Despite occasional veneers of permanence, closure, and stability, infrastructure architectures are always precarious achievements. The links between nodes do not last by themselves. They need co-creative management systems, which is yet another reason for building co-creative capacities jointly.

Development

Thanks to the World Wide Web, social media, and advances in mobile and interactive communications and information technologies, networked individuals around the globe are no longer passive and docile recipients of dispensed instructions and development assistance. They are active participants and collaborators in the value creation process and co-creators of solutions with a wide range of private, public, and social sector enterprises. On their part, enterprises are learning how to engage external and internal stakeholders and to harness their personal, peer-to-peer, and collective knowledge, creativity, and expertise for the purpose of engendering development together.

Development, as Nobel laureate Amartya Sen has argued, is about capabilities to engage with freedom's processes and opportunities.[201] This requires understanding the direct relevance of human capabilities to people's wellbeing and freedom and its role in influencing social change and economic production. Development refers, ultimately, to improvements in the conditions of life for people experiencing relative capability deprivation.

Development concerns trajectories of change, encompassing movement from circumstances of relative hardship and deprivation toward qualitatively improved conditions of life.[202] Whether development is pursued through interventions by external agents, such as development assistance agencies, or through initiatives of the "targeted" communities themselves, it is a process that must involve "engagement" of social actors. Indeed, in many developmental efforts, targeting implies a one-sided process, tending to be elitist, unaccountable (except to donors), and by definition distant from those they seek to help, no matter how well meaning or progressive the efforts may be. Often recipients end up being just that: on the receiving end of control rather than being engaged. Effective development is increasingly understood as a set of processes that reflect underlying social dynamics of the territories in which it takes place.

For a wider framing of capacity building, we must turn to a social ontology in which the structure of systems enables agency.[203] Structural, political, and resource obstacles are sometimes more decisive than absence of capacity in how communities develop. One cannot ignore the vital understanding that empowerment requires power over resources, power over relationships, power over information, and knowledge and power over decision making. Experts brought in from outside to build capacity tend to overlook that communities might already possess capacities. They also miss opportunities to learn from the very same communities in their zeal to engineer ways to address capacity shortages.

Capacity development has typically prioritized problems, "deficits," and strategies at the local level, since training for, measuring, and tracking capacity development tend to be manageable at that level. A perspective that privileges the local, however, comes with the risk of ignoring the diversity of the community itself, as well as opportunities to leverage ideas and solutions from communities outside the local. Note that community capacity is rooted in the meshwork of human capital, social capital, and organizational resources that is resident within and outside of that community, which can be leveraged to develop solutions to collective issues and thereby maintain and enhance the wellbeing of that community.[204] Community capacity can be tapped by various forms of social agency, ranging from individuals through organizations to civic networks, to obtain desirable community conditions and improve sustainability of community capacity itself.

There are many successful development initiatives that have been based on open, participatory, and collaborative engagement. For instance, in April 2011, the World Bank announced the winners of the first Apps for Development competition, which sought innovative technological solutions to development challenges related to the Millennium Development Goals (MDG). The competition was part of the World Bank's Open Data Initiative, which has made its catalog of development data available to anybody, anywhere in the world. The top winners include an application to visualize development indicators through maps and charts, a Web-based tool to measure the impact of global events on progress on the MDG, and an interactive application that explores human development. The popular choice award, determined by online public voting, is an application that takes data from the World Bank databases on a randomly selected topic and generates comments supported by pictures, videos, and maps to raise public consciousness about the MDGs. The World Bank's Development Marketplace for turning Ideas into Action is another example, "stepping up the pace of innovation to catalyze change in development" as noted by World Bank Institute vice president Sanjay Pradhan, as it rapidly expands the deployment of engagement tools on its online platform.[205]

The concept of enabling hundreds of exchanges—whether south-south, north-south, south-north (or even north-north following the development impacts of the Great Recession of 2008)—as countries seek to learn from one another to address global challenges like poverty and disease, climate change and environmental issues, and wars is indeed promising. These are just a few of the initiatives involving stakeholder engagement. They all involve some kind of platform (whether live meetings or online, or a combination of the two) where interactions take place. The following questions, however, must be asked:

- What are the engagement experiences of participants?

- What mechanisms exist for people to share their experiences?

- Can we (re)design the platforms and the environments they afford in which engagement happens by tapping into insights gained from participants' experiences?

- Can we open up the platform design process?

Across a wide range of issues from micro-credit to water management to education or minority rights, capacity makes a difference and develops in direct engagement with real-world problems and outcomes. However, it is not an input but rather the expression of people's collective ability to act and obtain outcomes in a domain, as well as the sustainability and evolvability thereof. As such, it corresponds to a measure of vitality and effective functioning in a human system. Because capacity is a living and lived phenomenon and about real-life experiences, it is both relational and intrinsic. Every living system has interactions with its environment, affecting and being affected by it to coevolve with other elements in the ecosystem in which it operates.

Economic development is the process through which economies are transformed from those where people have limited resources and choices to those where they have much greater resources and choices.[206] Given their potential role in promoting growth or employment, micro-entrepreneurs, managers of competitive firms, and investors are seen as critical catalysts of development. Further, many development economists assumed economic inequality for several years, given the acceptance of the so-called Kuznets curve, according to which there is a sharp rise in inequality during early phases of industrialized economic growth, followed by a subsequent decline thereafter.[207] There is now growing recognition that extreme income concentrations are not conducive to sustainable patterns of growth. An important component of the current economic development paradigm is much greater recognition of active participation of individuals, which, together with the discipline of competitive-like markets from a growth standpoint, provides checks and balances that limit predatory economic behavior and rising income inequalities. In addition to the achievement of higher incomes, development is now seen as intentions to reduce poverty, improve health and nutrition, prolong life expectancy, and afford opportunities for education.

Consider an example of mutual value creation in the cross-sector partnership between Swiss Re and Oxfam on Horn of Africa Risk Transfer for Adaptation (HARITA).[208] Swiss Re is a reinsurance company that was interested in addressing climate change through its corporate social responsibility arm. However, it was also a strategic move because climate change affects weather patterns, which in turn affect the insured products in their portfolio (e.g., flood, hurricane, crops). Oxfam is one NGO whose mission is to "create lasting solutions to poverty, hunger, and social injustice." Together, they created a framework for micro-insurance for crop farmers in Ethiopia. However, this was not something they could do alone. In addition to partnering with the government, they also partnered with other NGOs, which in turn had more direct relationships with the farmers. Community members, elected by their peers were instrumental to the design team in charge of designing the product and the evolution of it. In fact, one of the key innovation ideas came from a farmer: to allow the poorest farmers to pay for insurance premiums with labor, their only asset. Other partners also provided key inputs to the platform in order to develop a holistic risk management framework. HARITA had to tap into the Ethiopian government's program, which allowed citizens to earn cash or food in exchange for working on community infrastructure projects and, now, premiums. Another critical input was weather data that would form the basis for the index insurance and payouts. One of the partners trained a group of local farmers to collect the necessary weather data to become a reliable local source of information. HARITA evolved into an ecosystem of enterprises and platforms.

The private sector (i.e., Swiss Re and the local insurance company) benefited because it was learning about how to create and sell a viable product to the crop farmers, a market to which they have never had access before. By involving farmers in the design of the project, they were also able to come up with a solution that would be inclusive of even the poorest farmers—with future opportunities to grow in this market with other types of insurance, such as health. At least for Swiss Re, HARITA also helps them address the issue of climate change because it empowers farmers to try farming methods that will generate higher yields or be more sustainable.

There are also social benefits from this project. Insurance shifts the risk to an entity that can handle it better—something that the very poor desperately need but do not usually have access to. Farmers are usually very risk averse because they are afraid that trying something new could completely ruin a good crop that they need that year and possibly the next year to sustain them and their families. Crop insurance helps smooth out those very bad years, allowing farmers some freedom to take some smart-risk investments. Society as a whole benefits because these investments may result in higher yields or make land more arable, resulting in increased food production. Because there is more wealth in the community, the more they can spend on other important areas and, the sooner they can lift the community out of poverty. While programs like health, sanitation, and education are generally viewed as public goods and should be governments' responsibilities, governments often do not have the resources or the ability to tackle them, so creating an environment that is favorable toward the private sector, who may be interested in supporting these issues, is critical.

NGOs also benefit from this co-creative partnership because they are taken seriously as an important partner with a for-profit firm. Without NGO involvement, it would have been difficult, if not impossible, for Swiss Re to have created and sold a viable product in Ethiopia. Oxfam is able to work on a sustainable solution that is directly related to its mission of fighting hunger and poverty. In general, an NGO can also benefit in cross-sector partnerships because it does not have to find external funding for the project, which makes it more sustainable, while also developing skills it can use on other projects.[209]

It is not clear in scaling up this solution that it will continue to be a co-creative process. Because many of the stakeholders involved are local to the specific region in Ethiopia, Oxfam and Swiss Re would have to find new partners that work with the farmers on the ground. While Oxfam and Swiss Re may originally have conceived HARITA, it is the network of in-teractions and the linkability of engagement platforms across enterprises, which has co-creative potential, especially in the extension of services. The original nodal entities need not be the ones that continue to engage the farmers in co-creation. Potential solutions would likely have to con-tinue to engage NGOs that stay in the field. Through them, Swiss Re and Oxfam could learn what issues are developing that need to be addressed before they grow into bigger problems. NGOs could be incentivized to continue to be local access entities because they see the on-the-ground benefits the project has on the community. Depending on the level of cell phone usage in the area, HARITA can also continue to engage with the farmers using mobile platform–enabled solutions. For example, NGOs can bring in microfinance institutions that can provide funding for the smart-risk investments that farmers would now be more likely to make. Other

NGOs work on solutions for farmers that can be incorporated. While the network incurs some coordination costs, it is a benefit to the farmers because it limits the number of interactions they must have with different parties. Also, the co-creative process that led to the insurance scheme in the Ethiopian community may not work for other communities. For example, because the national government already had a program that allowed people to do community infrastructure projects to earn cash or food, they were able to incorporate that element in order to be inclusive of even the poorest farmers. To develop the capabilities to build these co-creative insurance initiatives in other communities and countries, Oxfam and Swiss Re would need to identify the critical elements that would serve as the basis of their new engagement platforms to enhance economic and societal development moving forward.

Systemic co-creation, then, has the power to transform relationships and social realities and enhance the quality of our human experiences. It can even widen the current structural limitations of funding for development—not only by thinking out of the box but by transforming the box itself—for example, enabling people from the grassroots groups not to have to depend solely on large donor agencies or even someone else's agenda. On the supply side, donors could have more freedom to choose from a network of capable organizations with a wealth of local knowledge and experience in development at the grassroots level. Ultimately, enhancing such freedom-centric development through co-creation thinking would enable individuals and institutions to converge on the collective realization of human potential and enhance the growth, productivity, and resilience of the ecosystems in which we live and the quality of people's lives.

Sustainability
Social responsibility in business has gained momentum, and private sector enterprises are playing a more active role in tackling economic development, environmental protection, and other social issues. This movement has required many private sector enterprises to work more closely with governmental organizations, nonprofits, civic groups, and consumers. An *Economist* survey noted that while "doing well by doing good" has become a fashionable mantra, few large companies can afford to ignore

corporate social responsibility (CSR). The survey concluded that done well, CSR "is not some separate activity that companies do on the side, a corner of corporate life reserved for virtue: it is just good business."[210] While co-creation can be a means for ensuring that private sector enterprises do social responsibility right, it is more than that. Co-creation takes CSR a significant step forward because all stakeholders have a say in and benefit from outcomes. Co-creation increases the social legitimacy of all enterprises, while simultaneously expanding enterprise value. Further, the co-creation-based view goes beyond CSR to transform the very enterprise of enterprise—by bringing together various stakeholders in enterprise capability ecosystems to enhance co-creative capacities. By expanding the stakeholder base of network value, co-creation taps into the knowledge of participants in the social ecosystem to create a freer flow of information, engage people more wholeheartedly, and enable richer, fuller stakeholder interactions—for example, donors who can provide not only financial capital to charities but also education and business expertise. The human experience becomes not only more meaningful for everybody, but in the process, co-creative capacities of agency are deepened, making them more sustainable.

Consider the stated corporate vision of ABB, the Switzerland-based leader in power and automation technologies: to help its customers use electrical power more efficiently and increase industrial productivity while lowering their environmental impact. ABB seeks to balance economic success with environmental stewardship, to the benefit of all its stakeholders. Like many other global organizations, ABB uses the guidelines of the Global Reporting Initiative, an independent organization that developed a sustainability reporting framework, in tracking and disclosing its sustainability initiatives and indicators.[211] As noted by Michel Demaré, CFO of ABB, "We want our employees to share a broader vision of the company's role in society, our responsibilities, and accountabilities to all stakeholders—not only to investors and customers, but also to their colleagues and local communities."[212]

This goal took shape in the desert areas of Rajasthan in northwest India, where ABB's Indian unit created an "Access to Electricity" initiative for several villages and households that were not connected to the power grid. The dwellings there are very scattered, and power requirements are low. But these desert areas have an average of 325 sunny days each year. ABB recognized that Rajasthan presented a unique opportunity for electricity generation through solar photovoltaic (SPV) panels, which convert solar energy into electricity stored in a battery bank.

With the help of an Indian NGO, ABB gained access to village members, including the village council, and provided them with a pilot SPV unit. The company was aware that villagers would have to view the SPVs as affordable enablers of income generation in order to be convinced of their value, and the company was also sensitive to the fact that villagers would want to be involved in the process of formulating the program, according to S. Karun, head of Sustainability for ABB India.

Through discussions with villagers, ABB understood they would be willing to make a one-off investment of about $125 toward the system (a third of the SPV lighting system price). The concept was to get them to experience how electricity would improve their lives and discover how it could help them earn more money. The average annual income of a family in these villages is around Rs 30,000 (about $750). A lighting system comprising a small (40WP) SPV panel, a low-maintenance 12V battery, a charge controller, and three compact fluorescent lamps would cost about Rs. 15,000 (around $375) per system, and it could run household appliances.

ABB entered into a private-public partnership with the government of Rajasthan, agreeing that the SPVs would be paid for in three equal parts: by the home owner, the government's Rajasthan Renewable Energy Corporation, and ABB. The company engaged villagers, NGO members, the state government, the supplier of the SPV systems, and a local organization for installation and maintenance of the systems in crafting the program. From 2006 to 2008, ABB deployed the system to approximately 1,100 households, touching about 6,000 people in seven villages in Rajasthan's interior.

The program has reaped substantial rewards for all parties. The main sources of income in the villages have traditionally been carpet weaving, animal husbandry, carpentry, basket weaving, shoemaking, and tailoring, and villagers were forced to stop working at sunset. Electrification has allowed them to work longer hours and increase their output. They can also take orders more easily through cell phones that the electricity has made available. The program has spawned a new business in the villages: the maintenance and repair of SPVs. ABB has trained SPV service technicians and now offers annual maintenance contracts at the nominal cost of less than a dollar a month.

Giving villagers a financial stake in the SPV units is what makes the program sustainable. When he visited one of these remote villages, Adam Roscoe, head of Sustainability for ABB Group, commented, "In [ABB's] other Access to Electricity models around the world, systems provided free were not maintained, whereas the ABB model gives the householder real ownership, and their investment in the equipment gives them an interest in maintaining it, thus enhancing the long-term sustainability of the model."[213]

By improving the economic outlook in the villages, the new system has also reduced migration to cities, a growing problem in India because of urban overcrowding. There has also been an increase in the daily attendance of children in schools of over 25 percent, including more female students, as evening studies and educational support have become available. The employment opportunities for local youth have risen through better education. The average income of many households, particularly those involved in weaving and tailoring, has increased by about 30 percent. Almost all households now have a cell phone, and women have more time to prepare meals because they can still cook after dark. There's even more social interaction in the village community because people don't have to rush back to complete their work before nightfall. As a result of their newfound empowerment, the Rajasthan villagers have also now become more actively involved in furthering the development of the villages while retaining their communal culture.

Sustainability refers to the capacity of a system to service current demand while still maintaining the potential to meet future needs.[214] A central theme of sustainability is that a system, process, set of objects, or range of values can be maintained at a certain level for a long period.[215] However, a relentless focus on optimizing a narrow range of values or a particular set of interests can seriously compromise the way the system generates value for the stakeholders. Local optimization of system components with disregard to other system parts has proven suboptimal when the world exhibits dynamic complexity.[216] Instead, the key to sustainability lies in enhancing the resilience of systems. This means there may be multiple stable states in which a system can exist, and it would have to cross a significant threshold to behave in a qualitatively different manner, implying a "phase transition" with a different structure and different feedback loops among its parts. Another core theme of sustainability is that systems unfold through a dynamic of growth, conservation, release, and reorganization, also called the adaptive cycle. Understanding the dynamics of the entire system critically depends on the recognition that these cycles operate and link across a variety of scales of time and space.

At the level of individuals, sustainability is a principle of framing, synchronizing, and tuning an individual's intensive resources, understood environmentally, affectively, and cognitively.[217] What is at stake in an ethics of sustainability is accepting the impossibility of mutual recognition (reciprocity) and replacing it with one of mutual specification (codependence). A present that endures is a sustainable model of the future. The anticipation of endurance, of making it to a possible "tomorrow," transposes energies from the future back into the present. This is how sustainability enacts modes of creative becoming.

Sustainability is about integrity and dynamism of systems in all their complexity and diversity of life forms and biological and physical processes, which have to be sustained.[218] Securing sustainable economic development within such a concept requires more than simply securing the stock of natural capital. It requires the more demanding objective of maintaining the diversity and complexity of systems, including those of human beings, while enhancing their value creative capacities.

In summary, co-creative ecosystems of capabilities whose value creation capacities are virtualized by leveraging capabilities of multiple private, public, and social sector innovation ecosystems:

- differentiate *governance* capacities in and through social communities;
- augment the *infrastructure* of agential capacities in and through business communities;

- effectuate *developmental* capacities in and through civic communities; and

- unfold patterns of *sustainable* capacities in and through natural communities.

Chapter 10 summarizes the key points and perspectives in embracing co-creation in enterprises, economies, and societies.

I O EMBRACING THE
CO-CREATION PARADIGM

This book is about *a fundamental expansion in the nature and means of value creation*. This expansion entails shifts in both the opportunity space and the resource space of value creation and how enterprises connect the two.

Traditionally, strategy has been thought of as mastery of the game of competition and its rules. The fact that there were generic strategies that firms could follow suggested that the game was familiar and the rules for winning were clear. Tools such as industry analysis and value chain analysis were built on the assumption that the goal of the strategist was to position the firm within the framework of a known game. But starting around 1990, the game of competition started to change. Major discontinuities, such as the deregulation and convergence of industries and technologies, rendered old ways of competing less and less relevant. Under the new circumstances, strategy is not a game with knowable rules and finite options. The goal of the strategist is to navigate through fog effectively.[219] A spirit of co-creative discovery is called for that involves experimentation, analysis, consolidation of gains, and further experimentation with ecosystem stakeholders. Strategy making has to thus become a joint process of co-creative discovery as enterprises create new opportunities together with customers, partners, and other stakeholders.

Consider, for instance, a health care enterprise. How should it compete in a coalescing "wellness space" where traditional industries and products interact? What does a product or service mean in the wellness experience space? How should it compete in a networked world where intelligence resides in software or on the Internet rather than in a hardwired motherboard or medical device? How does it compete when consumers are no longer mere passive recipients of products and services but active, informed, empowered individuals? How do managers cope when the very meaning of value starts to shift from products and services to the co-creation experience of individuals? How do enterprises engage stakeholders as co-creators of value? These were some of the new questions that conventional strategy frames had a hard time answering.[220]

The co-creation view, however, starts with interactions as the locus of value. As we discussed in this book, the co-creative enterprise is a nexus of platforms of engagements purposefully designed to jointly create and evolve value with stakeholding individuals. The co-creation paradigm of value creation goes well beyond the conventional goods and services value creation view of the past hundred years, where "demand" was conceived to be just "supply looking in the mirror," as it were. A co-creation-based view of enterprises is not about "build it and they will come." Rather, it is about *"build it with them, and they're already there."*

Co-creation can be applied to almost any type of innovation—from operational and product-service innovation to business strategy and management innovation. The co-creative enterprise is a formidable productivity engine that can pay for itself many times over, deepening worker engagement just as the quality movement and Six Sigma process-based practices increased worker productivity. In addition to cutting costs and improving efficiency, co-creation expands the risk-reward frontier. Most important, the co-creative enterprise is a growth engine. It enhances strategic capital and expands market opportunities. Co-creation draws innovative ideas from customers, employees, and stakeholders at large. It increases the capacity of enterprises to generate insights and take advantage of opportunities they might not have identified, while reducing capital intensity by using global networks and communities.

In the future, enterprises that do not embrace co-creation principles are likely to see an erosion of value. Collectively, the examples in the book demonstrate the universal applicability of a co-creation paradigm of value creation across a variety of industries and business domains; across the private, public, and social sectors; and in both developing and developed countries.[221] As managers begin exploring value creation as a co-creation with their peers, employees, customers, suppliers, partners, financiers, and other stakeholders, their thinking and actions begin to change, and they can elevate themselves to a higher orbit of value creation.

Ask yourself these questions:

1. How does the enterprise currently connect with customers and external stakeholders? Can it be engaged more co-creatively in these interactions? Where and how can interactions be made more co-creative?

2. What assets and resources—the product or service itself, mobile devices, social media, call centers, retail channels, websites, and communities—can be leveraged as engagement platforms? How can we generate better and more experience-based insights with customers and stakeholders through these platforms?

3. Where are the operational, product-service and business innovation opportunities for expanding value through the co-creation paradigm? Are there activities inside the enterprise that can be opened up to co-creation? With whom? How can the organization experience the innovation process with stakeholders?

4. Who are the different types of stakeholders in the enterprise ecosystem? How does the enterprise currently engage with them? What are the current experiences of individuals in the ecosystem as they engage with enterprise platforms and offerings? Can the enterprise build more meaningful experiences with them?

5. What social, environmental, and economic development activities is the enterprise engaged in? What types of stakeholder interactions can we change for the better? Can stakeholders be involved in different and new ways to expand mutual value?

6. Where and how can the enterprise contribute to and benefit from partnerships with other private, public, and social sector enterprises

in the social, business, civic, and natural communities–based ecosystem in which it operates? How can the enterprise enhance its social legitimacy and build trust with stakeholders?

7. Where and how can managers and employees inside the organization be engaged co-creatively? Where and how can new stakeholders be included in management processes? Where and how does the enterprise begin the process of change in the organization?

8. Where and how do we make the processes of strategy and decision making, and performance management more co-creative? How do we open up these processes, and to whom, inside the enterprise and its ecosystem?

9. How can new human resource engagements be designed to enable more meaningful employee experiences? How can we enhance and nurture a culture of co-creation inside the enterprise?

10. What organizational capabilities are needed to become a co-creative enterprise? How can the co-creative capacities of technical, social, and organizational architectures of enterprises be enhanced? Where and how can new and better platform linkages be enabled? How can the enterprise keep platforms alive in embracing co-creation of value consistently and across all functions in the organization and in the extended enterprise ecosystem?

Ultimately, building co-creative enterprises is not just about thinking outside the box but about "transforming" the box. This transformation results in a win more–win more approach to doing business that benefits the enterprise's employees, customers, suppliers, partners, financiers, and all other stakeholders. We hope this book inspires you to become a co-creator and your organization to become a co-creative enterprise. We conclude the book by summarizing some key aspects of co-creation thinking and escaping the past to co-create the future.

EMBRACING CO-CREATION THINKING

Co-creation is fundamentally a way of thinking about value creation that expands value in win more–win more fashion, together with individuals who are seen as both the means and ends of value creation. To summarize, co-creation thinking can be broken down into the following components:

1. Jointly creating and evolving value with stakeholding individuals;

2. purposefully designing platforms of engagements;

3. affording a variety of novel, personalized interaction environments;

4. meshing together ecosystems of capabilities;

5. augmenting creative capacities of enterprise architectures and management systems;

6. enabling and supporting individuated value creation, personally and in the social, business, civic, and natural communities in which individuals function;

7. connecting with the quality of actual experiences of engagements through the platform and of the outcomes of value that result;

8. using rapid experiential learning, insights, and knowledge to coevolve human stakeholder experiences of value;

9. building new strategic capital for enterprises; and

10. expanding wealth-welfare-wellbeing.

Enterprises must fundamentally stop thinking of individuals as passive and docile recipients of their offerings but must instead engage individuals as active co-creators of value. All entities that affect or are affected by the actions and outcomes of a value creation process can be co-creators. In other words, the more inclusive the engagement of stakeholders in the act of creating value (through engagement platforms), the better the results. Value is subjective and not only varies from individual to individual, but also within individuals in the context of their experiences in space and time. The meaning of value is thus a function of human experiences, and products and services are a means to this human experience-based embodiment of value. By definition, individuals are an integral part of creating experience-based value. Individuals must therefore be engaged as stakeholders in value creation on the same level as enterprises. Convergence of value creation based on individuals' experiences in economy and society necessitates that all enterprises, whether in the private, public, or social sector, must engage people both individually and collectively. Engagement platforms are both offerings and the means to create those offerings. Private, public, and social enterprises must build co-creation ecosystems of capabilities (in which engagement platforms are enveloped) centered on the wealth-welfare-wellbeing of all individuals.

Co-creative enterprises follow a simple principle: they focus their entire organization on the engagements of all individuals. They innovate and design engagement platforms to create mutually valuable experience outcomes together with stakeholding individuals. There are two equally important aspects to engagement platforms as a locus of co-creation: realizing assemblages of persons, processes, interfaces, and artifacts, purposefully designed as a system of engagements, and affording productive and meaningful interaction environments for stakeholding individuals as co-creators of experience outcomes. Engagement platforms can come in all forms, from live meetings, websites, retail stores, and cell phones to call centers, private community spaces, and open community spaces.

To get started, the technology does not matter as much as the philosophy that drives the engagement. However, larger-scale transformation and sustained co-creation typically require paying attention to the co-creative capacities of technical, social, and organizational architectures. The co-creation architecture of the co-creative enterprise rests on interaction and experience-centric capabilities and inclusivity, generativity, linkability, and evolvability among its myriad engagement platforms involving customers, employees, and all other external and internal stakeholders.

Stakeholders' experiences come from interactions in their environments. Stakeholder engagements must be designed in creative, intentional, integrative, and transformational fashion, and experiences must be configured around dialogue, transparency, access, and reflexivity. If we accept human experiences as the embodiment of value, then as change agents we have to design our management functions of the organization to change the nature of engagements such that they result in value-creating agencies of stakeholder relations, ideas, decisions, and offerings. We need to have an experience mindset rather than the conventional goods and services mindset. Since the value of experiences, by definition, vary from context to context, from event to event, and from individual to individual and are socially influenced, enterprises must create value together with individuals (customers and all external stakeholders, and employees and all internal stakeholders). The immense power of co-creation arises from the power of engagement platforms themselves and leveraging global network resources to harness the collective experiential learning, insights, knowledge, skills, and creativity of all participants in a mutually valuable manner that expands wealth-welfare-wellbeing.

The totality of human experiential outcomes (current and possible) in terms of novelty, variety, personalization, and the quality of co-creation experiences, transcends any enterprise's view of humanized value. In any organization, no matter how focused it is on the experiences of co-creators, there are insights to be gained through real-time visualization and dialogue about actual, lived experiences. These insights help enterprises learn smarter and faster and minimize the likelihood of not connecting with human experiences. Just the term *users* limits their potentially creative roles as stakeholding individuals, as well as the significance of their personal human experiences. The language people use often reinforces a mindset—in this case of design being enterprise- and product-centric, rather than agency- and experience-centric. The latter is what constitutes co-creative design and calls for viewing individuals as "co-creators" instead, which subsumes the "user" role (as when a person uses a product or service), and moves beyond to the "agential" role in the value creation process.

Co-creative design continuously expands the experience mindset of platform designers inside the enterprise, enabling them to gain insights through the lens of participants and thereby make more meaningful changes to their offerings and processes that augment mutual value. Co-creative design increases value creation efficiency and effectiveness in the long run. Co-creative design thinking is critical to the design of engagement platforms. Its art lies in simultaneously identifying innovative ideas and the people willing to mobilize themselves around them, both inside and outside the enterprise. The faster the enterprise can scale up this process, the more likely it is to get a truly transformative result. Ideas do matter, but the energy of self-selected groups of individuals providing the passion and energy to pursue them is even more important. Building a co-creative enterprise energizes the whole organization.

ESCAPING THE PAST TO CO-CREATE THE FUTURE

Any enterprise can start and sustain a transformation to value creation as a co-creation. The paths to transformation are many, representing a strategic choice to be made by each enterprise depending on its prevailing culture, management outlook, initiatives, aspirations, and leadership. Success is a function of the active involvement of managers and employees at all levels. The key point is this: *leaders at all levels must co-create the transformation path*. Of course, enterprises have been transforming for years, following numerous waves of process reengineering and change management techniques. All these approaches have advocated some form of mobilization, ranging from the benign need for "buy-in through involvement" to the larger-scale mobilization process of some corporate transformation models. So what does co-creation bring to the world of transformation? The answer lies in the role of the customer and stakeholder. In co-creation, the customer is an integral part of the team participating in the transformation of the enterprise because it is in his or her own self-interest to do so. As co-creators, they achieve a better experience and outcomes through co-creation engagements. This type of involvement means that the change process is itself co-created between the company and its stakeholders, and it does not proceed from some corporate blueprint of that change. As a result, the transformation process cannot be designed unilaterally or predictably as such—an occasionally threatening reality for corporate change agents who have been schooled for years in the structured change processes of quality, reengineering or change models. They must let stakeholders co-create the transformation path.

Of course, the greatest difference of all lies in the ultimate goal of the transformation, which is to allow the individual to co-create his or her own experience, not only in the change process but also in the eventual day-to-day experience that will result from the change process. The best way to get there is to use a co-created approach to transformation.

Successful change management is best achieved through engagement of those affected by change. A key role of senior management leadership is to enable organizational linkages between employee/internal co-creation, customer/community co-creation, and partner/network co-creation. Leaders in most established organizations need not attempt to move mountains but instead find "wellsprings" of co-creation opportunities that make strategic sense to them and build the requisite capabilities to evolve over time toward a co-creative enterprise. The key is the capacity to experiment, learn, and execute with supportive co-creative management processes. Managing innovation by everybody is a big organizational and social challenge. The technologies that enable the innovation co-creation process and that help achieve the innovations must be agile and capable of enabling co-creative interactions on a large scale. Leaders must adopt a distributed view of strategy involving a process of engaging multiple constituencies in the interactive resolution of complex issues. They must encourage the continuous co-creation of strategy across a wide spectrum of themes and supporting initiatives, launched between themselves and the people who have the most at stake with the company—namely, the customers and employees of the firm, with creative inputs from partners and other stakeholders. Companies increasingly have to redefine themselves away from single-company performance models toward ecosystem-based performance management systems. Joint performance models can be co-created through multistakeholder engagement platforms. If individuals are viewed at the center of performance management processes, co-created personal scorecards can be developed between key individuals and the firm. Individual goals can be defined and aggregated in "bottom-up" fashion into an enterprise's overall scorecard, which ultimately results in a more "bought-in" co-created performance management system.[222] An organizational capacity to learn, nurture, share, and deploy knowledge across traditional boundaries (both personal and institutional) is a major co-creation capability in strategic risk management for companies that can develop it.

As enterprises open up their innovation process to tap into talent from all over the world, this process can be made better and more effective by applying co-creative design thinking. The key is to view the innovation process as a co-creative process of engagements, together with stakeholders, and using the power of experience visualization to generate new insights about what aspects of offerings and experiences are of value. Going beyond crowdsourcing and mass collaboration, innovation co-creation builds the innovation process together with participants. Moreover, innovation co-creation recognizes the experiences of people and talent inside the enterprise as much as those of outsiders. Co-creation of innovation works regardless of whether an enterprise's resulting offerings are standard, customized, or personalized. By enhancing engagement experiences all around, co-creative innovation is triggered in the enterprise ecosystem.

Spurred by rapid advances in tools for collaboration, information networking, and communication, enterprises are building new types of social, business, civic, and natural communities–based ecosystems. These ecosystems let different entities come together to create value—often through a nodal enterprise that provides the leadership and facilitates execution. Members of the ecosystem share risks while combining competencies to create new innovations that each entity could not achieve separately. Some of these enterprises even connect the engagements of their stakeholders within the ecosystem. Each of the entities in enterprise ecosystem engages in multiple types of interactions. Making these interactions co-creative provides new pathways to expanding value.

Successful nodal co-creative enterprises enable platforms and bring capabilities and enlightened leadership, engaging vendors and partners on the one hand and end customers and users on the other. They focus on co-shaping interactions in the ecosystem through participant experiences. Nodal enterprises can take co-creation to new levels by linking upstream co-creation (the "production" of offerings) with downstream co-creation (the "consumption" of offerings) and transforming value creation on both the "supply" side and the "demand" side. Reaping the full benefits of co-creation across the ecosystem requires building engagement platforms that multiple types of stakeholders can easily plug into. By seamlessly connecting experiences across the different engagement platforms, new types of mutual value can be unleashed together.

The co-creation architecture of engagement platforms must emphasize the importance of social linkages of human capital inside the organization. For organizations to co-create a unique customer experience, they must co-create a unique employee experience inside the organization. Management co-creation inside the enterprise must support customer engagement. Linkages between external value co-creation and management co-creation inside the enterprise generate the capacity for continuous and resilient growth. Co-creative states of capability ecosystems in terms of governance, infrastructure, development, and sustainability, must coevolve toward expanding mutual involvement and shared building of joint solutions.

All stakeholding individuals must have a say in and benefit from outcomes. By engaging multiple stakeholders in continuous innovation of private, public, and social sector ecosystems, co-creation enables a more efficient discovery and development of sustainable growth opportunities. Enterprises can use co-creation to better manage the triple bottom line that balances economic success, environmental stewardship, and social progress. Co-creation ultimately enhances the social legitimacy of all enterprises, whether in the private, social, or public sectors. Co-creation in the citizen sector can energize the motivation of participants, especially volunteers, by enhancing their interactions and making their experiences more meaningful. Governments can become co-creative by moving from one-way systems where they hand down laws and provide services to citizens to a co-creative system where citizens, corporations, and civil organizations create mutual value together. To borrow Abraham Lincoln's words, organizations and institutions should be co-shaped by the people, for the people, and of the people, and, might we add, to create value together with the people.

Building effective ecosystems requires going beyond "doing well by doing good" to "doing even better for ourselves by doing well for others." By creating more value with others, the "win more–win more" nature of co-creation simultaneously generates enhanced wealth-welfare-wellbeing. Public, private, and social sector co-creation has the potential to balance the invisible hand of free markets with the visible hand of governments and civil society, together with stakeholder expectations of more responsible, responsive, and effective enterprises, and coevolving better states of governance, infrastructure, development, and sustainability.

Ultimately, co-creation has the power to transform our reality of the world. It is a "way of becoming" toward a world full of transformative possibilities. Co-creation can guide this personal, organizational, economic, and societal transformation. *Are we ready to co-create the change we want to experience personally and collectively in the world?*

REFERENCE MATTER

NOTES

PREFACE

1. See Prahalad and Ramaswamy (2000, 2002, 2003b, 2004a, 2004b, 2004c) for a discussion of an individual and experience-centric view of value creation.

2. See Ramaswamy (2006, 2008, 2009a, 2009b, 2010).

3. See Ramaswamy and Gouillart (2010a).

4. See Ramaswamy and Gouillart (2010b, 2011).

5. See also Ramaswamy (2011a, 2011b, 2012) and Ramaswamy and Ozcan (2012, 2013).

CHAPTER I

6. For an extensive array of cases, see Ramaswamy and Gouillart (2010b).

7. We use the term *enterprise* to refer to any private, public, or social organization of collective agency, without implying or adopting any ideological coloring the term may carry in public debate. Note that we use the term *agency* in its most general sense as the capacity of any entity, human or nonhuman, to act and bring about change.

8. Stakeholders are constituencies that can affect or be affected by the actions of enterprising entities.

9. See also Ramaswamy (2012).

10. We use the term *social sector* to refer to the third "citizen" sector that is defined in and of itself as being distinct from the private and public sectors,

and calling attention to its "socially valuable purposes" rather than being seen as *non*profit or *non*governmental.

11. See also Ramaswamy (2008) on the Nike case.

12. By *meshwork* we mean a network entailing heterogeneous agents and interaction potentials. See De Landa (1997). See also Gansky (2010) for applications to collaborative consumption.

13. Actual and virtual are aspects of reality. By *virtual* we mean the real that is not actual, as opposed to the popular usage of the word as in virtual reality. See Deleuze (1994) and De Landa (2002).

14. See Nike (2007).

15. See Story (2007).

16. See Nike (2012a).

17. See McClusky (2009).

18. See Nike (2012b, 2013).

19. See Nike (2009).

20. See Prahalad and Ramaswamy (2004b), Prahalad and Krishnan (2008), and Ramaswamy and Gouillart (2010b).

21. Note that the individuals on the "blue side" are those on the "yellow side" whose roles entail "organizing agency,"—that is, enterprises are entities of individuals that organize agency.

22. See Chesbrough (2003); Huff, Möslein, and Reichwald (2013); Howe (2008); Brabham (2013); and Li and Bernoff (2008).

23. By *co-creation platform*, we mean an assemblage of persons, processes, interfaces, and artifacts, whose structuring (design) of engagements intensifies jointly valuable states of co-creating actions.

24. See Ramaswamy and Ozcan (2013).

25. See Ramaswamy and Gouillart (2010a).

26. See Kennedy (2012).

27. We are grateful to Jay Rogers, CEO of Local Motors, for his insights based on a conversation with the first author.

28. See Ramaswamy and Gouillart (2010b) for several examples.

29. See Coase (1937, 1960).

30. See Porter (1980, 1985).

31. See Tapscott (1996, 2001) and Tapscott and Williams (2006, 2010).

32. This section is inspired by the earlier work of Prahalad and Ramaswamy (2003a). See also Ramaswamy and Ozcan (2013).

33. See, for instance, Penrose (1959) and Foss (2005).

34. See Hamel and Prahalad (1994).

35. See also Hitt et al. (2001) and Child and Faulkner (1998).

36. See Hamel and Prahalad (1994).

37. The dominant "all-or-nothing" view of property rights used to dictate an internal focus and ownership-control approach. More recently, however, access to competencies through global supply chains and other commons-based peer production methods (including what is popularly referred to as *crowdsourcing*) have come out of a granular view of property rights that recognizes property as a bundle of rights that can be disaggregated and claimed in various combinations by different stakeholders. See Ostrom (2001) and Benkler (2006).

38. See Prahalad and Ramaswamy (2000).

39. We thank Jørgen Knudstorp, CEO of LEGO Group, for his insights into LEGO's success in co-creation in conversations with the first author.

40. In September 2013, LEGO launched a much stronger and versatile third generation of Mindstorms, with more co-creative capabilities. Based on Linux, it is open for "hacking," thereby making a virtue out of what it perceived as a threat when the first generation was launched.

41. As much as LEGO—and some fans—loved the concept and idea of LEGO Factory, due to a lack of business momentum (smaller consumer base, coupled with the higher price) and the alternate opportunity of children's stories (e.g., Star Wars, Ninjago, etc.) that has drawn more children and business growth, LEGO Factory closed, although the virtual designer software was still available.

42. See O'Connell (2009).

43. See Lillis (2010).

44. See the glossary in our curated website (cocreationparadigm.com) for a theoretical definition of engagement platforms, capability ecosystems, and experience domains.

CHAPTER 2

45. In a territorial assemblage, *content* stands for "an intermingling of bodies reacting to one another," whereas *expression* denotes the "incorporeal transformations attributed to bodies" forming pragmatic/semiotic systems (Deleuze and Guattari 1987).

46. See Brown (2009) and Martin (2009) for a discussion of design thinking. For a discussion of *co-creative* design thinking, see the section "The New Frontier of Co-Creative Design," p. 141, in Ramaswamy and Gouillart (2010b).

47. See Hass (2008) for a fresh look at Merleau-Ponty's philosophy of creative expression.

48. See Joas (1996).

49. See Spinosa et al. (1997).

50. See Hallward (2006) for Deleuze's philosophy of creation. See also Page (2007) for a complex systems perspective on how difference begets creativity.

51. See Taylor (1993).

52. See Hall (1993) for a detailed explication of intentionality in Heidegger.

53. See Joas (1996).

54. See Gilbert (2010), List and Pettit (2011), Roth (2010), Searle (2010), and Tuomela (2007) for discussions on joint intentionality.

55. See Sherif (2010).

56. See Deleuze's adoption of Gilbert Simondon's notion of disparation (Toscano 2006).

57. See Bonta and Protevi (2004) and Nietzsche's concept of "will to power" (Porter 2006).

58. See Colebrook (2002).

59. See Latour (2005) and Barad (2007) for their concepts of mediation and intra-action, respectively, and Bradshaw (2013) for Apple's foray into wearable technology.

CHAPTER 3

60. By *co-creation domain*, we mean a stratum of involvements, events, contexts, and meanings, whose structuring (configuring) of experiences actualizes jointly valuable states of co-created outcomes.

61. See OnStar (2013).

62. See Nikulin (2010) and Habermas (1984, 1987).

63. See Garsten and De Montoya (2008).

64. See Heidegger's philosophy of technology (Sheehan 1998), and Benkler (2006).

65. See Velmans (2009).

66. See Gibson (1979).

67. See Ricoeur on narrative identity and agency (Mackenzie 2008).

68. See Jarvis (2008b).

69. Ibid.

70. See Gorton (2009).

71. See Jargon (2009) and Fitzgerald (2013).

72. See also Ramaswamy and Gouillart (2010b). We would like to expressly thank our colleague and co-creator Francis Gouillart for his unique contributions.

73. We are grateful to our co-creator David Richards, who spearheaded idClic, and for his contributions to this example.

74. See Drucker (1959), Argyris and Schon (1978), Toffler (1990), Senge (1990), Nonaka and Takeuchi (1995), Amin and Cohendet (2004), and Easterby-Smith and Lyles (2011).

75. See Buckman (2013). See also Prahalad and Ramaswamy (2004b).

76. See Brown and Duguid (1991), Lave and Wenger (1991), and Amin and Cohendet (2004).

77. See Easterby-Smith and Lyles (2011).

78. See Wilkinson (2011).

79. See also Hamel (2007).

80. See Coase (1937) and Simon (1951).

CHAPTER 4

81. By *co-creation ecosystem*, we mean a meshwork of social, business, civic, and natural communities, whose structuring (leveraging) of capabilities virtualizes jointly valuable states of co-creative capacities.

82. See Mathew (2009) and Starbucks (2009).

83. On this issue, Habermas (1998) may remain the standard reference for years to come.

84. See Badiou for a set-theoretic explanation of the difference between belonging and inclusion (Norris 2009).

85. See Young (2000).

86. See Deleuze and Guattari (1987).

87. See Bhaskar (2008).

88. See Castells (2010).

89. See Callebaut and Rasskin-Gutman (2005).

90. See Reid (2007).

91. Capability is the (affective) capacity to act and be acted upon in assemblages (through differentials). Capacity is a singularity in a meshwork. Hence, we can talk about capacity of a capability as well. See our curated website (cocreationparadigm.com).

92. See Prahalad and Krishnan (2008).

CHAPTER 5

93. See also Ramaswamy and Gouillart (2010b).

94. We are grateful to our co-creator Katsutoshi Murakami for his contributions to the Nestlé example.

95. We appreciate the efforts of Bimal Rath, then head of Human Resources, and Sanjeev Sharma in working with the first author to experiment with co-creation.

96. You can read about Jeff Jarvis's experiences and how he was just the "tip of the iceberg" on his archived "Buzzmachine" blog.

97. See archived discussions on Jeff Jarvis's "BuzzMachine" blog.

98. See Jarvis (2007).

99. See Tapscott and Williams (2007).

100. See Jarvis (2007).

101. See Fortt (2008).

102. See Jarvis (2007) and Jarvis (2008a).

103. See Yeomans (2009).

104. We are grateful to our co-creator Katsutoshi Murakami for his contribution to the Brother Industries example.

105. We are grateful to our co-creators K. K. Rajesh, who was involved with this initiative within HUL, and Manish Srivastava for their assistance with this example.

106. See SAP (2009).

107. We are grateful to our co-creator Yasuyuki Cho for sharing Wacoal's experimentation with opening up the product development process and his passion for and personal experience of co-creation.

108. We thank our co-creator Anders Gronstedt for his contributions.

109. We are grateful to our co-creators André Coutinho and Marcelo Alessandro Fernande of Symnetics (part of the Tantum Group) for their contributions to the SENAI example. We also thank Max Yogoro for his edits.

110. We thank Luis Eduardo and Andre Coutinho, co-creators of the RTMVP example.

111. See Levy (2008).

112. See Frigo and Ramaswamy (2009).

113. For example, see Nocera (2009), who was highly critical of the shortcomings of risk oversight processes at many of the failed financial services institutions.

114. We thank our co-creator Mark Frigo for valuable discussions on embracing co-creation thinking in strategic risk management.

115. See Frigo and Litman (2008).

116. See Frigo and Litman (2007).

117. See Hamner (2009).

118. See Weber (2006).

119. See Frigo (2013).

120. See Sharma and Mukherjee (2013).

121. See Chapter 10 of Ramaswamy and Gouillart (2010b).

122. See Ramaswamy and Gouillart (2011).

CHAPTER 6

123. See Ramaswamy (2006).

124. See Prahalad and Ramaswamy (2004b) and Ramaswamy (2006).

125. We thank Manjunatha Kukkuru for his contributions to this discussion of experience-centric architecture.

126. See Prahalad and Ramaswamy (2003b) and Normann and Ramirez (1998).

127. See Koppel et al. (2005).

128. See Infosys (2008).

129. See Gawande (2007) and Groopman (2007).

130. See UNM (2013).

131. See Salesforce.com (2013).

132. See also Prahalad and Krishnan (2008).

133. We are grateful to our co-creators Scott Kuebler, Chad Greeno, and Anthony Lodato for their contributions to the Freightliner example.

134. We are grateful to our co-creator Shomit Manapure for his contributions not only to the Ryder example but to the entire discussion of co-creation opportunities in the logistics business.

135. See Scott (2010).

136. See Scott and Davis (2007).

137. See also Prahalad and Ramaswamy (2004b) and Prahalad and Krishnan (2008).

138. See North (1990).

139. See Schumpeter (1942).

140. See Weick (1979, 1995).

141. See Tsoukas and Chia (2011).

142. See Baum (2002).

143. See Maturana and Varela (1980) and Magalhães and Sanchez (2009).

144. *Operational closure* refers to system operations producing and connecting to one another while staying within the system due to system-environment boundaries established everywhere and at all times. Moeller (2006) provides an accessible introduction to Luhmann, who is a key source on social systems. See also Argyris (1977) and Senge (1990) on "feedback loops."

145. See Scott (2010).

146. See Deleuze (1983, 1990) and Deleuze and Guattari (1977).

147. See Scott (2010).

148. See Cameron et al. (2003), Cameron and Spreitzer (2012), Lewis (2011), and Nelson and Cooper (2007).

CHAPTER 7

149. See Ramaswamy and Ozcan (2012) and Ramaswamy and Gouillart (2010b). See also Boynton and Fischer (2005) , Degnegaard (2010), DeGraff and Quinn (2007), and Denison (2012).

150. See Quinn (2012).

151. Naveen Chopra would like to thank his M&M core team of Mahendra Bhamare, Manish Saluja, Himanshu Gupta, and Sanjay Patel.

152. See also Ramaswamy and Gouillart (2010b).

153. We are grateful to Dr João Polanczyk, CEO of HMV; our co-creators André Coutinho and Rogerio Caulby at Symnetics; and Mathias Mangels at Tantum for their contributions to this example. See also Ramaswamy and Ozcan (2012).

154. See Nayar (2010) and Ramaswamy (2009b).

155. See Nayar (2009).

156. See Cook (2008).

157. We are grateful to our co-creator André Coutinho for his contributions to this example.

158. Triple helix is an economic development model suggested by the World Bank, where the articulation of three actors (government, private sector, and research centers/universities) is essential to build an innovative economy. Recently, triple helix has been extended to "quadruple helix innovation" involving citizens.

159. Sectorial chambers deal with core crops such as milk, coffee, cocoa, and rubber, among others. Thematic chambers work with strategic themes such as infrastructure, supply and logistics, cooperativism, financing/insurance/credit, international relations, and science development.

160. We are grateful to our co-creators Manjunatha Kukkuru and Manish Srivastava of Infosys Labs and to Dr. Sougata Ray of the Indian Institute of Management, Kolkata, for their contributions to the Infosys example.

161. See Infosys (2012).

162. See Shibulal (2012).

163. We thank Manish Srivastava and Sunil Maheshwari for valuable conversations on transformational change.

164. See also Ramaswamy and Gouillart (2010b) and Gouillart and Billings (2013).

CHAPTER 8

165. See Pryor (2005).

166. For the classical statement, see Marx (1977).

167. A good survey on consumption and consumer culture is Sassatelli (2007).

168. See Bagozzi et al. (2002) for a concise and rigorous survey of affect, agency, and value in consumer behavior.

169. See Bell (1973) for an early but influential statement of this thesis.

170. See Parry et al. (2011).

171. See Hardt and Negri (2000).

172. We are grateful to Pablo Armendariz, head of Innovation at Caja Navarra, for sharing the story of the bank's co-creation journey and his contributions. We also thank Sofia Medem of the Palladium Group for facilitating this process. See also Dávila Parra et al. (2008), which provides more details into CAN's individual-level analytics capabilities.

173. See Gardner (2007).

174. See Managing Director's Letter (2008).

175. See President's Letter (2008).

176. See www.agenda2020.org.br.

177. See also Brugmann and Prahalad (2007), Porter and Kramer (2006, 2011), and Senge (2008).

178. See Drayton and Budinich (2010).

179. See Mandela (2000).

180. We thank M. S. Krishnan and the Ross School C. K. Prahalad Initiative and its UIDAI MAP Project team of Nupur Bagaria, Sachin Chiramel, Tawruss Sellars, and Shelley Zhang. See also Ross MAP Project Report #12-300.

181. See UIDAI Planning Commission (2010).

182. See, for instance, Hawken (2007).

183. See Coase (2012).

CHAPTER 9

184. See Friedman and Miles (2006) and Fulcher (2004).

185. See Sen (1987, 1999).

186. See Blair and Stout (1999).

187. See Friedman (1962) and Jensen (2005).

188. See Freeman et al. (2010) and Ghoshal and Bartlett (1997).

189. See Sachs and Rühli (2011).

190. See the extensive economic, sociological, and anthropological studies of Mondragon in Bradley and Gelb (1983), Cheney (1999), Kasmir (1996), Thomas

and Logan (1982), and Whyte and Whyte (1991), as well as more recently published articles in Azevedo and Gitahy (2010), Campbell (2011), Corcoran and Wilson (2010), and Williams (2007).

191. See Lafuente and Freundlich (2012).

192. See Dixit (2008).

193. See Blair (2001).

194. We are very grateful and indebted to our co-creator Pratip Kar, who was a coauthor of this example.

195. See Perry (2001).

196. See *Digital Agenda for Europe* (2013). We are grateful to Richard Straub for his insights based on conversations with the first author, and we also personally thank Martin Curley and Bror Salmelin for their contributions.

197. See Curley and Formica (2013).

198. See *Living PlanIT* (2013). We thank Ian Taylor for his contributions.

199. See Graham (2010).

200. See Easterling (1999).

201. See Sen (1999).

202. See Hershberg (2001).

203. See Kenny and Clarke (2010).

204. See Chaskin (2001).

205. See Ramaswamy (2011a).

206. See Behrman (2001).

207. See Hershberg (2001).

208. The authors thank Ted London and Arianne Tjio for this example. See Doh and London (2012). See also London and Hart (2011).

209. See also Brugmann and Prahalad (2007).

210. See "A Special Report on Corporate Social Responsibility" (2008).

211. The authors are grateful to S. Karun for sharing ABB's environmental co-creation efforts as part of its sustainability initiatives.

212. Communication with the authors.

213. Communication with the authors.

214. See Walker and Salt (2006).

215. See Stephens (2009).

216. See Senge (2008).

217. See Braidotti (2006) for an interpretation following Spinoza, Nietzsche, and Deleuze.

218. See Capra (2002).

CHAPTER 10

219. See Mintzberg (1989).

220. See Prahalad and Ramaswamy (2004b).

221. See also Ramaswamy and Gouillart (2010b).

222. See Ramaswamy and Gouillart (2011).

BIBLIOGRAPHY

Please visit www.cocreationparadigm.com for a more complete set of references and additional aids to exploration.

"A Special Report on Corporate Social Responsibility." 2008. *The Economist,* January 19.

Amin, Ash, and Patrick Cohendet. 2004. *Architectures of Knowledge: Firms, Capabilities, and Communities.* Oxford: Oxford University Press.

Argyris, Chris. 1977. "Double Loop Learning in Organizations." *Harvard Business Review* 55 (5): 115–25.

Argyris, Chris, and Donald A. Schon. 1978. *Organizational Learning: A Theory of Action Perspective.* Reading, MA: Addison-Wesley.

Azevedo, Alessandra, and Leda Gitahy. 2010. "The Cooperative Movement, Self-Management, and Competitiveness: The Case of Mondragon Corporacion Cooperativa." *Journal of Labor and Society* 13 (1): 5–29.

Bagozzi, Richard P., Zeynep Gurhan-Canli, and Joseph R. Priester. 2002. *The Social Psychology of Consumer Behaviour.* Buckingham, UK: Open University Press.

Barad, Karen M. 2007. *Meeting the Universe Halfway: Quantum Physics and the Entanglement of Matter and Meaning.* Durham, NC: Duke University Press.

Baum, Joel A. C. 2002. *Blackwell Companion to Organizations.* Malden, MA: Blackwell.

Behrman, Jere R. 2001. "Development, Economics of." In *International Encyclopedia of the Social and Behavioral Sciences*, edited by Neil J. Smelser and Paul B. Baltes, 3566–74. Amsterdam: Elsevier.

Bell, Daniel. 1973. *The Coming of Post-Industrial Society: A Venture in Social Forecasting*. New York: Basic Books.

Benkler, Yochai. 2006. *The Wealth of Networks: How Social Production Transforms Markets and Freedom*. New Haven, CT: Yale University Press.

Bhaskar, Roy. 2008. *A Realist Theory of Science*. London: Routledge.

Blair, Margaret M. 2001. "Corporate Governance." In *International Encyclopedia of the Social and Behavioral Sciences*, edited by Neil J. Smelser and Paul B. Baltes, 2797–2803. Amsterdam: Elsevier.

Blair, Margaret M., and Lynn A. Stout. 1999. "A Team Production Theory of Corporate Law." *Virginia Law Review* 85 (2): 248–328.

Bonta, Mark. and John Protevi. 2004. *Deleuze and Geophilosophy: A Guide and Glossary*. Edinburgh: Edinburgh University Press.

Boynton, Andrew C., and Bill Fischer. 2005. *Virtuoso Teams: Lessons from Teams That Changed Their Worlds*. Harlow, UK: FT Prentice Hall.

Brabham, Daren C. 2013. *Crowdsourcing*. Cambridge, MA: MIT Press.

Bradley, Keith, and Alan H. Gelb. 1983. *Cooperation at Work: The Mondragón Experience*. London: Heinemann Educational.

Bradshaw, Tim. 2013. "New iPhone Chip Paves the Way for Apple's Wearable Technologies," *Financial Times*, September 12.

Braidotti, Rosi. 2006. *Transpositions: On Nomadic Ethics*. Cambridge: Polity Press.

Brown, John S., and Paul Duguid. 1991. "Organizational Learning and Communities-of-Practice: Toward a Unified View of Working, Learning, and Innovation." *Organization Science* 2 (1): 40–57.

Brown, Tim. 2009. *Change by Design: How Design Thinking Transforms Organizations and Inspires Innovation*. New York: Harper Business.

Brugmann, Jeb, and C. K. Prahalad. 2007. "Cocreating Business's New Social Compact." *Harvard Business Review* 85 (2): 2–12.

Buckman. 2013. *Buckman*. Buckman Laboratories International, Inc., 2013 [cited April 22, 2013]. Available from http://www.buckman.com/.

Callebaut, Werner, and Diego Rasskin-Gutman. 2005. *Modularity: Understanding the Development and Evolution of Natural Complex Systems*. Cambridge, MA: MIT Press.

Cameron, Kim S., Jane E. Dutton, and Robert E. Quinn. 2003. *Positive Organizational Scholarship: Foundations of a New Discipline*. San Francisco: Berrett-Koehler.

Cameron, Kim S., and Gretchen M. Spreitzer. 2012. *The Oxford Handbook of Positive Organizational Scholarship*. New York: Oxford University Press.

Campbell, Al. 2011. "The Role of Workers in Management: The Case of Mondragon." *Review of Radical Political Economics* 43 (3): 328–33.

Capra, Fritjof. 2002. *The Hidden Connections: Integrating the Biological, Cognitive, and Social Dimensions of Life into a Science of Sustainability.* New York: Doubleday.

Castells, Manuel. 2010. *The Rise of the Network Society.* 2nd ed. Chichester, UK: Wiley-Blackwell.

Chaskin, Robert J. 2001. *Building Community Capacity.* New York: A. de Gruyter.

Cheney, George. 1999. *Values at Work: Employee Participation Meets Market Pressure at Mondragón.* Ithaca, NY: Cornell University Press.

Chesbrough, Henry W. 2003. *Open Innovation: The New Imperative for Creating and Profiting from Technology.* Boston: Harvard Business School Press.

Child, John, and David Faulkner. 1998. *Strategies of Cooperation: Managing Alliances, Networks, and Joint Ventures.* Oxford: Oxford University Press.

Coase, Ronald H. 1937. "The Nature of the Firm." *Economica* 4 (16): 386–405.

———. 1960. "The Problem of Social Cost." *Journal of Law and Economics* 3: 1–44.

———. 2012. "Saving Economics from the Economists." *Harvard Business Review* 90 (12): 36.

Colebrook, Claire. 2002. *Gilles Deleuze.* London: Routledge.

Cook, Scott. 2008. "The Contribution Revolution: Letting Volunteers Build Your Business." *Harvard Business Review* 86 (10): 60–66+.

Corcoran, Hazel, and David Wilson. 2010. "The Worker Co-Operative Movements in Italy, Mondragon and France: Context, Success Factors and Lessons." *CSERP & CWCF.*

Curley, Martin, and Piero Formica, eds. 2013. *The Experimental Nature of New Venture Creation: Capitalizing on Open Innovation 2.0, Innovation, Technology, and Knowledge Management.* Berlin: Springer.

Dávila Parra, Antonio, Aranda C., and Arellano J. 2008. "Caja Navarra: Reporting Customer Profitability . . . to Customers." *IESE Business School Cases* (C-747-E).

Degnegaard, Rex. 2010. *Strategic Change Management: Change Management Challenges in the Danish Police Reform.* Frederiksberg, Denmark: Copenhagen Business School.

DeGraff, Jeffrey T., and Shawn E. Quinn. 2007. *Leading Innovation: How to Jump Start Your Organization's Growth Engine*. New York: McGraw-Hill.

De Landa, Manuel. 1997. *A Thousand Years of Nonlinear History*. New York: Zone Books.

———. 2002. *Intensive Science and Virtual Philosophy*. London: Continuum.

Deleuze, Gilles. 1983. *Nietzsche and Philosophy*. New York: Columbia University Press.

———. 1990. *Expressionism in Philosophy: Spinoza*. New York: Zone Books.

———. 1994. *Difference and Repetition*. New York: Columbia University Press.

Deleuze, Gilles, and Félix Guattari. 1977. *Anti-Oedipus: Capitalism and Schizophrenia*. New York: Viking Press.

———. 1987. *A Thousand Plateaus: Capitalism and Schizophrenia*. Minneapolis: University of Minnesota Press.

Denison, Daniel R. 2012. *Leading Culture Change in Global Organizations: Aligning Culture and Strategy*. San Francisco: Jossey-Bass.

Digital Agenda for Europe—European Commission. 2013. European Commission [cited May 27, 2013]. Available from https://ec.europa.eu/digital-agenda/en.

Dixit, Avinash K. 2008. "Economic Governance." In *The New Palgrave Dictionary of Economics*, edited by Steven N. Durlauf and Lawrence Blume. Basingstoke, UK: Palgrave Macmillan.

Doh, Jonathan, and Ted London. 2012. "Building and Scaling a Cross-Sector Partnership: Oxfam and Swiss Re Empower Farmers in Ethiopia." *University of Michigan GlobaLens Case Studies* no. 1-429-185.

Drayton, Bill, and Valeria Budinich. 2010. "Get Ready to Be a Changemaker." *HBR Blog Network* (blog), February 2. http://blogs.hbr.org/cs/2010/02/are_you_ready_to_be_a_changema.html.

Drucker, Peter F. 1959. *Landmarks of Tomorrow*. New York: Harper.

Easterby-Smith, Mark, and Marjorie A. Lyles. 2011. *Handbook of Organizational Learning and Knowledge Management*. 2nd ed. Chichester, UK: Wiley.

Easterling, Keller. 1999. *Organization Space: Landscapes, Highways, and Houses in America*. Cambridge, MA: MIT Press.

Fitzgerald, Michael. 2013. "How Starbucks Has Gone Digital." *MIT Sloan Management Review*, April.

Fortt, Jon. 2008. "Michael Dell 'Friends' His Customers." *Fortune*, September 4.

Foss, Nicolai J. 2005. *Strategy, Economic Organization, and the Knowledge Economy: The Coordination of Firms and Resources.* Oxford: Oxford University Press.

Freeman, R. E., J. S. Harrison, A. C. Wicks, B. L. Parmar, and S. De Colle. 2010. *Stakeholder Theory: The State of the Art.* Cambridge: Cambridge University Press.

Friedman, Andrew L., and Samantha Miles. 2006. *Stakeholders: Theory and Practice.* Oxford: Oxford University Press.

Friedman, Milton. 1962. *Capitalism and Freedom.* Chicago: University of Chicago Press.

Frigo, Mark L. 2013. *Strategic Risk Management* [cited May 26, 2013]. Available from http://www.markfrigo.com/Strategic-Risk-Management.html.

Frigo, Mark L., and Joel Litman. 2007. *Driven: Business Strategy, Human Actions, and the Creation of Wealth.* Chicago: Strategy & Execution.

———. 2008. *Return Driven Strategy* [cited May 26, 2013]. Available from http://returndriven.com/driven/index.html.

Frigo, Mark L., and Venkat Ramaswamy. 2009. "Co-Creating Strategic Risk-Return Management." *Strategic Finance* (May): 25–33.

Fulcher, James. 2004. *Capitalism: A Very Short Introduction.* Oxford: Oxford University Press.

Gansky, Lisa. 2010. *The Mesh: Why the Future of Business Is Sharing.* New York: Portfolio Penguin.

Gardner, James. 2007. "Caja Navarra: A Bank at the Centre of Its Community." *BankerVision* (blog), August 14. http://bankervision.typepad.com/banker vision/2007/08/caja-navara-a-b.html.

Garsten, Christina, and Monica Lindh De Montoya. 2008. *Transparency in a New Global Order: Unveiling Organizational Visions.* Cheltenham, UK: Edward Elgar.

Gawande, Atul. 2007. *Better: A Surgeon's Notes on Performance.* New York: Metropolitan.

Ghoshal, Sumantra, and Christopher A. Bartlett. 1997. *The Individualized Corporation: A Fundamentally New Approach to Management.* New York: HarperBusiness.

Gibson, James J. 1979. *The Ecological Approach to Visual Perception.* Boston: Houghton Mifflin.

Gilbert, Margaret. 2010. "Collective Action." In *A Companion to the Philosophy of Action,* edited by Timothy O'Connor and Constantine Sandis. Chichester, UK: Wiley-Blackwell.

Gorton, Lindsay. 2009. "Starbucks Revamps Menu with Healthier Fare." *Brandweek*, June 30.

Gouillart, Francis, and Douglas Billings. 2013. "Community-Powered Problem Solving." *Harvard Business Review* 91 (4): 70–77.

Graham, Stephen. 2010. *Disrupted Cities: When Infrastructure Fails*. New York: Routledge.

Groopman, Jerome E. 2007. *How Doctors Think*. Boston: Houghton Mifflin.

Habermas, Jürgen. 1984. *The Theory of Communicative Action, Volume 1: Reason and the Rationalization of Society*. Boston: Beacon Press.

———. 1987. *The Theory of Communicative Action, Volume 2: Lifeworld and System: A Critique of Functionalist Reason*. Boston: Beacon Press.

———. 1998. *The Inclusion of the Other: Studies in Political Theory*. Cambridge, MA: MIT Press.

Hall, Harrison. 1993. "Intentionality and World: Division I of Being and Time." In *The Cambridge Companion to Heidegger*, edited by Charles B. Guignon, 122–40. Cambridge: Cambridge University Press.

Hallward, Peter. 2006. *Out of This World: Deleuze and the Philosophy of Creation*. London: Verso.

Hamel, Gary. 2007. *The Future of Management*. Boston: Harvard Business School Press.

Hamel, Gary, and C. K. Prahalad. 1994. *Competing for the Future*. Boston: Harvard Business School Press.

Hamner, Susanna. 2009. "Harley, You're Not Getting Any Younger." *New York Times*, March 21.

Hardt, Michael, and Antonio Negri. 2000. *Empire*. Cambridge, MA: Harvard University Press.

Hass, Lawrence. 2008. *Merleau-Ponty's Philosophy*. Bloomington: Indiana University Press.

Hawken, Paul. 2007. *Blessed Unrest: How the Largest Social Movement in History Is Restoring Grace, Justice, and Beauty to the World*. New York: Penguin Books.

Hershberg, Eric. 2001. "Development: Socioeconomic Aspects." In *International Encyclopedia of the Social and Behavioral Sciences*, edited by Neil J. Smelser and Paul B. Baltes, 3592–97. Amsterdam: Elsevier.

Hitt, Michael A., R. Edward Freeman, and Jeffrey S. Harrison. 2001. *The Blackwell Handbook of Strategic Management*. Oxford: Blackwell.

Howe, Jeff. 2008. *Crowdsourcing: Why the Power of the Crowd Is Driving the Future of Business*. New York: Crown Business.

Huff, Anne Sigismund, Kathrin M. Möslein, and Ralf Reichwald. 2013. *Leading Open Innovation*. Cambridge, MA: MIT Press.

Infosys. 2008. Interoperable Healthcare Systems and their Practical Applicability. In *Infosys SETLabs Briefings on Business Innovation through Technology*. Infosys.

———. 2012. *Infosys and WPP Unveil the First Comprehensive Cloud-Based Platform that Simplifies Digital Marketing—Infosys BrandEdge™, In Partnership with Fabric, A WPP Company*. Infosys Limited, April 23 [cited May 2, 2013]. Available from http://www.infosys.com/newsroom/press-releases/Pages/cloud-based-platform-digital-marketing.aspx.

Jargon, Julie. 2009. "Latest Starbucks Buzzword: 'Lean' Japanese Techniques." *Wall Street Journal*, August 4.

Jarvis, Jeff. 2007. "Dell Learns to Listen: The Computer Maker Takes to the Blogosphere to Repair Its Tarnished Image." *Business Week*, October 29, 118.

———. 2008a. "Dell, Starbucks, and the Marketplace of Ideas." *BuzzMachine* (blog). http://buzzmachine.com/2008/04/21/dell-starbucks-and-the-market place-of-ideas/.

———. 2008b. "Hey, Starbucks, How about Coffee Cubes?" *Business Week*, April 15.

Jensen, Michael C. 2005. "Value Maximization, Stakeholder Theory, and the Corporate Objective Function." *Journal of Applied Corporate Finance* 14 (3): 8–21.

Joas, Hans. 1996. *The Creativity of Action*. Chicago: University of Chicago Press.

Kasmir, Sharryn. 1996. *The Myth of Mondragon: Cooperatives, Politics, and Working-Class Life in a Basque Town*. Albany: State University of New York Press.

Kennedy, George. 2012. "BMW Taps Local Motors Crowd-Sourcing Community to Design the City Car of 2025." *autoblog* (blog), September 20. http://www.autoblog.com/2012/09/20/bmw-taps-local-motors-crowd -sourcing-community-to-design-the-cit/.

Kenny, Susan, and Matthew Clarke. 2010. *Challenging Capacity Building: Comparative Perspectives*. New York: Palgrave Macmillan.

Koppel, Ross, Joshua P. Metlay, and Abigail Cohen. 2005. "Role of Computerized Physician Order Entry Systems in Facilitating Medication Errors." *Journal of the American Medical Association* 293 (10): 1197–1203.

Lafuente, José Luis, and Fred Freundlich. 2012. *The MONDRAGON Cooperative Experience: Humanity at Work*. Management Innovation eXchange, October 17 [cited February 17, 2013]. Available from http://www.managementexchange.com/story/mondragon-cooperative-experi ence-humanity-work.

Latour, Bruno. 2005. *Reassembling the Social: An Introduction to Actor-Network Theory*. Oxford: Oxford University Press.

Lave, Jean, and Etienne Wenger. 1991. *Situated Learning: Legitimate Peripheral Participation*. Cambridge: Cambridge University Press.

Levy, Emanuel. 2013. "Lucasfilm." *Emanuel Levy*. http://www.emanuellevy .com/popculture/lucasfilm-8/.

Lewis, Sarah. 2011. *Positive Psychology at Work: How Positive Leadership and Appreciative Inquiry Create Inspiring Organizations*. Chichester, UK: Wiley-Blackwell.

Li, Charlene, and Josh Bernoff. 2008. *Groundswell: Winning in a World Transformed by Social Technologies*. Boston: Harvard Business School Press.

Lillis, Tim. 2010. "Q&A with Cecilia Weckstrom of the LEGO Group." *Indirect Collaboration* (blog), March 4. http://indirectcollaboration.blogspot. com/2010/03/q-with-cecilia-weckstrom-of-lego-group.html.

List, Christian, and Philip Pettit. 2011. *Group Agency: The Possibility, Design, and Status of Corporate Agents*. Oxford: Oxford University Press.

Living PlanIT—Technology for Sustainable Cities. 2013. Living PlanIT SA [cited May 27, 2013]. Available from http://www.living-planit.com/.

London, Ted, and Stuart L. Hart. 2011. *Next Generation Business Strategies for the Base of the Pyramid: New Approaches for Building Mutual Value*. Upper Saddle River, NJ: FT Press.

Mackenzie, Catriona. 2008. "Introduction: Practical identity and Narrative Agency." In *Practical Identity and Narrative Agency*, edited by Catriona Mackenzie and Kim Atkins, 1–28. New York: Routledge.

Magalhães, Rodrigo, and Ron Sanchez. 2009. *Autopoiesis in Organization Theory and Practice*. London: Emerald.

Managing Director's Letter. 2008. In *Annual Report*: Caja Navarra.

Mandela, Nelson. 2000. *Speech by Nelson Mandela at the Inaugural Laureus Lifetime Achievement Award, Monaco 2000*. Nelson Mandela Centre of Memory [cited April 21, 2013]. Available from http://db.nelsonmandela.org/ speeches/pub_view.asp?pg=item&ItemID=NMS1148&txtstr=Laureus.

Martin, Roger L. 2009. *The Design of Business: Why Design Thinking Is the Next Competitive Advantage*. Boston: Harvard Business School Press.

Marx, Karl. 1977. *Capital: A Critique of Political Economy*. Translated by Ben Fowkes. New York: Vintage Books.

Mathew, Phil. 2009. "Starbucks Sets Eco-Friendly Goals for New Store." *Brandweek*, June 26.

Maturana, Humberto R., and Francisco J. Varela. 1980. *Autopoiesis and Cognition: The Realization of the Living*. Dordrecht: D. Reidel.

McClusky, Mark. 2009. "The Nike Experiment: How the Shoe Giant Unleashed the Power of Personal Metrics." *Wired*, June 22.

Mintzberg, Henry. 1989. *Mintzberg on Management: Inside Our Strange World of Organizations*. New York: Free Press.

Moeller, Hans-Georg. 2006. *Luhmann Explained: From Souls to Systems*. Chicago: Open Court.

Nayar, Vineet. 2009. "The Reincarnate CEO." *Fortune Brainstorm Tech* (blog), September 9. http://tech.fortune.cnn.com/2009/09/09/the-reincarnate-ceo/.

———. 2010. *Employees First, Customers Second: Turning Conventional Management Upside Down*. Boston: Harvard Business School Press.

Nelson, Debra L., and Cary L. Cooper. 2007. *Positive Organizational Behavior*. London: Sage.

Nike. 2007. "The Consumer Decides." In *Investor Days*. Nike, Inc.

———. 2009. Letter from the CEO. In *Corporate Responsibility Report FY07-09*. Nike, Inc.

———. 2012a. *THE NEW NIKE+ RUNNING EXPERIENCE: SMARTER, MORE SOCIAL, MORE MOTIVATIONAL*. Nike, Inc., June 21 [cited March 27, 2013]. Available from http://nikeinc.com/news/nikeplus -experience.

———. 2012b. *THE NIKE+ PLATFORM: Nike+ will be giving select developers access to resources below*. Nike, Inc., 2012 [cited April 13, 2013]. Available from http://developer.nike.com/resources.

———. 2013. *NIKE+ ACCELERATOR*. Nike, Inc., 2013 [cited April 13, 2013]. Available from http://nikeaccelerator.com/.

Nikulin, Dmitri V. 2010. *Dialectic and Dialogue*. Stanford, CA: Stanford University Press.

Nocera, Joe. 2009. "Risk Mismanagement." *New York Times Magazine*, January 2.

Nonaka, Ikujiro, and Hirotaka Takeuchi. 1995. *The Knowledge-Creating Company: How Japanese Companies Create the Dynamics of Innovation*. New York: Oxford University Press.

Normann, Richard, and Rafael J. D. Ramirez. 1998. *Designing Interactive Strategy: From Value Chain to Value Constellation*. Chichester, UK: Wiley.

Norris, Christopher. 2009. *Badiou's Being and Event: A Reader's Guide.*
London: Continuum.

North, Douglass C. 1990. *Institutions, Institutional Change, and Economic*
Performance. Cambridge: Cambridge University Press.

O'Connell, Andrew. 2009. "Conversation: Lego CEO Jørgen Vig Knudstorp on
Leading through Survival and Growth." *Harvard Business Review* 87 (1):
25.

OnStar. 2013. *Auto Security, Car Safety, Navigation System, OnStar.* OnStar,
LLC, 2013 [cited April 22, 2013]. Available from http://www.onstar.com/
web/portal/home.

Ostrom, Elinor. 2001. "Environment and Common Property Institutions." In
International Encyclopedia of the Social and Behavioral Sciences, edited by
Neil J. Smelser and Paul B. Baltes, 4560–66. Amsterdam: Elsevier.

Page, Scott E. 2007. *The Difference: How the Power of Diversity Creates Better*
Groups, Firms, Schools, and Societies. Princeton, NJ: Princeton University
Press.

Parry, Glenn, Linda Newnes, and Xiaoxi Huang. 2011. "Goods, Products and
Services." In *Service Design and Delivery,* edited by Mairi Macintyre, 19–29.
New York: Springer.

Penrose, Edith T. 1959. *The Theory of the Growth of the Firm.* New York:
Wiley.

Perry, David C. 2001. "Infrastructure Investment." In *International*
Encyclopedia of the Social and Behavioral Sciences, edited by Neil J. Smelser
and Paul B. Baltes, 7486–89. Amsterdam: Elsevier.

Porter, James I. 2006. "Nietzsche's Theory of the Will to Power." In *A*
Companion to Nietzsche, edited by Keith Ansell-Pearson, 548–64. Oxford:
Blackwell.

Porter, Michael E. 1980. *Competitive Strategy: Techniques for Analyzing*
Industries and Competitors. New York: Free Press.

———. 1985. *Competitive Advantage: Creating and Sustaining Superior*
Performance. New York: Free Press.

Porter, Michael E., and Mark R. Kramer. 2006. "Strategy and Society: The
Link between Competitive Advantage and Corporate Social Responsibility."
Harvard Business Review 84 (12): 78–92.

———. 2011. "Creating Shared Value." *Harvard Business Review* 89 (1–2):
62–77.

Prahalad, C. K., and M. S. Krishnan. 2008. *The New Age of Innovation: Driving*
Co-Created Value through Global Networks. New York: McGraw-Hill.

Prahalad, C. K., and Venkat Ramaswamy. 2000. "Co-Opting Customer Competence." *Harvard Business Review* 78 (1): 79–87.

———. 2002. "The Co-Creation Connection." *Strategy and Business* (27): 50–61.

———. 2003a. "The Next Practice of Strategy." In *University of Michigan Business School Working Paper Series*: University of Michigan Business School.

———. 2003b. "The New Frontier of Experience Innovation." *MIT Sloan Management Review* 44 (4): 12–18.

———. 2004a. "Co-Creation Experiences: The Next Practice in Value Creation." *Journal of Interactive Marketing* 18 (3): 5–14.

———. 2004b. *The Future of Competition: Co-Creating Unique Value with Customers*. Boston: Harvard Business School Press.

———. 2004c. "Co-Creating Unique Vaue With Customers." *Strategy and Leadership* 32 (3): 4–9.

President's Letter. 2008. In *Annual Report*. Caja Navarra.

Pryor, Frederic L. 2005. *Economic Systems of Foraging, Agricultural, and Industrial Societies*. Cambridge: Cambridge University Press.

Quinn, Robert E. 2012. *The Deep Change Field Guide: A Personal Course to Discovering the Leader Within*. San Francisco: Jossey-Bass.

Ramaswamy, Venkat. 2006. "Co-Creating Experiences of Value with Customers." *SETLabs Briefings* 4 (1): 25–36.

———. 2008. "Co-Creating Value through Customers' Experiences: The Nike Case." *Strategy and Leadership* 36 (5): 9–14.

———. 2009a. "Co-Creation of Value—Towards an Expanded Paradigm of Value Creation." *Marketing Review St. Gallen* 26 (6): 11–17.

———. 2009b. "Leading the Transformation to Co-Creation of Value." *Strategy and Leadership* 37 (2): 32–37.

———. 2010. "Competing through Co-Creation: Innovation at Two Companies." *Strategy and Leadership* 38 (2): 22–29.

———. 2011a. "Co-Creating Development." *Development Outreach* 13 (2): 38–43.

———. 2011b. "It's about Human Experiences . . . and beyond, to Co-Creation." *Industrial Marketing Management* 40 (2): 195–96.

———. 2012. "CoCriando O Futuro." *Harvard Business Review Brasil* 90 (6): 20–29.

Ramaswamy, Venkat, and Francis J. Gouillart. 2010a. "Building the Co-Creative Enterprise." *Harvard Business Review* 88 (10): 100–109.

————. 2010b. *The Power of Co-Creation: Build It with Them to Boost Growth, Productivity, and Profits*. New York: Free Press.

————. 2011. "Building a Co-Creative Performance Management System," *Balanced Scorecard Report*, 13 (2), March–April.

Ramaswamy, Venkat, and Kerimcan Ozcan. 2012. "CEOs Must Engage All Stakeholders." *Harvard Business Review OnPoint* (Fall): 10–11.

————. 2013. "Strategy and Co-Creation Thinking." *Strategy and Leadership* 41 (6): 5–10, Special Issue: The Value Co-Creation Revolution.

Reid, Robert G. B. 2007. *Biological Emergences: Evolution by Natural Experiment*. Cambridge, MA: MIT Press.

Roth, Abraham Sesshu. 2010. "Shared Agency." In *The Stanford Encyclopedia of Philosophy*, edited by Edward N. Zalta. Available from http://plato .stanford.edu/archives/win2010/entries/shared-agency/.

Sachs, Sybille, and Edwin Rühli. 2011. *Stakeholders Matter: A New Paradigm for Strategy in Society*. Cambridge: Cambridge University Press.

Salesforce.com. 2013. *Burberry's Social Transformation*. Salesforce.com, inc., 2013 [cited May 2, 2013]. Available from http://www.salesforce.com/ customers/stories/burberry.jsp.

SAP. 2009. *SAP Launches New Social Media Tools for SAP Community Network*. SAP AG, August 18 [cited February 18, 2013]. Available from http://www.sap.com/corporate-en/news.epx?pressid=11708.

Sassatelli, Roberta. 2007. *Consumer Culture: History, Theory and Politics*. Los Angeles: Sage.

Schumpeter, Joseph A. 1942. *Capitalism, Socialism, and Democracy*. New York: Harper & Brothers.

Scott, Tim. 2010. *Organization Philosophy: Gehlen, Foucault, Deleuze*. Basingstoke, UK: Palgrave Macmillan.

Scott, W. Richard, and Gerald F. Davis. 2007. *Organizations and Organizing: Rational, Natural, and Open System Perspectives*. Upper Saddle River, NJ: Pearson Prentice Hall.

Searle, John R. 2010. *Making the Social World: The Structure of Human Civilization*. Oxford: Oxford University Press.

Sen, Amartya. 1987. *On Ethics and Economics*. Oxford: Blackwell.

————. 1999. *Development as Freedom*. New York: Knopf.

Senge, Peter M. 1990. *The Fifth Discipline: The Art and Practice of the Learning Organization*. New York: Doubleday.

————. 2008. *The Necessary Revolution: How Individuals and Organizations Are Working Together to Create a Sustainable World*. New York: Doubleday.

Sharma, Samidha, and Shubham Mukherjee. 2013. "'We Like Our Attitude and We Will Reinforce It.'" *Times of India*, January 19.

Sheehan, Thomas. 1998. "Heidegger, Martin (1889–1976)." In *Routledge Encyclopedia of Philosophy*, edited by Edward Craig. London: Routledge.

Sherif, Mostafa Hashem. 2010. *Handbook of Enterprise Integration*. Boca Raton, FL: CRC Press.

Shibulal, SD. 2012. "Co-Creation: The Future of Innovation." *Business Standard*, June 25.

Simon, H. A. 1951. "A Formal Theory of the Employment Relationship." *Econometrica*, 293–305.

Spinosa, Charles, Fernando Flores, and Hubert L. Dreyfus. 1997. *Disclosing New Worlds: Entrepreneurship, Democratic Action, and the Cultivation of Solidarity*. Cambridge, MA: MIT Press.

Starbucks. 2009. *Starbucks Reinvents the Store Experience to Speak to the Heart and Soul of Local Communities*. Starbucks Corporation, June 25 [cited May 26, 2013. Available from http://news.starbucks.com/article_display.cfm?article_id=232.

Stephens, Piers H. G. 2009. "Sustainability." In *Encyclopedia of Environmental Ethics and Philosophy*, edited by J. Baird Callicott and Robert Frodeman. Detroit: Macmillan Reference USA.

Story, Louise. 2007. "The New Advertising Outlet: Your Life." *New York Times*, October 14.

Tapscott, Don. 1996. *The Digital Economy: Promise and Peril in the Age of Networked Intelligence*. New York: McGraw-Hill.

———. 2001. "Rethinking Strategy in a Networked World (or Why Michael Porter Is Wrong about the Internet)." *Strategy and Business* (24): 34–41.

Tapscott, Don, and Anthony D. Williams. 2006. *Wikinomics: How Mass Collaboration Changes Everything*. New York: Portfolio Penguin.

———. 2007. "Hack This Product, Please!" *Business Week (Online)*, February 23.

———. 2010. *MacroWikinomics: Rebooting Business and the World*. New York: Portfolio Penguin.

Taylor, Charles. 1993. "Engaged Agency and Background in Heidegger." In *The Cambridge Companion to Heidegger*, edited by Charles B. Guignon, 317–36. Cambridge: Cambridge University Press.

Thomas, Henk, and Chris Logan. 1982. *Mondragon: An Economic Analysis*. London: Allen & Unwin.

Toffler, Alvin. 1990. *Powershift: Knowledge, Wealth, and Violence at the Edge of the 21st Century*. New York: Bantam Books.

Toscano, Alberto. 2006. *The Theatre of Production: Philosophy and Individuation between Kant and Deleuze*. Basingstoke, UK: Palgrave Macmillan.

Tsoukas, Haridimos, and Robert C. H. Chia. 2011. *Philosophy and Organization Theory*. Bingley, UK: Emerald.

Tuomela, Raimo. 2007. *The Philosophy of Sociality: The Shared Point of View*. Oxford: Oxford University Press.

UIDAI Strategy Overview: Creating a Unique Identity Number for Every Resident in India. 2010. In *UIDAI Documents*: Unique Identification Authority of India (UIDAI) Planning Commission, Government of India.

UNM. 2013. *Project ECHO*. The University of New Mexico, 2013 [cited May 2, 2013]. Available from http://echo.unm.edu/.

Velmans, Max. 2009. *Understanding Consciousness*. 2nd ed. New York: Routledge.

Walker, B. H., and David Salt. 2006. *Resilience Thinking: Sustaining Ecosystems and People in a Changing World*. Washington, DC: Island Press.

Weber, Joseph. 2006. Harley Just Keeps On Cruisin'. *Business Week*, November 6: 71–72.

Weick, Karl E. 1979. *The Social Psychology of Organizing*. 2nd ed. Reading, MA: Addison-Wesley.

———. 1995. *Sensemaking in Organizations*. Thousand Oaks, CA: Sage.

Whyte, William F., and Kathleen K. Whyte. 1991. *Making Mondragon: The Growth and Dynamics of the Worker Cooperative Complex*. 2nd ed. Ithaca, NY: ILR Press.

Wilkinson, Adrian. 2011. *Oxford Handbook of Participation in Organizations*. Oxford: Oxford University Press.

Williams, Richard C. 2007. *The Cooperative Movement: Globalization from Below*. Aldershot, UK: Ashgate.

Yeomans, Matthew. 2009. "How Dell Got Out of Hell." *The Big Money* (blog), December 14.

Young, Iris Marion. 2000. *Inclusion and Democracy*. Oxford: Oxford University Press.

INDEX

Italic page numbers indicate material in figures and tables.